After It Rained

Also by Reta Evens Simons
It Rained at Harvest Time:
Memoirs of the Forever Prairie

After It Rained
Memoirs From the Prairie to Bryn Athyn, PA

Reta Evens Simons

EDITED BY S. LEIGH MATTHEWS

REASK PRESS

Copyright registration number TXu000523346
All rights reserved.

ISBN 978-0-9992672-1-9

First Edition: 2019

After It Rained by Reta Evens Simons

Edited by S. Leigh Matthews
Keneth A. Simons

Book and cover design by Dona Simons

Andri S. Muth has preserved and maintained original manuscripts, typed and electronic copies, as well as included photographs and illustrations.

Kathleen D. Simons typed the first copy of the manuscript from the original longhand.

Front cover photographs taken by Keneth A. Simons

Wedding and several other photographs by Richard Lynch

Glencairn, Cairnwood and cemetery photographs by Lara Muth

Reask Press
for more information visit: www.donasimons.com/reask

Prologue

Reta Evens Simons grew up on a farm on the Western Canadian Prairies in the 1920's. In this recently settled area, the schools only went through the eighth grade. When she was 14 years old, a traveling minister gave her the opportunity to go to high school in Bryn Athyn, Pennsylvania, on the other side of the United States.

Only because it rained at harvest time, was Reta's father willing to take the time for driving her across the border to catch the train in Montana before the start of school in the East.

Her destination, the small town of Bryn Athyn, in the Philadelphia suburbs, is unique in many ways.

In the 1960's Reta wrote the amazing true story of her young life. That first book, *It Rained at Harvest Time: Memoirs of the Forever Prairie*, includes her earliest years. Then she wrote this book, *After It Rained*, telling of her life in the East after she started high school in 1929. Here you'll find dramatic contrasts and changes that she went through coming from way out on the farm to affluent suburban Pennsylvania.

Included here are a few illustrations that Reta drew in the margins with the same ball point pen used for the original manuscript. Then, I've also included some drawings from a U.S. History notebook that Reta wrote and illustrated with pen, ink and watercolors in her high school years.

Reta lived in the town of Bryn Athyn at an important time in its history, not long after its inception. She witnessed the building of the town's castle, Glencairn, and then actually lived and worked in it. Her account of that time, place and the people involved is unique in literature. Few, if any, books about it exist. If you have read *It Rained at Harvest Time* you will recognize that the first chapter of this book is the same as the last chapter of that one.

The photos on the front cover were taken by Reta's husband, Keneth Simons. She sits by the Pennypack Creek, near where she lived, that is mentioned in these pages. The image on the back cover is an oil painting Reta did of grain elevators in Benton, Alberta around the same time she wrote the two books. I'm glad to have had the privilege of learning to paint beside her. She was equally gifted at painting, writing and as a creative seamstress.

The photographs included in both books have their own story. Reta carefully put her photos into scrapbooks. Almost all the photos survived a house fire in 1952. The old farm house that Reta, Keneth and two children had been living in burned to the ground. They were given three days to dig through the ruins before the last of the damaged walls were knocked down. Among the ashes they found soaking wet scrapbooks as firemen had hosed the house with water trying to put out the blaze. They spent days peeling wet photos off of black pages and hanging them on clotheslines to dry. My brother and sister both remembered this clearly. Then Reta carefully put them into new scrapbooks. My sister kept most of them, along with both books' manuscripts.

But I owned one small scrapbook full of 1930's photos, kept in a closet in my house in New Orleans. The levee break in 2005 after Hurricane Katrina filled the house with seven feet of water for weeks. Unlike most of my belongings, the scrapbook was on a high shelf and survived with only damage from dampness. Like my parents before me, I peeled some of the very same photographs off of black pages and hung them to dry. In creating this publication, I've spent time restoring them with varying levels of success. You can still see damage, the most pronounced burn found on the marriage license and the most pronounced flood effect on the photo of my mother and I on the Staten Island Ferry, which came from a slide.

After all the effort expended preserving these photographs, it is extremely gratifying to be able to include them here. Thanks to my sister, Andri, for maintaining most included materials.

I must also mention the great good fortune that I, and my Mother's words, have had from working once again with the gifted author/editor/educator S. Leigh Matthews. Many thanks to her. Most of all, I'll always be grateful to my mother for giving us her amazing history.

Dona Simons
Book and cover designer 2019

This book was written by Reta around 1965. She wrote the entire document longhand with illustrations. It was typed into the computer in 1986 and edited by myself in 1990. I attempted to leave her style unchanged, while making minor changes in grammar and punctuation.

Keneth A. Simons 1992

Preface

The house is quiet. Life has settled down, some. I often read that it is good to try something new.

My life has never settled down, except for very short periods, which has made it interesting. Given a choice, I'd rather have it so settled that I'd be free to choose an interest. As it is I snatch at things of the spirit only in odd moments. Having time to reflect helps me so much to grow.

All the arts are a challenge and pleasure to dabble in, regardless of a person's capabilities. Doesn't every young person dream of being a beautiful dancer or of pouring out his feelings in song? Most young people have a restless feeling, without ever realizing just what specific form to express it in.

Perhaps I'm out of date. The young today seem to do a large amount of expressing themselves. Some are wholly devoted to it in a very noisy way. This didn't happen in our day. Thoughts took the form of daydreaming and were tucked away for the future when we'd be "on our own."

Many years later, I can say I've read much and a favorite choice is stories of real people, how they lived and what they thought. Almost anyone's life is a good story.

I'd like very much to know how my poor mother grew up. Yes, poor Mother. She was an orphan. We all loved her as children, but felt sorry for her at the same time. Sad to say, we rarely respected her.

I'm oh so sorry now. She had much more than we realized until too late. But isn't this most often the case?

It took reading about someone who as a very little person loved to lie on the grass and watch the cloud pictures overhead, to remember how often I have enjoyed the same thing, but never thought to put it in words. You see, I grew up out west on a big, bare Canadian farm, not so big as western farms can be today, but because it rained one harvest day, my whole life was changed. At 18 this was a very romantic thought.

Now, a generation later, my only excuse for writing this is my children's interest in "things way back in Mother's time," or the "olden days" as we used to say.

Reta Evens Simons 1968

Reta, Keneth and Andri sorting through the ruins of the house in 1952

Contents

CHAPTER 1   1
    It Rained at Harvest Time..................1
    The Train Ride...........................6
    I Reach My Destination..................11

CHAPTER 2   21
    The D.'s................................21
    Schoolmates.............................25
    Eleanor's Home..........................26
    Each Week...............................28
    Pleasurable Things......................33
    At School...............................36
    Sunday..................................38
    The End of the First Year...............39
    Dancing Class...........................42
    The Second Year.........................43
    After A While...........................46

CHAPTER 3   51
    Townspeople.............................51
    The Big Families........................54
    Activities..............................55
    The Summer of 1930–31...................58
    Maxine..................................66
    Scarlet Fever...........................68
    The Third Year in Bryn Athyn...........69
    Mrs. Heath's............................71
    Mrs. Rose...............................73
    Steel Pier..............................83

Chapter 4   87
Senior Year in the Dorm..............................87
Sandwiches..96
Those Awful Sophomores of 1932................102
Boys..105

Chapter 5   111
The Senior Class......................................111
The Seashore..113
A Special Picnic.......................................117
Stan's Wedding.......................................118
Graduation...120
Glen Tonche...124
An Interim..132
Home at 18...133
Fun at Home..136

Chapter 6   145
Things Not to be Forgotten.......................145
March..147
Back to Bryn Athyn..................................150
Cairnwood..153
The Mountains..164
Di, Lib, and Gwen....................................170
My first Vacation.....................................171

Chapter 7   177
Some Young Men....................................177
New York...180
Irene...181
Christmas at Cairnwood...........................183
Young People...186
My Twenty-First Birthday.........................187
Boys and Problems..................................190
Glencairn...202

Chapter 8   211
    My First Double Date..........................211
    Keneth Simons.....................................213
    In the Meantime..................................217
    Keneth's College Friends....................218
    Gypsy Vacation....................................220
    More Keneth...222
    A Visit to Gay's....................................227
    That Man..229

Chapter 9   235
    The Anchorage....................................235
    Betty's..237
    Odds and Ends...................................238
    The Fall of 1939.................................241
    The Simons Family............................243
    Thanksgiving......................................251

Chapter 10   257
    Wedding Clothes................................257
    Apartment Hunting...........................261
    The End of 1939................................263
    Wedding Plans...................................266
    Our Wedding Day..............................269
    The Honeymoon................................272

Pen and ink drawing from Reta's high school U.S. history notebook

Pen and ink drawing from Reta's high school U.S. history notebook
The Nina, the Pinta and the Santa Maria

Chapter 1

A farmer won't give up harvest time for anything!

Winter came soon in the Northwest, and the season wasn't long for planting, growing and ripening. Some years might have had a very early snow before harvest was finished. If the temperature stayed low, and the snow was light and dry, harvesting was still possible but difficult. Rain or thaw meant a halt until the grain dried out. Dampness damages wheat, lowers its grade. This was more likely to happen with the new combine. Wheat stalks took longer to dry because they were fully ripened. There was also a longer handling time at this crucial stage. The farmer with a combine might be waiting for the wheat to ripen at a time when the old-fashioned man had wheat pouring safely into a granary. So every bit of daylight had to be used, once combining started. With shorter twilights this time of year, the days went all too fast.

I pondered the chances of ever leaving home. Dad still didn't talk about it. I got the feeling that perhaps my plans were all in vain. As harvest progressed and time ran out, the feeling grew stronger. I became anxious. We didn't push Dad. If he'd made up his mind, he wasn't likely to change it, but fussing could change it for the worse. I clung to the hope he'd take me sometime very soon, unsure myself as to what the right time was exactly. He had done what was needed up until now.

From the time plans started, I'd wished and hoped for an early harvest, knowing that otherwise there could be a problem. Dad didn't worry about getting places or being on time, but I did. He might even decide, "Why bother about any of it?" His most likely thought was that the particular leaving day wasn't that important and who knew how long it would take to get to Pennsylvania anyway? He'd never think to ask. It didn't matter that much to him when the train ran!

In trying to understand Dad, I would say he was strictly the boss at home. Aside from that, he tried hard not to get involved with anyone. He was not a participator, but rather a limited onlooker of life. The wishes and feelings of others became less and less important to him as he grew older. He could not understand why he had no friends. Being strongly opinionated, when he wanted to do or say something, he did. You can be sure that, if the school I was hoping to attend had not been a religious one, he wouldn't have been the slightest bit interested. Educating girls was foolishness! But religion did mean everything to him. When he was told that attending this particular school would assure his girls would stay in the Church, he was in favor of it.

On the first of September, as harvest neared its end and nights were cold and frosty, I finally asked him if I was to go. A trip to the city of Calgary was still a must for fingerprints and a passport picture. Then I had to be taken south, down across the U.S. border. The law stated that no one under sixteen was allowed to cross unaccompanied by a parent or guardian. I was only fourteen, so I had to depend on Dad. Getting to the border was the part that worried me most. It seemed one thing too many; maybe he'd object and leave me stranded! When I asked him directly, he said, "Oh, if it rains sometime, I'll take you," and no more. Rain wasn't likely to happen at that time of year, when frost had already come, but I hoped. Most of harvest was over. I had a strong feeling that, if we didn't go about the time intended, I'd never be allowed to go at all. From experience, I didn't leave anything up to chance. We were accustomed to looking out for ourselves.

Luckily, one morning about two days later we woke to the sound of rain! It rained at harvest time and my life was changed forever! Inside me crept an exhilarated feeling, not to be voiced, but something of the sort that is had when hopping out of bed early to find a beautiful day awaiting. Everyone was aware of the portent when they heard the rain. Mom was especially quiet.

My sisters got up and dressed, ready for the day. Dad seemed just the same as on any other morning. He went about eating his breakfast. When he'd finished, he started putting everything in the car. Mom looked sad.

There were no lingering farewells. Dad stepped up on the running board and into the car. I got in on my side, and we drove off very matter-of-factly. Because we were headed west for Calgary, which still seemed like Canadian home territory, I didn't yet realize the finality of it all. The idea of seeing a city was new and absorbing at the moment.

We drove and drove across the prairie. Suddenly the city was before us – the first city I had ever seen! The houses were so close together. How could anyone build that near his neighbor with all the space about? There were no sprawling suburbs. The city sat on the landscape like a box. Once into it there was no mistaking the main street.

Soon we had arrived and Dad was intent on looking at everything. I asked, "Please, can I get my hair curled for the passport picture?" I was fully expecting to be refused. He didn't say a word. Did he feel that with this landslide of wants, needs and doings for me, what was one more? By this time he probably felt a little like the father of the bride!

He appeared to know nothing about the city. After parking the car, he went walking down the street, gazing at its wares as keenly as I did. He never asked directions, but would hunt until he found the place by himself. He was looking for some kind of building where they gave you passports. We passed a beauty shop. I hesitated and then walked in. Dad followed. "Yes, the lady could do my hair now," and Dad sat down to wait. And wait he did, far longer than I'd thought possible. She lifted my heavy hair to do one layer of waves, and then another and another, with a curling iron. My neck was stiff and tired by finishing time. When she'd finished with the last top layer and I looked in the mirror the awful result almost brought tears!

My hair seemed to stand out straight from the sides, not at all flat and pretty like Florence Moore's had been. The woman brushed and patted it, to no avail. She looked perfectly pleased with her accomplishment. I didn't utter a word, and what more could she do anyway? I'd have liked to wash it out then and there, and felt we'd wasted a lot of time. She sold us a heavy, string net cap with ribbons to tie under the chin. This was for sleeping to keep the waves from getting "spoiled"!

With the picture taken and a stamp on the passport, we were ready to leave. The wonders of the city were glimpsed in passing but lost in the hurry to get going. We headed straight south for the first Montana town to be found across the border. It seemed like an endless trip. Never had I been on such a long ride. The country became more barren, and there were no farms. We saw an interesting thing: a rattlesnake curled up by the side of the road. Dad stopped the car and got out to look at it. The tail raised in a dull rattling whir, and I acted as mother would have, saying, "Dad, come back in the car."

After more miles of desolation, the border went by almost unnoticed. I'd expected a wire barricade and big gates, flags and something very important, maybe guards with guns. Dad had been quiet the whole trip and when my line of chatter about everything seen had about run down, we came to two very little piles of stone and cement. There was one on each side of the road. I asked what they were. Dad slowed the car and on a visible patch of cement on the north side was printed CANADA, on the south, U.S.A. What a letdown! After all the fuss made about crossing the border there was no one to stop us and no one to even talk with. Would we be caught later?

Further on the road skirted the rim of The Badlands area. We stopped the car to gaze below into a colorless, small version of the Grand Canyon. Varying strata of earth ranged from almost white to black. Not a blade of grass, water or any living thing was seen. Interesting but not pretty.

Sixty miles beyond the border, a small town came into view. We reached the railroad tracks and a little station on its outskirts. HAVRE was printed under its eaves. The building was somewhat better painted than the one at Benton. Dad took the suitcase out of the car and we went inside. A man behind a grill-covered window sold him a long pink ticket, folded every so often on black dotted lines. The money he handed back to Dad was given to me, thirteen fat silver dollars. Now not only did I have some money of my own, the new purse was heavy with it. Then dad gave me a hurried goodbye hug and stated something like, "Don't exaggerate too much." He believed that was a frightful American trait. Out the door he walked, into the green Chrysler car and he drove away.

I carried the suitcase to the long bench against the wall, sat down, and suddenly felt completely deserted. That was the first moment I stopped looking ahead in a dreamy sort of way, and realized what was happening right now. It produced a terrible, lonely and unsure feeling, and I got a great big lump in my throat.

I sat for a long time, in a heap, thinking of home. Then the stationmaster stepped out of his cubbyhole. This was a bit scary, and I wondered how "safe" he was. Mom's "Never trust any man" came to mind. Glancing at him, he looked kindly. He told me that the next train coming was not mine, and it only had a couple of cars. He went on to say that, because the tracks were not very straight and level, this small train rocked and rolled. So the local people had nicknamed it The Galloping Goose. He asked where I was going in Pennsylvania. Sakes, didn't he know? Hadn't he sold us a ticket all the way there? Thinking this, I answered, "Bryn Athyn." "There's a beautiful cathedral there," he remarked. It was news to me, but the fact sounded in keeping with Dad's religious talk and gave me a safe feeling about my destination. I'd never been near a church and still didn't know the school was to be a religious institution.

The little train came and went; no one got on.

When it was almost too dark to see, I got up to look out of the window. There was no sign of a town, and nowhere to get any supper. There was nothing to do but sit down again and wait some more. Soon it was very dark outside, and the stationmaster again came out into the big room. Now what? More worry! He said he was leaving now and that the next train to come along, at about 10 p.m., would be the right one. "Will you be all right?" "Oh yes," I said.

After he left, the place was most lonely and I'd gladly have gone back home. It was late to be up, and I was tired. Never having been alone in my life before, being lonely was the hardest part. Feelings of uncertainty and worry came over me, or perhaps it was anxiety. The man's little grilled room had no light in it now, and the clickety-clack of the telegraph, which had almost seemed like company, had stopped. All was very quiet. The waiting room's one light hung from a cord, with a small green glass shade over the bulb. The outside world became frosty white, but the waiting room contained a small coal stove, so I was not uncomfortable.

Finally, I heard the noise of a train. There was a lot of huffing and puffing, and I went outside to watch and to be ready. The lighted windows came sliding up to the platform. Some went by before the train stopped. I had no feeling left at all of starting on a wonderful, new adventure. The only feeling now was one of pure relief.

A man in a dark suit and a very official-looking cap, stepped down from the train and helped me up with the suitcase. Then the train started moving.

THE TRAIN RIDE

I had never before seen a passenger train, and now I was inside one! It wasn't as pretty as I'd pictured it. There was no one to say where to sit, and so I chose an empty seat in the corner. The conductor had left the suitcase and walked down the aisle and out of sight. A whistle blew. Soon he was back and asked for my ticket. He tore off a piece and handed the rest back to me, then disappeared again.

A person would feel less alone on a raft in the middle of the ocean than I felt on that train! The car was almost dark. By craning to look about I could see one or two people slumped down in their seats. Were they asleep? Bed was the only place to sleep! Besides, how could I watch my belongings if I were asleep? There was the suitcase to keep within touch and the pocketbook with all the jingling money.

Mom hadn't tried to give me advice about the future. She had said long ago, "Trust no one you don't know" and "Trust no man." In the time before leaving home she'd added, "If you are ever stuck, look up the Traveler's Aid." Now the unknown void held a note of security, with my knowing there was someone somewhere to be depended upon.

After staring out of the window into the darkness for what seemed like hours, I decided I should get some sleep. A large boil had just healed on my arm. Another boil was brewing almost on the end of my nose for everyone to see. Oh, horrible luck! I always felt ugly anyway. Then, too, my feet were cold. Wouldn't it feel good to take those uncomfortable new shoes off and tuck those cold feet under me on the seat? But, "people don't take off their shoes in public."

After much experimenting, the seating problem was solved. I found it quite comfortable to sit in the corner of the seat, with my feet stretched across the suitcase, which was standing on edge on the floor. This also guaranteed that no one would run off with the suitcase while I slept. Next, I found that I was warmer when I took the coat off and draped it kitty-corner to cover more of me. Has anyone ever taken a coach ride in winter and not had cold feet?

Now, what to do about the purse? There was so much money in it! It made such a noise when it moved! I was afraid of being robbed. I devised a way to take care of that. Putting an arm through its short-handled strap and pulling the purse up safe under my armpit, I could rest in peace. The next day another trick was discovered after watching someone else. By reversing the back of the seat ahead, two seats faced each other. This made a big, square, comfortable space. The suitcase was still on the floor to fill the gap between the seats, and the coat was over all. I rode this way for four nights and three days!

A man who looked like a conductor came down the aisle three times a day carrying a large, flat, steel basket. In it were sandwiches of bread and meat, or bread and cheese, with no butter. Most times he came by I bought a sandwich. I didn't do it every time because I didn't know how long the trip would last. I didn't want to run out of money. The sandwiches seemed very expensive. I bought the ham ones because they were meat. At home, we only ate very brown cooked meat. I'd not had cheese or ham before – such pink meat! There was drinking water at the end of the car.

I knew we were headed for Chicago, that dreadful gangster city, headquarters of the notorious Al Capone. Richard had talked about that. The idea gave me the shivers! Every so often I asked the conductor where we were, so as not to miss the right place. By the second night I hunted up the string granny cap to put on after the lights were turned down. This kept my hair-do from getting tangled. Gradual changes took place outside the window. The most wonderful change was seeing trees, lots and lots of them. There began to be fields with other crops besides wheat. Some gardens were mere patches. Dad's machines would scarcely be able to turn around in them. Nothing different had happened inside the train, except a few more people had been picked up. Then we arrived at Minneapolis-St. Paul, which the conductor called The Twin Cities.

The train stopped in the darkness, on what seemed to be a trestle over water. The passengers began to stir. I raised the blind to take a peek, and saw two men directly below me. One pointed his finger at my window and both went into gales of laughter. Embarrassed, I ducked from sight. Women weren't seen then in caps and curlers. Still, I couldn't see what was all that funny. Maybe they were laughing at my red, bulbous nose and wondering why such a one would bother with a cap for tidy hair. Oh dear, again? A new day dawned and the next time the train stopped we were in the city of Chicago. "You have to get off to change trains, this one doesn't go any further," explained the conductor.

To go back:

Before I left home, an older girl who lived in a place called Glenview, near Chicago, had written to me, saying that she was going to school in Philadelphia too. She described her looks and said she'd wear a red flower and meet me at the station in Chicago. I thought, "How nice," but didn't know what to write because I'd no idea of when I'd leave home or of how to make such arrangements.

Farmers, at least at home, were apt to wait and see what happened. Dad never planned ahead. He went to town when he needed something. Years later this trait was exasperating when we tried to pin him down on his proposed visits. He preferred to wake up some morning and feel like coming. The first we'd know about it would be his arrival on the doorstep, which often meant a rapid rearrangement of the household.

At the last minute, as it turned out, this girl wrote again to say that her sister had decided to get married in Bryn Athyn and that she was leaving ahead of schedule for the wedding. Another girl would take her place and meet me. Lois Nelson was the girl and Bea Synnestvedt the sister who got married. I gave up thinking about it after that.

So, the train rolled into Chicago. As we moved past the city, everything seemed speeded up. There were more houses flying by the window. Many passengers had been picked up at Minneapolis and now were fussing with their bags and standing up. Dozens of railroad tracks ran alongside and then we pulled in under the cover of a big shed.

I followed the conductor as he carried my suitcase down the aisle and put it outside at the bottom of the steps. People were everywhere, and everywhere there was confusion. A big black man in a red cap picked up my suitcase. I snatched it away from him! Imagine trying to steal my bag in broad daylight, and right from under my eyes! His color was startling too. With a firm grip on the suitcase, I walked quickly in the direction everyone else was going. This led to a cavernous room. Shoes clicked on the stone floor. It had a very high ceiling. There were a few desks, over by the walls. Stopping a few feet inside this room to gaze up at the tall ceiling, I noticed the stupendous variety of people. Some of them were strange colors!

Wondering where to go next, I carefully looked around the room. There, above a desk, was a huge sign. Across its face was printed "Traveler's Aid." While hesitating, I saw a tall girl with a red flower on her shoulder standing under it! I walked over, still uncertain, until she started asking questions. Sure enough, she was the replacement for the girl who was supposed to meet me. Our meeting like that was pure dumb luck.

She led the way up wide stone steps to a place called a Rest Room, where her mother was waiting. The mother was resting, lying down on a long bench with a shawl over her face and head. When we spoke to her, she sat up, with the shawl still over her head. She said she was "going to rest a bit longer." There was food in a paper bag, which the two of us sat down to eat.

This all had a strange air about it. I felt impatient, and couldn't eat much. I was anxious that I might miss the train that was to take me East. However, being on solid ground for a while felt good. The world didn't wobble when I got a drink of water, and there was a respite from the noise of the clacking wheels. The girl asked to look at my ticket and said, "It's too bad we're going on different railroads. We'll have to meet in Philadelphia." I had a ticket on the Baltimore and Ohio. The other girl, Luelle Starkey, was riding the Pennsylvania.

Again I was riding alone on a train, feeling as if I'd been going on forever this way. Such a long way to go. The scenery had become prettier all the time. So had the houses, with flowers and green bushes snuggled up against them. Nowhere at home were there green lawns, or flowers planted around buildings. Houses out there were stark and bare, and usually surrounded by bare earth.

Whole fields of corn could be seen from the train's windows. Whatever did they do with it all?

Then came the mountains and, best of all, the Horseshoe Curve around the sides of a river. These mountains weren't huge rugged rocks jutting into the sky, like the pictures of Alberta's Rockies. I wouldn't have called them mountains at all, but rather big hills with their rounded tops and soft coverings of trees. The river at their base was a disappointing muddy color, but with trees hanging over its very edge, it was a lovely sight. This was the best scenery of the trip, but I was too tired to appreciate it. My nose was a major problem. If only it could be bandaged to hide the boil! Also it hurt. At least this ride didn't turn out to be as long as the previous one. Next afternoon I arrived in Philadelphia.

When I walked down the train steps, there was that same girl, wonder of wonders! Again we were in a great big maze of a railroad station. I was very disappointed. I thought that this train would let me off right at the school! "No," said Luelle, "the school is twenty miles further and on another railway." This idea was most distressing. It's lucky she was there to cheer me up.

Having been a Senior at the school the year before, Luelle knew the ropes. When she looked at my ticket in Chicago, she'd known I had the longer route on the B&O whereas she'd ridden the "Pennsy." She had gone to a lot of trouble in Philadelphia to stay in town to meet me. I was too tired to care. I guess that, without her help, I would have sat in that railway station and waited for another day! I was so tired, so dirty, and my nose hurt. I hurt both inside and out. Inside I was full of anxiety and uncertainty, going further and further away from those familiar, simple things at home. So I dumbly followed the girl, who was wonderful because she seemed to know just what to do.

I REACH MY DESTINATION

After walking in eerie, underground, cement passages, upstairs and downstairs, we boarded a much smaller train. Sitting side by side we did some talking for about an hour and arrived on the five-o'clock mail train in Bryn Athyn.

Apparently the arrival of this train was the occasion for a social outing! Men arrived from work in the city and wives were there in the family car to meet them. Some walked. Only men drove cars at home. Many young people met, some as dates strolling down from the dormitories to collect mail from home. There seemed to be too many people about for such a small station. The tan and brown station building sat in a hollow, near a creek. Roads led out in several directions. One road went directly up a steep hill, one went over the creek on a bridge, and one went along on the level.

It was September 7, 1929. I had arrived on the last day students were expected to come for school. This was a happy accident; no one back home had planned it that way! Almost everyone left the station quickly. Luelle spied a young man she knew by name, Andy D. He'd been sent to look for me!! She took off. I looked up at that big blonde with his hands stuffed in his pockets. He wore light tweed knickers with buttons fastening them just below the knees. It sure looked funny to see a man with no pant legs on his trousers. He wore a short-sleeved shirt with bare arms. He picked up the suitcase and carried it for me. My, that was kind of him! He looked so nice! I promptly got a "case" on him that lasted a long while, about two whole years. He never paid the slightest attention to me. I suppose that first look had been enough. To explain where I was going to stay:

I found I wasn't going to live in a dorm like everyone else, and I was quite disappointed. The big Depression following the stock market crash had just started. A half-dozen homes in Bryn Athyn needed domestic help. These people had asked the school for girls to live in and earn their board. I had been chosen as one of these unfortunate girls.

Much later, when I asked the people who housed me how they picked me out, they said theyd chosen me from the list because they knew nothing of that section of the country nor of my family. They thought it would be interesting to have me. What I suspect is that they knew I came from a farm and thought I would be used to hard work! And work hard I did! Their time schedule for me was almost impossible. I was rather proud of myself, as I was the only one in this experiment to stick it out. I not only lasted through the first term, but stayed for three whole years. There wasn't even enough money to go home for vacation.

When I got off the train that day, I saw how fancy everyone was dressed and how pretty everything looked. I pictured going to work in some big place and being a servant, like Mom talked about in England. I didn't mind a bit. Mom, being English, felt people should know their place. But I did have a lonely feeling when I thought of not knowing a living soul in town. The only one I had met, Rev. Iungerich, had moved to Pittsburgh.

Walking up the hill, the young man had nothing to say. I was embarrassed and acutely aware of my appearance. I was also thinking how warm this country was for the time of year. Left behind at home were heavy frosts and cold. I wore a bulky, brown pleated wool skirt and long-sleeved sweater. They were warm enough at home. Here they were much too hot and scratchy. Besides they looked awful! With no permanent pleats, they were a rumpled mess.

Glancing up at this blonde giant again reminded me of how much smaller and skinnier the people at home were compared to what I'd seen in the USA. Going up the hill a ways, we took a footpath over the side as a short cut. There sat a little white house with a pink rambler rose over the door. Stepping into the living room, I saw a tall, dark-haired woman with no welcoming smile on her face. After one look at me, she half swooned onto a couch with arms outspread, and said, "Ye gods, another child to raise."

This sounded mighty like swearing, so I was rather leery of her.

I thought of my mother with her hugs; she would have said of this woman, "She was as cold as a cucumber."

Andy, who was her brother-in-law, left at once. There I was with this awesome woman! While still standing in the same spot inside the door, I took a good look around the living room. At least there were fabulous sights to see. On the floor was a soft green carpet, slightly the worse for wear, but to me, elegant. There was a brick fireplace. What was that for? I could hardly wait to see a fire in it, although that must be dangerous. There were such soft places to sit down!

Almost her first words to me were, "I guess you know all the facts of life, coming from a farm." I asked what she meant and she said, "You've seen animals born." I was shocked. At that moment she didn't appeal to me at all! The question wouldn't have seemed so bad if she had asked it at some quiet later time. As an opening comment, it was shocking!

She saw me looking around the room and asked what was so interesting. When I mentioned the soft places to sit down, she told me that the couch was called a "davenport" and pointed to a big "easy" chair.

Then she led me down a tiny hall. There was a room where several pieces of furniture were painted gray, and an iron bed. The table was for study and the dresser had a mirror. This was to be my room, all to myself! I was thrilled! The next door to this was the family bathroom. A bathroom inside? The idea was somewhat hard to fathom all at once. And everything in the room was white. Boy!!

Then there was the pure wonder of running water. You turned on the tap and water came out! She stood watching me wash the baby's bottle a few hours later. After running the tap (the spigot to her) till the bottle was half full, I shook it, then carefully poured it over the nipple. Her watching made me uneasy until she said, "How wonderful to be so careful and not waste water." They had to pay for it!

In the kitchen was a small white stove. By merely lighting a match, a flame popped up for cooking. The flame could be regulated to any height you wanted with a little white handle. The brown wooden icebox in the corner was full of many different foods. Lights went on all over the house by pushing little buttons.

It took me days to discover all the wonders of this place. This little home was one of the smallest and poorest in the town. Yet, to me, it seemed like living in the lap of luxury. The contrast with my home, as regards physical comforts, was extreme.

The people here were another story. They did not make me feel wanted, or at home. They kept me at arm's length. I felt they preferred it to be that way. Thus began a long period of living on my own, trying to understand how these strange people thought, talked and dressed. The woman's very standoffish manner made it hard for me to ask questions. Instead, I watched everything carefully to learn how. I could never guess what dress was right for what occasion. At home there had been only one dress for all occasions!

During the first few days I went to church, a tea party and later a football game. Each situation presented a problem. It was bad enough not knowing what to say, let alone not knowing how to look. Young people learn pretty fast what others are wearing. Besides, I had the problem of a very limited wardrobe, with many items missing. Take shoes, for instance. Those brown laced-up Oxfords didn't look very dainty for tea! I noticed that some girls wouldn't even wear them for school. In those days there was not the selection of style, color, and size that there is today, but there was some choice. Black was usual for winter, navy for spring and white in summer.

I cried into my pillow at night but didn't want to go back home. If you asked me, I couldn't have told you why I cried. Perhaps it was "growing pains," as Dad might say, or perhaps it was the sudden, drastic change in my way of life. Maybe it was being plumb worn out at night. Probably it was a little of all of those.

The bad part was that the Mr. of the house caught me crying. Their rooms were all upstairs on the other side of the house, but he crept around at night. Even though I was careful, he heard me crying. He asked me to come out to the living room, where I got the dickens. His long, boring lectures were the usual: "You don't appreciate all that's being done for you, etc., etc."

After the first few days of settling in and being allowed out some, there was no free time and much too much to do. They had three small children and she ran a beauty shop in the basement of the house. They allowed me only eight minutes to walk to the school, which was at least a mile away. There were many rules, and they were strict. It was rough after my relatively carefree life on the timeless prairie.

I literally did all the work in the house, and they were fussy people. She did not cook one meal while I lived there, nor make a bed, nor vacuum. Woe betide me if she ran her finger over a baseboard and discovered dust!

The job I disliked the most was the hand wash. There were mountainous amounts of this. There were the usual delicate clothes, her nighties, slips, etc. The whole family's nasty cotton socks were washed by hand so they'd last longer. Babywatching was perpetual. When I was there, I booked the appointments for the beauty shop and swept up the hair promptly after she cut it. I also washed the towels from that shop.

When the six o'clock train from the city arrived, I was to keep watch in the kitchen. When the top of the Mr.'s head appeared over the hill, supper was to be dished up. We must sit down to eat the moment he arrived.

Every job I did involved clock-watching. I lived in a perpetual state of anxiety. At home there had been no rules. Here everything was governed by rigid rules. After doing the supper dishes and hurrying the three children through their baths, there was little time left for studying. My light must be out by ten. With so much to learn in school, I had a terrible time keeping up. So I resented his lectures, and him.

Not a word did I ever say back. I think he went out of his way to catch me crying. The third time this happened and the usual lecture began, I cried louder so as not to have to listen! Next day, I overheard him say something to the effect that I was a psycho. That was the end of my crying, for good (to this day I can't cry). I'd just be feeling sorry for myself. I didn't understand why he crept silently about the house. Why did he do it? More than once he startled the wits out of me. Was he expecting to catch me doing something I shouldn't?

Another thing that was new to me was their sarcasm, such a nasty form of communication. However, it too was accepted, though rather uncomfortably, as another of the ways of these people. Very soon the words "subtle" and "hint" were added to my vocabulary. This further complicated a life that was already too complex.

Being subtle apparently meant beating around the bush. When this was done, one had to ask additional questions to find out what was intended. This was done gingerly by both parties. Even then, they never gave a direct answer. The educated rarely seemed to be patient with gaps in another's knowledge. Hinting was just as bad. It meant you were doing or wearing something wrong. You had better think of something else! But what? Why didn't these people come right out and say what they meant?

Things were much simpler out West. People were what they were. They looked pleased or displeased with their children. They came right out and said what they thought. These subtleties wasted so much time! One had to worry and puzzle out an answer to some obscure situation. Chances were it was an uncomfortable and unsure answer.

In spite of all this I was quite happy. In many ways I felt lucky to be there and looked forward to each new day. I learned much more than they guessed. They were hard-pressed financially, and busy folk themselves. Besides, they were just not outgoing people; they were too wrapped up in their own problems.

After supper on the first night I arrived in Bryn Athyn, two smiling girls, Joyce Cooper and Alice Fritz, appeared to take me to the dorm. It was a custom for all B.A. girls to collect there on opening night, to meet and greet old students and newcomers.

My hair had been brushed and my face scrubbed free of all the train soot and cinders. Something new called a Band-Aid was pasted on the sorest part of my nose.

Those girls looked so pretty dressed in summery cottons. I felt dowdy in the rumply, pale brown woolies I wore. Everyone was happy and friendly, but I sat in a corner. They all seemed to know each other and could talk of so many things I knew nothing about. I felt so strange in a new land. One woman, a teacher named Wertha Cole, came over to talk. She was soft-spoken and kindly in her manner. She looked so pretty in a white silk dress with lavender feather-stitching on the collar and cuffs. She'd made it herself, she said. I thought only poor people sewed! I went home feeling that I had had a wonderful time.

For a long while, I enjoyed the dances. I felt lucky to be an onlooker. There was one unusual happening. While I was sitting on the sidelines, a handsome older fellow came across the room and asked me to dance. I felt sure he'd made a mistake, had gotten too close before realizing, and then was too polite to back off. Everyone here was so quiet in their ways and manners, I couldn't tell. I quickly replied, "Oh, I can't dance, thank you." The lively square dances at home were a far cry from these formal waltzes and foxtrots. He politely sat down and asked a few questions, in a friendly way, before leaving.

One of the two girls who'd taken me to the dorm saw this happening and afterward rushed up to ask, "Do you know who that is?" It must be someone important, judging by her excited voice! "That is the bishop's son," she said. I could forget that one! My general premise was that all handsome people were for each other. Better to try for friends in one's own category.

I soon found out that I was unpopular with the boys and considered a wallflower, whatever that was! Anyways, I went to every school dance and had a delightful time. When there was an extra of "all the men left" in a big circle with the whistle blowing every so often to change partners, I jumped up to join the circle. The rest of the time there were other wallflowers to sit beside and visit. They became nice new friends. As time went on, the one thing I yearned for was a chance to visit with other young people. School dances were the only opportunity for a break from constant work.

People talked about a "Depression." Dad used the word often, meaning little hollows on the surface of the land. What did these people mean? I came to know what was meant, in a vague sort of way, but could see no signs of it. How could these people talk about hard times? They didn't know how good they had it! But I kept very quiet about the poverty at home as a matter of family pride.

Everyone had so many different kinds of clothes and varieties of food, the likes of which I'd never seen before. Outside every window, lovely things were glimpsed. Bright green lawns, flowers and bushes, that everyone at home would have said were "awful pretty." All houses had paint on them. None were of bare, beat-up boards like our house. How wonderful the trees looked.

When I told Mrs. how I'd like to run and put my arms around one, to see and feel how big it really was, she thought I'd lost my mind. She was very prosaic and remembered my saying that all her life. I wrote home to tell Richard all I saw and did. He answered and said I exaggerated.

Down by the station was the prettiest tree-lined creek, the Pennypack, where water ran rushing over the stones. It seemed so big to me that I thought it must be a river! The day after I arrived, I went back to the station to take a peek and to see if my trunk had arrived. It had. I hurried home to tell the Mrs. and she gave me instructions as to how I might get it: "Go up the road a piece, to a certain gray house, and ask the man there if he will go and get it." She carefully said his impossible name, Doren Synnestvedt, which I repeated all the way over. When the door was opened by a woman, I could only stand there, having plumb forgotten that awful name! Collecting a few wits, I asked if her husband was home? "He is not," she said and closed the door.

Late the next afternoon, when the list of chores was done and the lady of the house not yet home from visiting, I again walked to the station. The weather was very warm and I needed the cooler things in that trunk very badly. There must be some way of getting it moved! I had worn that woolly sweater and skirt for a solid week, plus the four nights of sleeping in them on the trains.

The tall stationmaster, Mr. Clayton, was a pleasant man. Looking into the grilled window, I could see him busy tapping out code on his clicking telegraph machine. Soon he came to the window, and I asked to see the trunk. He went outside and unlocked the storeroom door. He looked very surprised when I asked him to get my trunk out.

He then hurried back to his noisy little room. I hoped that someone would come along to help with the trunk. Nobody did, so I started dragging it, which was slow and hard. Worst of all, the cinders were scraping the bottom and the green paint would be ruined. So I stood it on end to inspect the damage and to rest a moment.

Suddenly I looked up to see dozens of men, yes, dozens, pouring down the hill, walking two by two. They seemed to have appeared out of nowhere. When I resumed trying to push my trunk up the hill, not one of them offered to help. Every last one went right on past me. What helpful people! They must be fine fellows! Later I learned that these were the artisans and craftsmen who worked on Bryn Athyn's beautiful Cathedral. They were catching the 4:30 train into Philadelphia.

After standing the trunk on end, an idea popped into my head. Why not try rolling it instead of dragging it? So I pushed it up on end and pulled it clump, down, end over end, across the station yard, diagonally across the road, up the hill and across the field. I maneuvered it up the front steps and finally into the house, and into my room.

The effort had been worth it. When the lady of the house arrived home for supper, I'd had a bath and was wearing a thin green dress with short sleeves. She asked who brought the trunk and I told her. Again she swooned, in her make-believe fashion, onto the couch and said, "Ye gods," in an unpleasant voice. It seemed to me she was awfully fond of that expression!

At school the next day, a number of people knew about my adventure with the trunk. Some mentioned the fact. Even the redheaded principal of the Boys' School, Karl Alden, came through the dividing, swinging doors to shake my hand and say, "You'll never fail in life." I could not understand him. Instead, I cringed with embarrassment, thinking they'd feel I knew no better. What I had done seemed to me to be conspicuously unladylike! I had contemplated waiting until after dark, but I needed the clothes!

Thus, I left a sea of farms and tumbled into a new, fascinating world of doctors, lawyers and merchant chiefs.

Pen and ink drawing from Reta's high school U.S. history notebook

Reta's mother, Rose Evens, with Purp back home on the farm in Canada in 1929

Chapter 2

THE D.'s

I arrived in the midst of a family with three children. The oldest was a boy in second grade. Next came a girl in kindergarten. The youngest was a baby boy, not yet two years old, in diapers and with a bedtime bottle.

The Mrs. ran a beauty shop in a room in the basement. The Mr. eked out a living as a draftsman. Once or twice I helped him out. He could do wonders with his draftsman's angles and squares, but he couldn't draw the outline of a small Scottie dog! It was to be used as a trademark on something, so he brought it to me to draw.

They seemed like such a cold family. I grew up in a family which thrived on hugs, and they were sorely missed here. There was lots of table talk, with the father doing most of it. Rarely was there laughter, and they had no sense of humor. When they did laugh, it was over unlikely sorts of things. They seemed to be afraid of showing any warmth. Their talk was very educational to me.

Mr. was a tall, dark, nervous sort of man. At least he moved that way. He was active and alert. Mr. was very much the head of his household. He talked in a firm voice, and his facial expressions completely reflected his moods. Much of the discipline with his children was done without his ever saying a word. He did the same with me. A scowl meant things weren't so good. Raised eyebrows were almost praise. I can't remember being out-and-out praised for anything!

I was happy enough if everything seemed to be satisfactory. Most instructions were just handed out as orders. The Mrs. was particularly good at this.

Mealtimes were about the only times everyone was together, and they are what I remember the best. My favorite meal was Sunday breakfast. Before this I must tell you about Saturday night.

Over the hill is a small town called Huntingdon Valley (such a nice name!). The houses and stores are right next to Bryn Athyn. No one could tell where one stopped and the other began. Huntingdon Valley ran along Second Street Pike, which was macadam. The next town south was called Bethayres. It had its own railway station. A bus ran through the middle of B.A. on the Pike and picked up passengers who rode to those trains. Bethayres had more trains than Bryn Athyn, and the trains had bigger engines. After the train station there was only open country.

In Huntingdon Valley was a group of stores with parking in front. These stores were almost attractive, but very run down and old. Architecture was a sort of old English. There was Brown's drugstore, rather narrow, that went way back. It was all dark woodwork and poorly lit. A counter, right inside the door, had all sorts of spouts and handles to push down. From these came goodies, like delicious toppings for ice cream.

In back was a musty place where secret drugs were mixed, with dark bottles and potions on shelves. These were paid for over a dark wooden counter.

To the left was an ice cream parlor, with a big dirty window looking out onto the Pike. In there were little round tables with twisted wire legs and four twisty wire matching chairs around each. A colorless, "blah" room, with nothing pretty to see, but what goodies could be ordered! It took me several years to learn all about this!

Above this drugstore was a labyrinth of dark little rooms where people lived. Mr. Brown, the druggist, and his wife lived there. Mr. Brown seemed old to me. He was thin, and his head protruded forward from his shoulders, which made him look as if he were anxious to please. He was sharp-featured, with a fair-sized nose and gray hair, very thin on top. He parted it on the side and over the top went very long strands of hair that slid down over his brow. Mrs. Brown was well built, not really fat, but buxom and rather motherly looking. She had soft-looking gray hair, with a knot at the back of her head. Neither of them ever looked really neat and tidy, nor as if they ever saw the sunshine. Both were kindly, gentle folk.

Next to Brown's was a hardware store, run by a Mr. Reichard. He stocked lots of nuts and bolts and such. His store was a part of the drugstore building. Across the Pike was the American Store, which sold food. Almost everyone bought groceries here. On that side of the street and down the hill a little, was another store called Clayton's General Store. Mr. Clayton was a brother of Bryn Athyn's Station Master. Mr. Clayton delivered groceries, so his prices on food were a little higher than those at the "Acme" (American Store). The American Store closed at 9 p.m. on Saturday. 8:30 p.m. found the Mr. at our house putting on his coat to sally forth to the Acme. He went to see what bargains could be had to feed his family for the next week.

He came home bustling and full of little tales. He had suggested that this or that item wouldn't keep over Sunday, or that it wouldn't be sold on a slow Monday. This way he talked the price down and got bargains. He was always pleased with himself and always did all the shopping. It was fun to see what he came home with. Sometimes the vegetables were half spoiled.

My favorite meal was Sunday breakfast. Sunday morning, we had half a grapefruit, a fried egg, a piece of bacon, and one dozen soft rolls. The rolls came in a square, all baked together, and we each had two.

When I had the table all set and everything was ready, I went to the foot of the stairs and called the family. This was first call for breakfast, which meant the grapefruit was ready for eating. Second call meant that the bacon was on to cook. Last call meant "you'd better come." Mr. always came clippety-clop down the stairs at once, and the kids scurried along with him. "Mother" brought up the rear.

This call routine was the procedure for each meal. He worked in the city and caught the 6 p.m. train home to B.A. Supper had to be timed exactly. My orders were to "start dishing up when you see his head coming over the hill"! Of course, before that time I would have collected the children, washed all their faces, and combed their hair. That was the sort of life we lived!

After being seated, saying grace, and unfolding the white table napkins from their rings, he would carve the meat at one end of the table. The plates were then passed to the other end, where she served the vegetables.

Conversation would begin, perhaps with discussion of a train wreck. Then there would be long, gassy descriptions of the B&O Railroad, how the big steam engines were run, where they ran, etc., etc. Sometimes he stopped to ask if anyone knew what line ran through B.A.?, or some such question. Then he would be off again for a spell. We all sat very quietly and listened dutifully until it was time for seconds. I found it somewhat interesting!

I soon learned that he wasn't very happy if I accepted when asked if I'd like seconds. I always accepted anyway. That look came over his face, with his forehead puckered. It gave me nary a qualm. Everyone else took seconds, unless it was something the children didn't like. I figured he wouldn't ask if he didn't want to serve me! The trouble was I got the feeling he was stingy, rather than actually hard-pressed!

They became more affluent in later years. They still seemed to me to be stingy. As a wedding present they gave me four Pyrex custard cups, those ugly, cheap glass bowls from the five-and-dime.

Monday morning was school time. Their house was situated in such a way that there were two ways one could go to school. The best and nicest way was to follow the path further up the same hill the trunk had been rolled over. This led to a macadam path, and so to school. The other way was up the back road, formally named Alden Road. It was unpaved and narrow. When anyone passed in a car, there were nothing but mud ruts to step into along the sides.

I was allowed 8 minutes to walk to school. This meant I must use Alden Road, unless I hurried more than ever. When I was feeling extra independent, I walked home the other way! The other way went up a very pretty hill. I'd like to have a house built there some day. The sun coming up on it in the morning was so pleasant, with all those beautiful big trees!

SCHOOLMATES

There were about eight girls in my class at school. Half of them lived on Alden Road. Being freshmen, we were all newcomers to high school. Four doors up, on Alden Road, was the only other out-of-town girl in our class. She also was working for her board. Her name was Dottie Echols.

It was 1929. Skirts were short. The sides of dresses ran straight up and down. Skirts that started below the hip line were full. Heels on dress shoes were high; on everyday shoes, about an inch. No flat shoes were worn. Keds were only for gym.

Dottie was the cutest one in our group. Two girls had long ringlets down their backs, a couple wore big buns on the backs of their necks, and several had bobbed hair. Dottie's black hair was bobbed, but it had a nice bit of wave with spit curls on each side of her cheeks. She had big brown eyes and a pronounced southern accent, as she came from Alabama. Her skirts were as short as possible, and she swished them as she walked. She chewed gum, was talkative and friendly, and was a real "flapper."

Since I had no evening slippers when I came, someone gave me a secondhand pair, of black satin. They were round toed and spike heeled, with a strap around the ankle and a perky bow on the front of this strap. I treasured them. Telling Dottie about them was a mistake. She borrowed them all the time "just to wear," and they soon looked past their best. Anyway, they seemed to suit her better than they did me!

The boys swooned over Dottie! She was a flapper girl in appearance and performance. She lasted only a few months and was sent home. In the meantime, the rest of us learned how the "other half" got around!

Next up the road lived Tryn Rose, the daughter of Don Rose, the famous newspaper columnist. She was the oldest of twelve very lively children, though they hadn't all arrived yet at that time. Tryn was friendly but somewhat reticent.

A bit further up lived a redhead with long silken hair that she wore in a bun. She was a bashful, blushing maiden, and her mother had been an Alden. Eleanor Cranch had two older brothers (both away) and a younger sister. Her father had remarried after her mother died, and she lived with a strict stepmother and the stepmother's two children. Eleanor soon became a fast friend, though I felt I often shocked her and tried hard not to.

Almost across the road from Eleanor lived an old man, her grandfather Alden. He had a long snowy white beard and white hair. He walked up Alden Road to school each day, bent over his cane. He was most friendly, but to be avoided if possible. When I tried to pass him, I was caught! Conversation started, and I just couldn't take off in the middle of a sentence! Staying with him meant being late for school. Alden Road was named after him. He was in charge of the school book room.

Then there was Peggy Cowley, who was a whimsical, smiling, rather dainty and quick little person. She lived in a little house with an old maiden aunt who was quite stocky and got around her house on a cane. She was "Tanny" and pleasant to all.

Peggy wasn't very interested in studies, but she found people absorbing. She liked everyone she saw and enjoyed each moment as it came along. She lived a hand-to-mouth existence. She and another classmate carried on long conversations in gobble-de-gook talk and seemed to have much fun doing it. The very words were a wonder to me. No, it wasn't pig Latin. They went through that stage, too. This was "whambie doodle," "doop de daddle," and what more I'll never remember. Aside from Dottie and one other girl, the girls in our class were mostly wallflowers who didn't get bids to dances. At the end of freshman year, there were six of us.

ELEANOR'S HOME

School lasted from 8 a.m. till 12:30 p.m. Two afternoons a week we had gym for three-quarters of an hour. The D.'s, where I lived, asked if I could be excused from showers so that I'd be home sooner. The school said, "No."

I was allowed to go to church every other Sunday. They never went, so I didn't see why I couldn't go each week. I asked to go a couple of times and received a firm answer of "No," so gave up.

Every Sunday night was my time off if I wished to go out. They sometimes asked me to stay home if they had an invitation. They had almost no social life, so this was not a problem.

About once a month, Eleanor asked me to her house for Sunday night supper. I was allowed to go after the children were fed. This was easy, as the standard supper was cold cereal with sliced bananas.

I never got used to Eleanor's house, nor felt at home there. She herself was such a dear girl, and I much appreciated the opportunity for a change. I never could decide whether she invited me just to be kind, or whether she liked seeing someone a little different from herself. We had nothing in common but our age!

There was a certain rigid feeling about the members of her household. None of them had any spontaneity. Her father was precise in his actions and meticulous in his speech. He looked like a rabbi, with his black goatee and round rimmed glasses.

Her stepmother was large and methodical, with a rather long face. She had a sick little boy who needed constant care. He lived to be about eight years old and never got off of his bed. At this time, he wasn't very old. His sister Ruth had dark curly hair and was a couple of years older. She was always in bed by the time I came.

We ate very plain suppers in front of the fireplace. The house wasn't a big one. It was dark as a cavern inside, even on the brightest days. The living room had much woodwork, all very dark, almost black. The upper half of the walls were a dull color, too. The one or two windows had the blinds pulled down. This protected the dark plush-covered furniture with its crocheted covers on the arms and back. The mother crocheted things as we sat. Never once did Eleanor and I have a chance to talk alone about school or anything. I supposed she wasn't very interested. The talk centered on her father asking me questions. He asked how crops were raised, how was the weather at home, and that sort of thing. There was never, never any fun talk.

I found that Eleanor and her sister Marion were terribly good girls. They jumped up to do any of the work, never talked back, and were polite in every way. Some girls were beginning to wear just a trace of lipstick, but only to dances. Not these girls! This was forbidden, along with face powder. Their hair wasn't curled, and their dresses were most plain. They wore old-fashioned petticoats under their dresses.

Eleanor had a terrible time at gym. Naturally the girls commented out loud on her old-fashioned ways. Perhaps that was why Eleanor understood my first reaction to gym and showers.

Downstairs at school was a cement-floored locker room with a couple of showers. We arrived in our clothes. We all had little metal lockers where we kept our ugly blue gym suits. We chose our own lockers.

Upon going down there the first time, I was most chagrined! There were all the girls busily undressing and getting into their gym suits. This wasn't the worst part! After gym they undressed all the way down to their "skinnybares"! And in front of all the other girls! Each one did have a short pongee silk robe, or the equivalent, to wear while standing in line for the showers.

There were lots of extra lockers, so I carefully chose one in a back corner where I could undress in relative privacy. This worked a time or two, and then I heard someone say, "What's the matter with her?" At that I gave up and joined the group. I never entirely gave up the feeling that a bit of privacy was more comfortable.

EACH WEEK

The woman I lived with was called "Dear" by her husband. He didn't mean anything by it, it was just a name. I could call her that, too, and most often did, but it was not easy to get used to. She never smiled or was sweet or easy, so the name didn't seem to fit, but I respected her.

She had been brought up as a very well-to-do young lady. A chauffeur drove her all the way to school in Bryn Athyn from Michigan. She was oldest in her family of four girls. While she was down at school, her very independent mother produced a boy, years younger than the girls. This very much surprised the father as she didn't tell him about it till the last minute! The father lost all his money in the crash of '29.

The man "Dear" married was one of seven sons with two sisters. Theirs was a very rigid household. The parents worked hard to see all the children were well educated through college. Much against their wishes, "Mr." fell in love with "Dear" and married her while both were young. So, he didn't go to college. He was the only one in the family without a college education.

He had a small salary, so they did not have an easy time trying to make ends meet. That's why she started the beauty shop in the basement. I arrived just at the time this was getting underway. They did all the work of building it themselves.

A black woman with light brown kinky hair came one day a week to do the wash and most of the ironing. In addition, there was a mountainous amount of work to do. And their standards were high!

"Dear" worked in her shop most of the time. When she didn't, she usually flopped down on the living room couch, tired out, with the blinds pulled down, to rest. She then liked me to sit on the couch with her feet on my lap and rub the bottoms of them. I did it, I'm sure, hundreds of times. When I was liking her, I didn't much mind. I never all the way liked her because she didn't seem to encourage that feeling at all. Much of the time I did it because she asked me to, and I kept my own thoughts. She shut her eyes and rested, so conversation was no issue.

Time went flying by, and everyone was very busy. I did not complain about my lot or even think about it. Years later any number of people did ask me "if you really worked that hard there? Perhaps it only seemed so because you were so young...?"

I am getting ahead of my story. These remarks came about because of happenings I knew nothing of at that time. I did work very hard there, but I already knew about effort. This work was really more glamorous than farm work! Besides, these people were very organized, which I liked, to a degree. The hard part of their life was the lack of affection and the rigidity of everything. There was no unbending or exception to their ways of living or doing. They were inclined to be sarcastic much of the time, a trait I find detestable.

The Great Depression was under way. Herbert Hoover was the Republican president, and things were bad, I was told.

I jumped into my clothes in the morning, set the table, and got breakfast. I called the family to eat, then dressed the children for school. The table was cleared and as many dishes washed as possible, leaving those 8 minutes to get to school!

I arrived home at lunch with no extra time spent on the way. They couldn't pin me down as tight on that because class might be out a bit late. There on the kitchen wall was the day's menu. Lunches became quite standard. Monday would be "Pigs in Blankets", made up of toast spread with peanut butter, a couple of strips of bacon, and a cream sauce poured over it. Tuesday, the day the wash woman came, was always baked beans, lettuce, and tomato.

There was one phone in the house, in the kitchen. While I was at home, I answered it. I booked her hair appointments. I was then expected to keep track of such things as haircuts. If one was booked at 3 p.m., then I was to be downstairs at 3:25 p.m. to sweep up the hair. If there was a run on shampoos, extra towels had to be washed.

Right after lunch, she went upstairs to rest. I washed dishes, got the kids at homework, or found where they were going to play. In other words, I baby watched all day.

There were certain days for certain big jobs. If the living room needed it, it was vacuumed more often. Monday all the beds were changed. They put all their socks and stockings in a cupboard in the bathroom, plus her slips and undies. These I had to wash out by hand so they'd last longer. Every week I resented doing the children's heavy, dirty socks and wore out my knuckles. I did his socks, too. They were not made of nylon in those days but of cotton. He was forever getting holes in the heels and toes. These I had to darn. Tuesday, after the wash woman left, I put away the ironing and finished what was left undone. There always was some. Then buttons had to be sewed on. I hated Tuesdays, but I didn't have any time to think about it.

Then there was cleaning. All the dark furniture was dusted with an oily cloth every day. This I whipped through. The baseboards were supposed to be done, too, but some days there just wasn't enough time. Sure as shooting, her finger would take a swipe on some unlikely baseboard, and she would make a little sarcastic speech. That one failing action was at the top of my list to show how picayune and thoughtless she could be. She expected the moon on a silver platter. It became a standard resentment, but I never dwelt on it in the hustle of work.

I did every bit of cooking. There was no time spent learning. A pie might be on the menu for supper. In the drawer was a cookbook. If it didn't turn out this time – and they would be sure to let me know – it might next time, as I became more familiar with the art.

I got welcome help from Mr. at Sunday dinner time. He mashed the potatoes and took great delight in making the gravy in the roasting pan, smooth and tasty.

After supper dishes were done and the kids undressed, I could study. This would sometimes be as late as 8:30 p.m., and 10 p.m. in bed was a strict rule. School was rough going, and there was no chance to sneak up late. He'd be right there. Later when I became a bit bolder, I snuck a book under the pillow to glance at early in the morning, when I could drag myself awake.

One of the first big jobs was to try and bring order out of chaos in the one half of the upstairs which was the children's bedroom. The other half was the parents'. This upstairs was very roughly finished. The sloping walls were covered with a cheap Celotex. Bits and pieces drifted down like sawdust constantly.

Around the room were scattered dozens of children's magazines such as *St. Nicholas*. There was no clothes closet. Under the small eaves were broken toys, clothes, and storage. There was also storage space under the eaves in the parents' room. The children were forbidden to look in there. One day their oldest boy got in and found his father's rifle. He pulled the trigger and shot a hole through the roof! All I can say is, it was the luckiest thing for me that his father was home at the time. The boy was his responsibility!

Next door lived the Burt Smiths. They were known as the "Birdie" Smiths, as that's what Mrs. Smith called her husband. They seemed a pleasant, happy family. Before supper, the mother went outside and called her children, "Ivy, Westy, Fady and Deany." This gave my people fits. Long after I left working at the D.'s, Mrs. Smith stopped me to say she remembered that she never saw me but that I was constantly running to school.

One thing I must mention at this time was my money setup. The few dollars that I had brought from home lasted for months! After they were gone, the D.'s gave me twenty-five cents a week. Mr. was the one who handed this out each Saturday night, and it was not a happy occasion. The first time this happened, he announced that it wasn't that I earned it but that he just gave it to me! Each time it seemed so grudgingly given that I hated to take it. But I needed it, for toothpaste and to write that one letter home every week. I also used it to buy pencils and paper for school.

I heard them talk about being so poor but couldn't see how. They had such an awful lot compared with us back home!

One time at the table, Mr. told me I ate so many slices of bread a day, that times 365 was so many, and that was fifty loaves in a year. Think of the cost! I got the feeling I was overwhelmingly in their debt, so was anxious to work as hard as I could. Never having been paid for work, I had no idea what it was worth. I pictured doctors, dentists, draftsmen, etc., anyone trained in a skill, as being the only ones worthy of money.

Up the hill a piece lived Mrs. D.'s sister. She had a family of three children, too. She came to the beauty shop once a week to have her long black hair washed and marcelled. She had married the son of one of the town's wealthy families. Because of the Depression, his income wasn't as good as usual, but it was still very good indeed compared to the D.'s.

I wasn't very fond of this sister. She seemed spoiled, and every time she left Mrs. D. was unhappy and said things to her husband at supper. A typical conversation would be about the sister having a new purse, which Mrs. D. never failed to notice. When asked about it, the sister would say, "Oh, I picked it up for $5." In those days, that was a lot for just a purse, and to me it seemed like a fortune. I could see Mrs. D. was unhappy because she couldn't afford a purse like that.

Sometimes the sister went off to Atlantic City for the weekend and stayed at the Traymore Hotel. Then Mrs. D. was positively green! And I can see why, to some extent.

What I objected to, even then, was the way the sister told these things to someone who had so much less. She didn't give you the feeling of sharing her pleasurable experience, but that she just enjoyed the contrast and often wished wished for something bigger and better. She was known all around as a dissatisfied woman.

What I liked about that family was the fact that I was occasionally allowed to go baby watch when they were stuck. They had nice children. Their house seemed amazingly bare for people who talked so fancy. When they came back home, the husband never failed to say, "Hold out your hand," and into it he dropped a fifty cent piece, with a smile.

PLEASURABLE THINGS

The D.'s had very, very little social life. In spring and fall, they went several times for a short automobile ride right after supper, to see the countryside.

With dishes empty on the table, Mr. would say, "Let's go for a ride tonight." We'd all jump up and soon be in the funny little, noisy, square black Ford. Papa and Mama in the front seat and the three kids and me in back with the little one on my lap. Mrs. would suggest we see such and such a place, "the rock garden will be at its best," etc. In the fall, it might be a drive down the then beautiful Creek Road to see the colored leaves. Mr. pointed out poison ivy. There was very little of it then.

When we got back home, I had to rush to get the dishes washed and the kids bathed. I bathed them all. Mr. had to correct my use of the word bathed. He pronounced it "bath-ed."

When school began, there were football games on Friday afternoons. Often, I was allowed to push the young one up the road in a stroller, with the other two along, and attend the game. Mrs. didn't seem very happy about that. She once remarked that she allowed it because she couldn't have people thinking she never let me out!

It was a nuisance always trying to keep track of those lively kids at the game when everyone else was parading around arm in arm, eating and talking. It took a year before I thought of this contrast, but then I felt lucky to get out at all!

The high school girls learned football songs which everyone sang at the games. The more we lost ground in the game, the more we sang! I was told this was to help school spirit and to inspire the team to get in there and fight.

In the fall, everyone seemed to be raking leaves. These were heaped up in piles in front of their houses and burned. They were like little smudges of incense! The damp, heavy weather became clear in the fall, with blue skies, and one felt nice and peppy. By this time, I'd thoroughly adopted B.A. and felt very much at home there. For many years the smell and sight of burning leaves, and the sound of football games, gave me a happy feeling. This was my favorite time of year because I remembered my first settling in at Bryn Athyn.

Before we knew it, Christmastime came. I managed to get something from the five-and-dime for each member of my family at home. I enjoyed doing this. Christmas was in evidence everywhere. There were pine branches cut and tucked above windows and on fireplaces. There was a beautiful set of red candles on the table. I'd never seen a candle before! The parents gave each child a very nice Christmas gift. They also seemed to have dozens of aunts and uncles who gave gifts as well. The wonder to me was the fact that these same children had toys left over from the last Christmas, and they didn't seem to play with them. In fact, they were often bored.

I remember being surprised when they liked something I made for them with paste and paper. With all these fancy toys, they still liked something simple.

For Christmas they gave me a thin little oval silver pin. That was most thoughtful and frivolous, and I enjoyed it much more than I would a practical gift.

There wasn't anything special to eat. The family was invited to Mr. D.'s parents' for Christmas dinner, and I was to go, too. This made me a little uncomfortable. I considered the D.'s to be very much above me, socially. When there were guests at the D.'s household, I had always eaten in the kitchen and felt I belonged there.

What an experience that dinner turned out to be! When we arrived, there was a big table, all set with sparkling silver and glass. The grandmother was a big woman, not fat. She was a no-nonsense person, as also was the grandfather. He was positively forbidding! He was tall and slender, with spectacles and a big nose. His face was very expressive, but he didn't say much.

After formal hand shaking, we sat in a living room that seemed to be full of tall sons. He had 7 of them and 2 daughters, some married at this time. The D.'s had the only grandchildren. They served a drink. The drink turned out to be awful-smelling whisky. Horrors! A "den of iniquity"!

Before long we all sat down at the table. In front of us were tall glasses on small plates full of the most awful-looking stuff I had ever seen. They all oohed and aahed. While I watched, each picked up a fork and up came a dripping, slimy bit of the gray mass. This awful-looking thing was popped into the mouth with relish! Ugh!

After I watched in stunned silence, someone nearby looked my way and said, "Oh, you are not eating your oysters." By this time everyone else was through. Mr. D. proceeded to tell me to pick up my fork and do thus and so. As if I hadn't seen. So, one by one, I managed to get those revolting things down. The real wonder was that I kept those down that had gone before! I had looked forward to doing no cooking on Christmas day. At this point I'd have gladly gone home to cook! No one said, "You don't have to eat them." It was wretched to be delaying the party till I finished; besides, everyone was watching me.

A huge baked turkey came next, with cranberry sauce, mushrooms, and all the fixings. The meal ended with wine and pies. All of this was new to me, but the oysters had ruined the day!

After dinner there were more dishes to be washed than I'd ever seen before. Grandmother stayed at the washing till the last ladle and pot was done.

Then everyone exchanged gifts, and the grandmother gave me a pale green knitted rayon (like underwear) nightie. I felt very much like an intruder, the only one not in the family, and so was taken completely by surprise to be given a gift. I loved that lady from then on. She was a woman of few words, knew her own mind, but was always quietly kind to me.

I took that nightie home in its box. It was put in my bottom dresser drawer. I took it out of the box periodically to admire it and its tiny little ribbon rosettes. During the year, I only wore it once in a while till it got a used look. It was the only pretty nightie I had for the next ten years. Money was needed for other things.

AT SCHOOL

At school, the one beastly subject was Latin. I was told it would help my vocabulary, but, to this day, I deny that. Our Religion teacher was a very learned minister named Dr. Hugo Odhner. He was wasted on freshmen! Back then no one wrote papers or was graded for religion class, so we fooled and talked through his classes.

You should have seen my hair during this time! Mrs. D. thought it should be bobbed, so it was. I hated such straight hair, so each night I wet a chunk on each side and stuck bobby pins in it to make a wave. When there was a dance, Mrs. D. gave me a free marcel. "Free advertising," she said. I enjoyed the night off to attend the dance as a wall flower and to talk to classmates, most often. I jumped up and joined every circle dance.

Going to the dance was most amusing. Part way around "The Loop" of houses on the hill above the D.'s lived the principal of the Girl's School, Miss Buell. Her name was Rita, too. Such a funny little old maid, we all thought. She wore dresses all of a sort in some kind of "nothing" style. She carried her purse by its rather long handle, flapping against her legs. When she walked, she was half bent over and swayed from side to side. Shall we say she wasn't graceful? Her hair was messed up all over the top of her head and fastened with hairpins. It was carefully done but didn't look it. I liked her very much. She listened to every word you said and spoke back slowly as though each word were considered. She also taught English, I thought well.

To get to the dances, we out-of-town girls had to be chaperoned, which seemed ridiculous to us. So, Miss Buell would meet Dottie and me at the top of the hill and walk us to and from the dance. We went promptly, since it was mighty nice of her to give up her evening.

Besides the dances, there were two outstanding social events for me that year. They were close together. The senior girl, who was supposed to meet me in Chicago and didn't, was Lois Nelson Boyeson. She and her roommate invited me to come to the dorm to see it and to stay overnight. As a birthday present, I was allowed to go.

It seemed like the height of fun to live among a bunch of friendly girls who ran their own lives, decorated their own rooms, etc. Lights out was at 10 p.m. Then the house mother came in with her flashlight and said, "Be quiet."

I went to sleep early; I slept like a log in those years. One night someone started shaking me and talking. When I managed to get an eye open, Lois said, "Come on, get up." It was still pitch-black night outside, and I was annoyed at being disturbed, and for what? When they finally talked me into getting up, there was a little white baker's cake. It was covered with coconut and had a candle on top! I was 15 years old, and that was my very first birthday cake! But how could I eat in the middle of the night? No way! Lois must have been disappointed after all her carefully made plans.

There was lots of other food, too. All I managed to eat was a bit of cake. Most memorable was the roommate who sat on her bed and ate her cake over the wastebasket. If she got a bite of cake, that was OK; if there was any coconut in it, she spit that into the wastebasket. She hated it, she said, and we giggled over watching her. It was midnight and Lois had to keep reminding us to be quiet or Miss Burnham would show up, and she would be "campused."

The party was a nice idea, but at that time did not appeal to me at all. Lois called herself my "grandmother" and periodically looked me up in school to say, "Hi." She never again asked me up for a night of midnight feasting!

In the class ahead of me was a tall, pretty, smiling girl. Her locker in the hall, where we kept all our school books, was next to mine. Here we visited between classes, to collect books for the next class. She had soft brown hair and lovely ringlets over her shoulders. She wore different colored velvet ribbons around her hair, fastened with pretty silver hairpins. She behaved like a real lady. One day she invited me to come to her house for Sunday dinner. When I come to think of this, it must have been soon after school opened.

I was picked up in an especially nice, big car, and so was Dottie. This girl's name was Gay P., and when I saw her house, I could hardly breathe let alone eat. It was a mansion, and it scared me stiff!

The man, a chauffeur, drove up to a covered door, jumped down and let us out, while Dottie rang the doorbell. We walked down a big long hall, past a music room. Me oh my! There was a most beautiful, curved, wide, wide stairway coming down from a balcony.

I was glad Dottie was along. She chewed her gum and talked away, quite unimpressed.

After a while, we went to the huge dining room and sat down. The only food I remember being served, by waitresses no less, was corn on the cob, another first. What in the world did one do with it? I knew it was incorrect to use one's hands to pick up food from the plate. How else could that be managed? It took a long time to serve everyone. Finally, I saw that the others were going to pick the corn up. I hadn't yet been told that, in this situation, one watches the hostess!

We finally got through dinner without my upsetting anything. Whew! Then Gay took us to the music room where she played the piano. One piece was a dreamy thing played as a waltz. It was called "Carolina Moon," and I thought it was very pretty. Not Dottie, she liked the other one, a fox trot called "Yes Sir, That's my Baby." I thought it was horrible and was surprised that Gay even played it. Dottie even said, "Play it again." Watching her tapping her feet to it, I decided that this was a good example of how different we were.

SUNDAY

Before going on, I will tell you how the usual Sunday was spent at the D.'s. They left me feeling rather bleak and flavored my Sundays for many years. I still am not fond of Sundays, so maybe the effect lingers on.

The breakfasts were always the high point of the day because of the bacon, the grapefruit, and the presence of rolls instead of bread. All three items were food treats, new to me.

After that, gloom seemed to settle in.

I did like going to church, but they talked there of getting rid of one's evils. I couldn't think of any evils I had! They talked of not stealing and of not lying. I didn't steal. I didn't lie. I wasn't jealous of anyone. I didn't swear. It was all very hard to understand! There was lots to do up until church time. So, I just enjoyed going to church because I got out of the house till noon. It was a beautiful church, too.

On the Sunday when I stayed at home, I caught up on work and even sometimes got in a bit of much needed study, if the kids behaved. Sometimes I was asked to wash their little white dog, Rags, who got so dirty. She was cute and fluffy and so white afterwards. I didn't much enjoy the job, nor cleaning up the tub afterwards. The whole room smelled so.

The D.'s sat in chairs, laid on the couch, and quietly read the paper.

It was a day of rest for them, and I'm sure that they really needed it. As a young person, I didn't feel I needed rest. The long afternoon was most often spent with the blinds down. They played that awful, slow, dismal classical music on the radio. While she relaxed on the couch, she most often liked to have her feet softly rubbed. It was boring! The kids never seemed to know what to do with themselves, either.

Sunday was the day I wrote the weekly letter home. I put it out to be mailed on Mr.'s Monday trip to the station. Each time they saw my letter, they questioned what I had written. Often sarcastic remarks were made. As a result, I wrote only about school. I knew I'd look guilty if I wrote anything about them!

THE END OF THE FIRST YEAR

School closing time came after what seemed a very short year. It was a busy and interesting year, and I was quite happy. School wasn't satisfactory because, under those conditions, I couldn't manage to get good grades. But I loved all my classmates!

I adopted the D.'s as my family, as much as I could, and took their idiosyncrasies along with everything else. I almost got the feeling at times that they liked me, and I hung on to that. Their children were quite obedient. They were rather strict with them, and I never saw any physical display of affection. I gave a child a hug once in a while, but the little girl always objected.

That first year basically set the pattern for the next three years.

June came and all the other out-of-town students went home. I felt as though I had lost a lot of friends! I had no money to take the train home. The awful Dust Bowl era had struck there. After leaving home, I never again got any money from Dad. He just didn't have it. In other words, after age fourteen, I was on my own in every way. I never went back home again, except to visit. It became a very remote place. I was completely out of touch with what went on there. There were times, when I saw other families together, that I wished I belonged somewhere to someone!

Really it was lucky for me the D.'s needed someone the year round or I don't know where I'd have gone! Summertime in B.A. was delightful. With all the school pressure off, everything seemed easier. The mornings were filled with work, but there was free time each afternoon. I spent this time with the children, not alone.

About a mile away, there was a small stream which was dammed up to form "The Pond." The Pond was privately owned, but the whole town swam there in the summer, and that's where 4th of July picnics and swim contests were held.

Each afternoon, when there was no rain (it seemed to rain an awful lot here compared with home), the young mothers went to the pond to swim with their children. When the fathers arrived home from the city, they too donned bathing suits for a quick dip and to pick up the family. No one had a second car.

I went swimming with the three children and most often got a ride both ways because of the young one. The D.'s car sat at home because they were so close to the station. Down here many women drove cars, which none did at home.

The pond became quite a social center. By the second year, some sand was dumped on the edge. This cut down on the mud collected on feet and clothes getting into and out of the water.

Lying beside the pond were two huge logs. We were told others were in the bottom of the water. We were told they were there to be aged. They were going to be used as beams in the Cathedral, that beautiful church I attended on Sunday.

After a little perpendicular bank, the water dropped off to unknown depths. I didn't know the first thing about swimming, so I kept right next to the edge when in with the children. Soon the D.'s taught me how to kick my feet and doggy paddle. I never had any time to swim by myself. I stood for hours and hours holding those kids under their middles so they could learn to kick and paddle.

Their parents checked on how they did at quitting time. When the children got blue with the cold, they had to be played with to keep them out of the water for a bit.

My turn came when the parents arrived to pick us up. I only got a five-minute lesson. The only reason they bothered with me was to have someone who could swim to take care of and teach their kids. They made it clear I wasn't there for my own amusement. I wished many times for a half hour all to myself to enjoy the water. Anyway, it was nice to be able to cool off in the hot and unfamiliar weather.

I will state here that never during my stay with the D.'s did I feel sorry for myself. But every so often I had wishes. I wished I could be free to run up the road to visit a friend some afternoon. I wished I didn't have to always hurry so on the way to school. Others seemed to visit on the way.

When I began to get supper ready, Mr. said to plan everything I'd need so that the refrigerator door would be opened only once! This, he said, saved electricity. He caught me sometimes having to open it several times and scolded. I wished I didn't have to worry about it. Years later, when I was trying to understand the source of some of my hang-ups, I came upon this memory. I realized one day, in my own home, that I got a tight feeling every time I went to the refrigerator! I also then came upon many other habits that were subconscious. It came about, I figure, from all the rigid rules learned at that first job.

After growing up with none of this organized living, it was my first training and it "took" completely. There was no other way to follow orders and live there, and I never thought to question any of it. Many habits can be learned at that age in three years. I never once talked back but felt like it a few times toward the end of my stay time. By then I knew something of how other people lived.

I wished for something decent to wear sometimes. By then I'd grown out of all my clothes and became aware of what others wore. Most often we wore skirts and blouses to school. I had only the one skirt I arrived in and no money to have it cleaned.

A story about clothes:

Mrs. D.'s mother came to visit from Detroit at the end of the first year. She saw that I had no clothes, so she said that she'd send a box of her used ones, with perhaps some from her friends. Maybe some would fit or I could make them over. A box arrived but not addressed to me. When Mrs. D. opened it, she kept all the pretty things. They hung in her closet as she had no time to make them over for herself. I was left with almost hopeless stuff.

The next year when her mother visited, she asked enough questions to find out about this. After that, she addressed the boxes to me and created a very uncomfortable situation. Even so, many of her things I tried to redo still had stains on them. I tried to hide these when I wore these clothes by holding my arms glued to my sides, down to my elbows, for shaking hands!

DANCING CLASS

When school opened again, Mrs. P., Gay's mother, offered the whole school a dancing class one night a week. This went on for six weeks. Mrs. P. gave these classes to the school every year as a treat, and they were wonderful, especially for those who hadn't learned to dance before. The class lasted from 7 to 9 p.m. and was known as "Miss Miller's Dancing Class."

I can still see Miss Miller. She was not young, not old. She looked smart in her always-black crepe dress and high heels. She had short black hair, rather close to her head, not fluffed out, with a bend or two of hair that was almost a spit curl.

She was pleasantly authoritative and never wasted words. She lined the girls up on one side of the room and the boys on the other. She would say, "Now slide-together-step, slide-together-step," out there in the middle. First she did it with her back to the girls, for us to follow, then turned around to face us while the boys followed. It was the Box step. When set to music it became a waltz or a fox trot. No one did any other steps at all. Miss Miller always pointed her toe out in such a ladylike way when she demonstrated.

At the last class, there stood a big vase of pink roses. Around each rose was pinned a white slip of paper with a girl's name on it. For the last dance of the evening, each boy chose one of those beautiful flowers, unpinned the name, and danced with the girl. Then he could walk her home.

Guess who got mine? That big handsome blond fellow, Andy, who met me at the station when I arrived in town. I was thrilled, but he wasn't. Going home from school, I walked the same route he did. I always hoped he'd walk with me. I don't know why, outside of the idea. I guess I was scared of him. I couldn't talk, so it was no fun for him.

Next door but one from Andy lived another fellow, in his class at school. He was much shorter, a pleasant fellow, and his name was Keneth Simons. I scarcely noticed him! Most often, if the two of them were together, they sort of walked with me as the path was only wide enough for two. So it was both of them or nothing, and I was not happy about this. They never bothered to walk me all the way home, which made me feel very inferior. Some boys loved walking girls home! Others were polite and walked them home, like it or not.

THE SECOND YEAR

The second year was almost like the first. One new thing was an invitation to join a sorority called the "Alpha Kappa Mu." The dorm girls had one called the "Deka." The AKM was for B.A. settlement high school students. I looked forward very much to joining.

First there was a week of what they called "initiations" that seemed most stupid. Having been told it showed one's good sportsmanship, I put up with it.

Each member in my class had a list of orders to follow. Some of mine were:

> 1. Say "hello" to every boy you see.
> 2. Part your hair in the middle, all week, for school.
> 3. If you go to the football game, take the dog Rags on a leash. (He was a nuisance, along with the kids.)
> 4. Wear two stockings, each a different color.

And there were more. One was to run around the table three times before sitting down. This one was cut out by the D.'s.

Then, on Saturday night, two girls came to collect me for the big trial. By this time, I had to write a paper explaining why I wanted to join the AKM. This must be read aloud. I sweated over it. I hadn't the faintest idea why anyone joined unless it was to have fun. To read it aloud was misery.

But the evening was the best fun. The two girls came with a big cloth as a blindfold. I was led under and around bushes, on the road and off. We walked and walked.

Finally, we came to a door and down steps to a concrete floor. "Stay down on the floor and be quiet." They left. All was quiet as a tomb except for a very loud ticking alarm clock. I stayed there a long time. During this time, I was to think of why I wanted to belong. Every order must be obeyed or we'd be banished from the club. I took all these things seriously.

When the two girls came back, we stooped here and stood up there and went through what seemed, by the sound, like a labyrinth of caves. We ended in a room where we heard other people. There, all kinds of things went on. "Put your right hand into this bucket of worms, now open your mouth and swallow this one." I was most uncertain as to whether or not this was real. A short piece of cooked spaghetti feels like a worm!

At last, the blindfold was taken off. There in a semi-circle sat everyone, with the president of the club in front of a single candle.

Gay P. was president that year. Much later I learned that all this had taken place in the basement of her house.

I certainly enjoyed being initiated more than when next year came along and I had to help initiate someone else. All the girls, as they became members, bought pins. They cost something like $3.50 and I, of course, couldn't buy one but was told I could belong anyway. I'd been a little anxious about that. Gay, one day, said she'd lost hers and had to order a new one and then had found her old one. "Would I like it?" I was happy as could be to have one and wore it always to school. Years later, when I woke up to many things, I decided that had been her nice way of giving me a pin!

The next night there was to be a supper at Francie's house, to welcome all new members. It was a most delightful affair.

I must tell you about Francie. She was adopted by two maiden ladies of the town, the Bostocks, and raised in a big house where they had grown up. She was compactly built, but not fat. She had a round face and short blond hair with bangs across her forehead, like the little kids. She had bright blue eyes and was different. She was fascinated with everything and had funny little pert remarks to make with expressive hands. She was full of ideas and made them work. She was a doer and tackled all sorts of different things. She was unorthodox in a nice way. She splattered up decorations with color combinations that made others shriek. Nowadays they'd be more easily accepted. She said she couldn't draw, but she drew little boxes, connected together. One couldn't miss the person she drew this way! The same went for clothes. She was an outstanding individualist, and everyone was fond of her. She was as cheery as could be, too. She positively bounced around.

When we walked in to supper at Francie's house Sunday night, the big table was all set so prettily, with our names on little place cards. It was most eye-catching because Francie had a salad at each person's place. On a big green lettuce leaf was a pear, with the round side up. On this were little raisin eyes, a red mouth with a chocolate cigarette that was a bit shocking to the chaperone, and I don't know what all. They were very carefully done and attractive.

The AKM had meetings about once a month, usually at recess. I sometimes got to them. The big thing of the year was to be a school dance put on by the AKM. We did the decorating for it, although I can't remember the occasion. At this time dances were held on the third floor of the old Elementary School building, called de Charms Hall. I do remember that our affair was a "Harvest Dance," with corn shocks around the room. Everyone came in barn dance skirts and blouses.

One day Francie showed up at the D.'s and asked what I was going to wear to the dance. She then produced a creation she had made. Such a wonderful thing to do! It was in our club colors: orange cotton, with blue ribbons as drawstrings on the neck and sleeves. It was a costume and made that way, but nevertheless wonderful.

Gay's big brother was going to take me. This was very nice of him, but I felt that I was a terrible dancer, though I was learning.

AFTER A WHILE

During the first couple of years at school, I felt I'd caught up on many things and knew most everyone in town on sight. They were all friendly, wonderful people.

There was very much an order to things. Crops didn't run their lives, nor did the seasons, but the people set their own particular dates.

School opened with everyone back in town. Some parents drove students to school from Pittsburgh or Chicago to save money. Perhaps one or two students from Pittsburgh went home for Christmas holidays, but that was all.

I was the only student from far away who came for four years of high school and didn't go home once during that time. When school ended each June, I went through a short spell of feeling as one must in "no man's land."

After about six weeks of school, when the leaves of beautiful fall colors had about disappeared for the year, there was a town celebration known as "Charter Day." This celebrated the granting of a charter to our private school. All who could, and especially alumni, came back to B.A. to celebrate a couple of days. Most of them stayed in private homes.

Friday morning started with the group collecting at school. All banners presented by each graduating class came out from under their covers. We lined up in double file, headed by the professors in their long black gowns, with colored scarves for their various college degrees. Then we marched to the church.

In the afternoon a football game was played against our favorite opponent, George School. Not being a large school, our few football players worked hard to win. My freshman year, 1929, we finally beat George School. There was great excitement in the town! The score was painted on the road in one place and there was much cheering. We sang all our football songs.

At night a big dance was held for all the town, with the banners hung around the room. By then the Assembly Hall was built, and it seemed so big we'd never fill it up. It seemed almost impossible to decorate it for our club dances.

During the evening all four of the boys and girls clubs collected, one club in each corner of the Assembly Hall. We sang our sorority songs all together. The music of them all blended into one theme and it was a stirring occasion.

The next night was the Charter Day banquet put on by the ladies of the town. School students didn't go to that.

The next fun thing, nothing to do with school, was Halloween. They did not hand goodies out to children. Trick or Treating came along later. There was just a mischief night, and no one knew what might happen. The most unpleasant thing was having windows soaped up. Cutting pumpkins for windows and tables was fun.

Our Mr. D. was grim-looking and stayed close to his front door with a pop gun. The kids were onto him. His front porch had more handfuls of corn thrown on it than any other in town.

Then, in November, came Thanksgiving. It always seemed to come too late, way after harvest time. Down here one could easily relate to the original Thanksgiving because we lived on the East coast where the Pilgrims had landed. Such good things were available here in the fall! So many yards overflowed with their own grapes, berries, all kinds of apples, squash, and pumpkins. All the colored leaves and squashes made it seem that there was an abundance of variety and more than enough for all.

Then came the first snow. So gently it fell and no blizzards afterwards. The little creeks kept right on running. The trees were bare, and often the ground was, too. Some years the snow covered the ground for longer times than others but never for the entire winter, as it did at home.

The creek that was known as the Pennypack, running beside the town, might freeze over for a spell, and most anyone would enjoy turning out for skating.

Sledding was one thing the young people did that was extra much fun. I was allowed to go once or twice each winter, at night. The road that wound up the hill from the station was perfect for sledding. It was fairly steep, with one sharp turn, hence a little, exciting hazard. Half the time we got this far and landed, rolling over and over on the opposite bank. If the corner was negotiated successfully, one went down the hill and over the railroad track to end up on the bridge. Almost everyone brought their sleds. Those without one piled in layers on someone else's. This made it even harder to maneuver the corner, but there was all the more fun and noise! Chances were, all ended up at someone's house for cocoa afterwards.

Christmas came, and I sent big boxes home. Several people had given me old clothes to send. I was hard pressed to find the money for the postage. One year, I received a memorable gift for my family. A very nice, well-to-do lady, who was a patron of the beauty shop, sent down lots of long, soft wool undies. She had bought them for her children, who wouldn't wear them. On top we packed a few sprigs of pine, dime store hard candies sprinkled through, and a bow of red ribbon.

Then came the Christmas holidays and perhaps some of the above-mentioned sledding.

I saw and heard my first talkie. It was *She Couldn't Say No*. I saw about one movie per year.

Easter came, and in no time it seemed school was closing. This meant some people wouldn't be back next year, and yet it had been nice knowing them while we could. Bryn Athyn's college then was so small, maybe 3 or 4 in each class.

Drawing from Reta's high school U.S. History notebook

Back home on the farm
Reta's siblings Bea, Mabel, Ted, Bill, Leslie, Margaret and Irene

Written on back of photo: Reta Evens. Age 16 years. Bryn Athyn, Pa., U.S.A. (She made this evening dress herself) (Pink roses in the background)

The AKM 1930? Reta seated, third from left

Chapter 3

TOWNSPEOPLE

Bryn Athyn was a planned town. It didn't start because it happened to be in a place that grew out of an industry, or because it was convenient to a railway, or any of the usual ways in which a town begins.

In the city of Philadelphia, in the late eighteen hundreds, there was a church founded on the teachings of Emmanuel Swedenborg. Some of the members decided to split off on their own to follow their particular interpretations of Swedenborg's teachings. This group became known as "the Academy." One of their principles was the religious education of children. For this purpose, they founded a distinctive school for educating the young. There were several prime movers in this direction.

The leader was a man of means, and he chose the site for the town. This was Mr. John P., Gay's grandfather. He bought a large amount of land in farm country. At that time, there were only a few old Pennsylvania stone farmhouses in what is now the borough of Bryn Athyn.

N.D. Pendleton was the white haired, dignified, soft-spoken bishop when I came to B.A. His older brother W.F. Pendleton, who was the previous bishop, had died. There was a young bishop (de Charms) who took over after N.D. died.

Reverend Alfred Acton, who was not a bishop yet, taught young men for the ministry. Mr. Louis Pendleton was a gentle, dignified, small old man who was easy to talk to. He walked with a cane. We'd read his book *The Wedding Garment*.

Rev. Enoch Price was a gentle, dignified, old white-haired man who still taught language, I think Latin, at school. I sometimes met him leaving his "four square" dark red stone house each day on the way to school. Mr. Charlie Doering, also a reverend, taught religion but was known primarily for his ability in math. He was the man everyone wrote to if they wished admission to school. He was capable and alert.

The girls' principal, Miss Buell, lived on "The Loop". She had replaced the original one, Miss Alice Grant, who retired only about a year before I came. Miss Grant still lived just behind a big old Inn, since torn down, that was on the point of the loop.

There was a smaller building, an old farm house known as the Inn Annex, where a number of people rented rooms or apartments. This was bought by two very nice ladies. One was the bishop's secretary, Mrs. Rennels. The other, Anna Hamm, was a faithful school teacher for many years. I'm told classes were held there when the town was new.

Around the same loop lived other school teachers, unmarried, who took over the homes their parents had built. One was Miss Margaret Bostock, who adopted Francie and taught 8th grade. I always wished I could have been in her 8th-grade class. She was very enthusiastic and took the children on field trips. I can remember hearing that they went to visit Crystal Cave, and I would have loved to have gone along.

Miss Erna Sellner lived almost across the street from Miss Margaret. They were buddies. She taught more than one generation and upon retiring was still very active at 80.

Miss Lucy Potts was a first-grade teacher, most sweet, soft spoken, and dearly loved by the children. She must have taught three generations and was still alive at 90. (Note: These two wonderful ladies had taught my husband and later taught my children.)

Most Bryn Athyn people at that time lived around The Loop or on Alden Road. There were a few other places, like College Park and Cranchville, with a house or two.

Rev. K.R. Alden was the redheaded principal of the Boys' School and headmaster of the boys' dormitory. He lived there in an apartment but when older moved into a house on The Loop.

Mr. Wilfred Howard was a science teacher. He lived in the big house that was next to the Cathedral.

Old Colonel Wells, whose wife had died, lived in a big shingle house on the spot where Bob Asplundh later lived. He had a mustache and a pointed white goatee. He marched at the head of the 4th of July parades on his horse, kept in his backyard. He was Mrs. Rose's father.

Near him lived Mr. Reginald Brown, who also taught at school. He married one of the Pendleton ladies, a daughter of W.F. They had one daughter, Rosamond, who was a friend of Francie's. She was an outdoor type. When I came, she was a senior.

Rev. Wm. Caldwell lived on Alden Road. He taught second-year religion and was the editor of the *New Church Life* magazine for many years. He also married a Pendleton, one of W.F.'s six or seven lovely daughters, and they had two daughters of their own. The youngest was a pal of Rosamond's, and they had great fun shooting bows and arrows though she was dainty and looked a lady far removed from places like the woods and outdoors. When my husband was a child, he played Robin Hood with these two girls.

Don Rose lived on Alden Road. He had at one time taught at the school but then worked as a columnist for the Philadelphia newspaper known as the *Ledger*. He was well known for his large family of twelve children and his column "Stuff and Nonsense."

Rev. Wm. Whitehead also lived on Alden Road.

Rev. Emil Cronlund lived across the Pike from the school. He preached often in summer but regularly made his living as a chiropodist (foot doctor). While a senior, I went to him a number of times to have corns removed that had been caused by cheap, ill fitting shoes.

Rev. Hugo Odhner lived on top of the hill in a funny tall house on the way from the B.A. Station to what was then the Huntingdon Valley Bank. He was a ponderous man with a Swedish accent and taught first-year religion. His wife had been Constance Waelchli, daughter of the minister whom everyone loved and who visited us out West.

The second year in school, one of my classmates lived with the Odhners. Her name was Olena Fine. Her circumstances were very like mine. Her family lived in Oregon. Her mother had spent a year in B.A. She was of Swiss descent and pioneered West in her day, too. Olena and I discovered she'd lived only 40 miles from us at one time. She seemed to enjoy reminding me in front of others about some of the rough living one did out West. At that time it was embarrassing, but she became a very good friend.

She lived at least a year with the Odhners and "Aunt Connie" Odhner sort of adopted her. Later on, she still visited them from time to time.

THE BIG FAMILIES

Bryn Athyn people had a reputation, locally, of having large families. Heading the list were the Raymond P.'s. These were Gay's parents. They were arduous church members and tireless in their efforts to foster the New Church school.

Harold P. was a brother who owned a fine, big stone house very near Raymond's. He had built a private swimming pool, the only one in the town at that time. Mrs. Harold P. came to the shop to have her hair done. Once or twice, I was invited to take the D.'s children to swim there in the summer. Such pure pleasure!

Bishop W.F. Pendleton's big white colonial house on Alnwick Road, the back side of The Loop, had only daughters living there when I came. There were any number of them. They lived in Southern style and were most gracious ladies. They had only one brother, who looked most elegant when he came to dances in his major's uniform, sword, and white gloves. He died young, soon after I got out of school.

Mr. Charlie Smith lived on The Loop near the old Inn. He also lived a handsome life and had a home full of grown sons, most of whom were married when I came. He took up the offering at Church in long black tails.

Up the same hill as Hugo Odhner was a big stone house where lived the Paul Synnestvedts. He and Harvey Lechner were patent lawyers. He had twelve children who built nice homes. On their land was also a handsome stone building housing a music studio. This family was devoted to music and their concerts were given there.

Mrs. Cara Glenn was a widow who lived up the Pike in a big dark tan stucco house known as Glenhurst. She had had one son, Gerald, who died, leaving a young family. She also had at least six daughters who ran wonderful homes. Everyone loved this family, and Granny Glenn, as she was known, was a mother to many. I knew her well before she died and thought her wonderful, as did everyone else. She did not like people fussing over her when she became feeble in body. She never got feeble in mind! She wished to "wear out, not rust out," to quote her. She was Mrs. Raymond P.'s mother.

When the apples from her small orchard were ripe, she packed them in baskets and took them to those who could use them. The family had quite a time telling her she was too old to drive.

ACTIVITIES

The town back then was very closely knit, and everyone knew everyone else. Growing up in this atmosphere was a wonderful thing. I'm sure it wasn't just youth or idealism that made us think there was good feeling all about.

Friday suppers were held in the Auditorium on the third floor of de Charms Hall. Dances and plays were also held there.

About 1930, the Assembly Hall was built. This, to us, was huge. It was especially good to have bigger gym facilities. Now Friday Suppers and all big social gatherings were held there.

The town was partial to Gilbert & Sullivan, and some prize performances were given. There were a number of good singers; outstanding to me was Mrs. Lucy Waelchli. She could thrill anyone with her portrayal of Katisha in *The Mikado*.

Teaching first-year art and coaching the football team was an outstanding fellow. His name was Fred Finkeldey. He was our gym teacher during winter when calisthenics were in order. He was as lithe as could be and barked out his orders. The kids thought him wonderful.

He produced a most impressive pageant for the Church Assembly. Everyone in school was involved. This was an enormous undertaking, with only a naive and inexperienced group of kids as performers. It was the story of Joseph. Where he collected his setups, etc., I don't know. Probably he did it all himself.

I knew almost nothing then, and I'm sure he wondered where I came from!

I tried out to do an Egyptian dance with some other girls. It was very tricky, with hand movements, standing partly front and hands sideways to resemble the Egyptian pictures. I gave up on that! I couldn't master it.

Next, he put me in the cymbal section to lead a group on stage. My music timing just "isn't," so that idea was given up even faster. In the end I *did* do something useful! I worked on the dancing girls' filmy costumes of white voile and gold with flat girdles. They were handsome, and I wished I could have been one of the dancers.

The procession of Pharaoh, with the wolf head men beside him with tall fans, was very dramatic. Some of the Psalms were sung, and they were beautiful.

When home at 5 o'clock, children often collected in front of the radio to listen to a make-believe series called *Buck Rogers*, the man of the future. Our jets now look for all the world like his dreamed-up ones.

In school we had a music class once a week after Chapel. This was led by Mrs. Bessie Smith. We learned to sing many songs and sometimes practiced church music. It was great fun. All boys and girls attended and gave Mrs. Smith more than she could handle at times. Then the principal, Rev. K.R. Alden, had to sit in and watch the boys to keep order. K.R. also loved singing.

He collected the high school into a "Whittington Chorus." The chorus sang in the balcony at church. The highlight for this group was the caroling on Christmas Eve, no matter what the weather. We tramped from one end of town to the other, and it was the greatest fun. Some years were clear and bright, some snowy, but always this was a big outing for the girls and boys. We sang till we couldn't any more.

Such fun to see all the beautiful decorations and happy people. Bishop de Charms' was a home we always went to. After each stop, we went in for goodies. Most often we sang inside because of the temperature and the long walks between.

The Raymond P.'s gave us huge, fat, and delicious oranges to take home and enjoy. The Harold P.'s had handsome cookies. That was the first place I'd seen and tasted Springerle. When the D.'s asked what we'd had, I said something like dog biscuits. They didn't appeal to me at all.

We also stopped at the Charlie Smiths'. We'd be led into their dining room with a big sparkling chandelier hanging over the large punch bowl. Mr. and Mrs. Smith were jovial hosts, he in his cutaway tails, which gave me the feeling that he lived graciously.

Something outstanding happened to this Whittington chorus. The Philadelphia Orchestra looked for a group to sing part of "Die Meistersinger" for a concert. I believe Stokowski himself came to hear us sing in church. He liked what he heard and sent a young associate conductor out to help train us.

The night before the performance, we went in to the Academy of Music in Philadelphia for a rehearsal with the great man himself. We lined up across the front of the stage and sang a bit for him. I was almost next to him. He suddenly dropped his baton, picked up a pencil, snapped it in two, and, holding the two pieces an inch or two apart, said, "My God, can't you see what it's like when you all breathe at once?" Stunned silence!! We were all awed to pieces anyway and trying to remember to do our very best. No one had mentioned such a problem. Well, we got a good practice in before the big night, and it was all a thrill.

I couldn't say how we sounded. But I can say that with that big orchestra behind us the whole place seemed filled with music, and we gave the performance all we had.

I remember making a long pale pink crepe dress with a blue narrowish velvet ribbon at the waist.

Besides the Charter Day dance, the grown-ups went to a big New Year's dance that was just for fun. The high school students' most exciting bit was they could stay up baby watching or get up and turn on the radio to hear them chime in New Year's at Times Square, New York. We looked forward to being grown up and celebrating New Year's in their fashion.

The strictly alumnae Theta Alpha was going strong and did things for the school. They gave an honorary scholarship and handed out awards. Some of it seemed unfair to me because the awards always went to those who had lots of time to study!

The Women's Guild wasn't as big in those days. I think they ended up taking over some of the duties of Theta Alpha. I knew very little about them then. I was intrigued one day to hear a couple of the ladies discussing how the Guild could deliver some coal to a family in need. "Would they be touchy about it?" Seemed silly to me. If someone was having a hard time, momentarily, how wonderful to be helped out! No one at home would have worried about *that* problem, and I didn't like the sound of it at all. If they had to do that kind of talking about it, I hoped the Guild never had to help *me* out!

Another thing the town had then were hucksters. There were two men who had trucks with boards out the sides and roofs and flaps that they could pull or roll down over their produce bulging out the sides. Lined up along the sides and overflowing inside were all the fruits and vegetables of the season.

Mr. Robinson was one. He was considered a little more upper class and was quite careful about everything. Some said he was a bit more experienced. The other was Frank Pastore, an Italian. He was loquacious and a busy little man. He liked to bargain, too. Stuck in his account book here and there were Bible pictures. He raised young tomato plants that could be bought. Things were sure made easy for people down here. He was a delightful person to know. His eyes sparkled with life.

THE SUMMER OF 1930–31

Winter and summer saw little change for the family I was staying with. Their only change was a week or sometimes two spent at the cabin of his parents at the Delaware Water Gap.

For me, summer was a big change. I felt like the only outside student left in town and, as far as I know, I was. Things were easier because of more work time. I got along fine with the children but didn't feel I was the "governess" sort. Sometimes I felt very bound by them and would have liked to be free.

When I was told we were going to the Gap on a vacation with the family, I was most anxious for the time to come. I don't know whether the D.'s enjoyed it or not. You could never tell with them.

One Saturday morning, with everything packed in the old black Ford, we took off. It was a seventy-five mile car trip. It seemed a long ride, but most all of it was very pretty along the way. They discussed whether to go up the Jersey side or the Pennsylvania. This seemed like a big discussion.

They were the sort that got in the car and drove like the dickens. The only thing they seemed intent on was breaking their own record of last time, or that of some other member of their family. Woe betide any one of the kids who said that he needed to stop!

There was one place we sometimes stopped on the way up. Just as the highway hit the first sight of the Gap, there were a couple of cages on the side of the road with bears in them. The kids begged to stop; so did I. Most often I just kept quiet. It being my first trip and first vacation likely had something to do with their stopping. It was fun to see a real live black bear like we'd seen in books. By this time, I was beginning to believe in books and things people talked about as concrete things that existed somewhere, for sure.

Mr. had told us of how the Delaware River cut a gap through the mountain, so it was exciting to see when we got there. That first sweep through the mountain on its curving road and the scenery there is still a thrill to me.

After a time of following the river on a small road, snuggled at the bottom of the mountain along the base of Blockade Mountain, we turned off to follow a trail of a road. It was steep and turned abruptly back on itself. There was talk of, "Would the car make it? Was the road washed out?" Everyone tensed up and the accelerator was pushed all the way to the floor.

The road was awful! It looped back and forth up the mountain, with rocks to be watched out for. We in the back seat clung to the seat in front as we bounced and lurched up and up this awful, steep mountain. My, it was scary. The trees crowded us on the sides, which helped make us feel safer. If the car slid, at least it couldn't tumble down the mountainside. I wished we'd never have to go down it again. I didn't relish looking to the side to see where we'd been. Looking straight ahead was enough. Best of all would have been to get out and walk.

We came to one stretch of road that was almost level. An iron pipe came out beside the road with water running from it. This was "the spring," and all drinking water was hauled in pails to the cabin from there, which was quite a distance.

On we went until, in front of us, in the midst of the thinning trees, stood something akin to a log cabin and a fort. The turret on one end made it look like a fort. It was built of weather-blackened boards, and it looked lonely. By the back door was a rubbly pile of rocks with weeds growing here and there among them. I was promptly told that perhaps there were copperheads and rattlesnakes here. It was always skirted by everyone.

Right up to the back of the house were lovely, woodsy trees. We walked through these to the "little house."

Across the front of the house was an open porch that looked down on an almost clear grassy patch with blueberry bushes here and there. "Don't ever pick a blueberry without first seeing if a snake is entwined in the bush." They could keep their blueberries!

The place was encircled by the woods. There were no views. It was a wilderness, but a nice one, though the trees were not as pretty as elsewhere nearby.

We all jumped out of the car, staying clear of the rock pile. That side of the house, on ground level, had the kitchen door. There were the grandma and grandpa to greet us. They were polite, not effusive. Both very tall, the grandma always looked very sure of herself and grandpa very stern. They were awe-inspiring.

We walked in the screen door and my sakes! It was worse than back home on the farm! And they *chose* to live this way.

The place they ate in was not a big room, and it was almost completely filled with a bare board table with benches on the sides.

The floor was just earth. How good that felt, barefooted on a hot summer's day.

Adjoining this was the kitchen, with an enormous black iron stove, a table to hold the dish pan, and cupboards of sorts. In the back wall was a slat door that opened into a square hole in the earth. In there were shelves and canned food. The kitchen floor was also earth. By the eating table was a set of stairs going up to the living and sleeping quarters and the porch overlooking the yard.

In the middle was the living room with a fireplace, a rocking chair, and other places to sit down. The most noticeable thing was that the living room floor sagged a bit in the middle. It was covered with layers of straw mats. It all had a pleasant, lived-in feeling. With a fire at night to take off the chill and the lamps lit, it was a cozy place.

On one end was the grandparents' room, a big bedroom with a wood-burning stove. The other end of the living room had several bedrooms and cots. Along the far wall was a door leading up more stairs to the turret room that gave the place that fort appearance. I'm sure this would have been anyone's favorite room.

I cannot remember where we all slept. I know several of their unmarried young sons were in and out. Mostly they were there for weekends, back from college and jobs. Among them was the youngest, that tall, sturdy blond one I liked.

Down the mountain was a place called Karamac Camp. Lying in bed on Friday and Saturday nights, we could hear the dance music drifting up. One piece that became familiar was "I'm Confessing That I Love You." The sons disappeared down there till the wee hours and slept late the next day. They said little if anything about it. I was all ears to hear how much fun it must have been, but those fellows lived to themselves.

Every day we walked down to the river for a swim. They said it was a mile but, especially coming home, it felt like ten. I've never, never liked mountain climbing, and to me the swim wasn't worth it. The water always seemed too cold, and there were warnings about poor swimmers getting caught in the current. I did not enjoy it.

Right near our swim place was a train bridge on a high trestle. Those boys had no fear. They were off roaming the cliffs of the mountains or something else as dangerous. One day, I saw three of them walk out on the bridge and climb to the top of the structure. Standing straight and tall in a row way up there, what did they do but jump into the river below! It was fascinating to see what happened next, even though I was afraid to look. What was so surprising was how they came down so straight, to splash in the river below, and then they bobbed up so fast, just like corks. They would then swim down the current to shoot over the rapids. They all seemed in such strapping good form, and no wonder. I'd have hated to be their mother, but she never seemed to give it a thought.

Grandmother was not given to chit-chat. She was quiet-spoken and I liked her very much, from a distance.

She spent much time down in the kitchen cooking mountainous amounts of plain but delicious food. When enough blueberries were collected (which I came to do often), she baked big, tasty blueberry pies. Old grandfather liked these. For his birthday, a big pie was baked with a partially-used candle from the church alight in the middle.

I felt terribly like a fifth wheel unless I kept busy. I worked all the time there, just like at the D.'s. I set the table and cleared, and everyone helped with dishes.

In the evenings, I could read or go to bed. It was quiet, usually. With grandfather so stern-looking, I went to bed very early. I'd have been in the way otherwise.

The second summer was just about the same. There are three things I remember about that summer.

After supper one evening, I was sitting on the floor watching the fire when grandpa from his height looked down and said, "Boo!" quite suddenly. I'm sure I jumped (if one can jump while sitting) six inches off the floor from fright. But I smiled back and he laughed. From then on, I figured he was human and not so different after all. He was not a talkative person anyway, but a dignified older man.

Their house was about three-quarters of the way up Blockade Mountain. On the top of the mountain was a lake I'd heard the sons speak of. It was bottomless, they said, and they called it "Sun Fish Lake." They sometimes hiked up there for a swim. None of them sat still enough to be interested in fishing. In fact, I'd not seen or heard of fishing as a hobby.

One afternoon, three of them decided to see if they could find the trail up. I was longing to go and see it, too. Grandmother read my thoughts. She suggested I go along. The proposal met with silence. Next, she said I was *going*. Each had a bathing suit and towel rolled up. Her boys did not talk back, but anyone could see they did not want me "for nothing."

They started off at a lope, with me bringing up the rear. That's the way it was the whole hot, dry way. They must have had a good sense of direction. Only once in a while was there the slightest sign of a path.

I hurried to keep up to them, but many times they were out of sight amongst the trees. After feeling a bit lost for a while, the first time this happened, who should come back but the youngest to make sure I'd not lost the way. As soon as he saw I was alright, he hustled back to his brothers. This made me think he was all the nicer and at the same time feel he wouldn't care to have me know this. For a while I almost regretted going but did appreciate the outing so kept to it. I'm sure they hoped I'd give up.

The only thing they'd said the whole way, and that was at the start, was to watch out for rattlesnakes. Glug. Sure enough, about half way up, the only time I saw them all, they were standing around a rattlesnake they'd killed.

By and by we came out of the woods to see a lovely, still lake. It was surrounded by trees, with rocks tumbling down into the water in little spurs. Some of the rocks were pretty big.

They disappeared around one of these to change into their bathing suits. I went the opposite way to find a big one. Every few minutes one of them would holler, "I'm coming around." I'd just get started undressing when they'd holler. Then I'd get dressed again. This went on for a while, then I heard them splashing around. Then I rushed into my bathing suit and did manage a swim. They were way out in the lake and having a grand time.

Going back down the mountain was easier, but I still went it alone. It was the only time I ever saw that lake, and I'd like to see it again. It was so unspoiled.

The other thing that summer which was miserable to my way of thinking had to do with getting food. It happened that there were no young men there during the week and someone had to be errand boy.

They lived on the New Jersey side of the Gap. Down the mountain and across the river on the Pennsylvania side was the town known as Delaware Water Gap. It was a fairly lively little town then and something of a resort. At least there were souvenirs to be bought at a couple of places. I especially wished I could buy one of those little pillows filled with balsam fir needles. They smelled so good.

The town looked very old-fashioned, and absolutely outstanding was a building looking like an old house with a balcony all the way across the front. It was painted gray with white trim. Across the front in big black letters were the words "Rapps Bakery." What they baked was unbelievably good. One could always buy big fat loaves of white bread. These always tasted like they were fresh from the oven. The only other treat we bought was an occasional batch of sticky buns. Many other good things were displayed. I think it was due to this bakery that I had to go more than once. The bread was so good it didn't last.

Grandmother gave me a small change purse with money and a list of food. It was quite an experience to be left with the decisions of what to buy, and I wasn't too easy about it.

Down the mountain I walked, keeping to the road. Rocks and snakes were something I'd as soon not tackle in a shortcut. Then across the long bridge and into the town to look for the stores. I'd have liked time to loiter on my own, but there was no chance of that. It was a long way back. When I'd finished, the bakery was the last stop. They gave me a sticky bun as a snack.

With a big brown paper bag on each arm, it was a mighty weary, long way back. My first stop for rest was when I hit the mountain. That was to rest my arms, not my legs. It got so's I wanted to stop oftener and oftener. When I finally reached the spring and had a drink of the cold water that ran out of the pipe, that was the last stop.

I could tell that the grandmother had worried about me. She'd never say so, but she was right there to meet me when I got back. I sure didn't enjoy going, but I knew she had no one else. I had the feeling that she appreciated my going. It also gave me the feeling I was earning my keep. I didn't get my twenty-five cent allowance when I was up there because "we were on vacation."

There was one spot that was sheer delight, and I was sorry we went only a time or two. As mentioned, the trees came right up to the back of the cabin. Through them, if one could find the way, was a spotty trail, hard to find, that went off at an angle from the house. It went on down the side of the mountain, through some lovely evergreens and clean, clear woods of moss, stones, and ferns. There was rhododendron, too, and mountain laurel. There were cliffs along the way and, beside a rather big one, the path curved around to the base of it. We were in a steep little valley. High above, hemlocks whispered. Down there, there was no sound from the still, quiet trees. At the base of the rock wall was a startlingly clear pool of water, and from it ran a fast little stream known as Dunnfield Creek.

The creek slid over bright moss-covered boulders and splashed into little pools of water. There was a whole series of these before it gurgled, brook-like, over other stones on the way down the mountain. Even so, it all had a hushed tone to it, and the whole beautiful sight seemed almost hidden between two mountains. The sun splashed down only in spots here and there. The first glimpse of it made a lovely memorable picture.

After coming around the corner of the rock, almost in front of us, was a rather small scalloped pool, and *just* below the surface, it seemed, was the bottom. I put a foot down to take a step into it and found myself up to my neck in the most frigid water I've ever been in. I fast climbed out amidst much laughter.

The children were below the pool enjoying the stream, and I joined them in their fun. We sat down on those soft mossy boulders and slid down into what we called "bathtubs," and on down a spell further till the mossy stones were no more. Then back up to try it again. There were a series of small waterfalls above the pool, but I never had the chance to explore them.

MAXINE

The third time the family planned on going to the Gap for a couple of weeks, I found myself left behind. I don't know why, unless it was a matter of space, or perhaps they wanted time to themselves. It was many years before I saw the Gap again.

For those two or three weeks, I was invited to stay at Bishop de Charms' home. Mrs. de Charms was a client at the beauty shop, and no doubt that is where these plans were laid. Mrs. D. needed a rest, I was told. She did work hard and being sociable wasn't her forte. It was wearing for her, to talk while she worked.

I was told about this at the very last minute. Suddenly, with no time to prepare, I found myself in a very fancy house with very important people.

Staying with the de Charms was a young niece of theirs, within a year or so of my age. She was perhaps close to fifteen, I was sixteen. She looked and seemed much older. This was Maxine. She had short jet-black hair and big brown eyes. Her figure looked rather matronly and she had a wonderful, cheery personality. I had not known her at all before this.

Maxine belonged to a big family of jolly, noisy people who lived next door to the de Charms. Her mother fascinated me. She was a big lady, and her eyes rolled when she told you tales of "her day," no matter what they were. "Don't you know?" was a favorite saying of hers, and then she'd roll her eyes heavenward. The dresses she wore were enormously big patterns of bright-colored prints.

Maxine was a lady in every way. She went to live with her aunt because she was unwell with a liver disease. She *never* complained, and the only sign of trouble was the yellow cast to her skin.

I moved in one evening. Maxine and I shared a room that was as pretty as could be. We each had our own twin bed. Such lovely soft beds and fancy things, like silky bedspreads. Upon newly arriving there, we talked into the night, as girls do. She told me to press a finger on her arm. The indentation stayed for ever so long. "See," she said, "that is because I have this liver trouble, and I'm not going to live very long." She never mentioned it again. Maxy and I talked and giggled. She was lots of fun.

In the morning no alarm clock; we just got up when we woke up. Such a delicious luxury! We went downstairs for breakfast, and there sat Bishop de Charms at a rather small round dining room table. It was soft and white, with the cloth way down the sides and set with pretty things. Mrs. de Charms was bustling cheerily in the kitchen cooking bacon. We could have bacon and grapefruit any morning, or a slice of cantaloupe. We went to the kitchen to choose what we would have and to offer help. Then we sat down together. What a wonderful place! The conversation was pleasant. The bishop told little quiet stories and everyone seemed so happy. Mealtime was a treat all around when everyone was together.

Mrs. de Charms gave a dinner party. The table was enlarged with many extra leaves and set with sparkly things. Maxy and I waitressed. Each day we helped with this and that, dusted the living room, but there were no hard and fast, from "minute to minute" jobs.

In a few days the de Charms took off on a trip, and I gathered that this was part of the reason I'd been invited. I was to keep Maxine company while they were away and help her to remember to take her medicine.

We had a wonderful time cooking our own meals, keeping the house tidy, and visiting her mother. Maxy had to avoid eating some things, which I let her worry about, and she was good about this. Her diet didn't seem to restrict us so's one would notice.

We went to bed on time but often talked. It was a gay and carefree time, though we were happy to see the de Charms come back. They told us all about their trip and interesting little things.

All too soon this carefree time was over, and I went back to the household of the D.'s. I came away feeling I knew why everyone liked the bishop so; he was the kindest person I ever met.

Because of my very booked schedule, I saw Maxine only a minute or two at odd times. She sometimes went to school and sometimes to church.

In a few months she did die, and I felt a haunting loss for some time. Her funeral was the first one I ever went to and going to the graveyard was the saddest ordeal. In those days there was often the open grave, and one watched the earth shoveled on after flowers were laid on the casket.

Maxine had told me she hadn't long to live. I did believe her but chose to put it out of my mind as much as possible. When we were having a jolly time, it was hard to believe she lived so comfortably with the idea. Being young and interested in everyhing, time went by so easily.

SCARLET FEVER

One episode that happened at the D.'s left me feeling they were not very kind people at all. Sure, I knew they worked and worried and had very little money. So it was with me. But one day the Mrs. got sick. She often spent extra time up in her bedroom with a headache or was tired. The shades were always down, so I was used to her not feeling good. I felt that she lived in too much gloom. This time she didn't just go up for the afternoon but stayed there, and the next day was no better. I was taking all her meals up on trays. It was so dark in her room I could scarcely see her. This went on for days. Then I woke up one day feeling miserable. She'd begun to feel better but was still in bed.

By the next day, I had a nasty fever and felt too awful to move. Mr. decided to call the doctor, who'd been several times to see Mrs. The doctor was a buddy of theirs; they occasionally visited socially. He lived about six miles away, in Glenside. I never liked him. He was dark, fat, and rather florid. His talk was pretty loose.

When he came, he first spent time upstairs with the Mrs. and then came down to my room. By this time, I was covered with a rash and had a temperature of 102 degrees and a sore throat.

He said I had scarlet fever. I had already had it at home, but he said I'd gotten it again from so much proximity to Mrs. D. The house was always so closed up, too, and I'd spent a lot of time rubbing her back, etc., and had run my legs off doing everything else besides.

I had been there almost two years and was never sick before or after this one time.

The Mr. was annoyed as could be at my being sick and asked, "When can she get out of bed?" "Tomorrow," the doctor said.

I'd been in bed only one day.

So next morning into my room the Mr. came with that tense, screwed-up face and said, "Out of bed and to work." I was covered with a rash and still had a terrible time standing on my feet. He stood there watching me till I was steady, waiting for me to get to the kitchen. My head reeled, and he said, "You've got nothing but a rash."

I think I hated him at that moment for being so inhuman and wished we could change places for an hour or so.

This episode convinced me that they did not care one bit about me as a person but only about the work I could do. It wasn't a good feeling, and I felt they didn't deserve the devotion I had given them. It was the sort of thing that made me begin to realize it is a hard, cruel world. I realized that they needed help and couldn't spare me the time to be sick, but they could at least have spoken kindly! I never felt the same about them again and began to hope the day would come when I could find another way to live.

THE THIRD YEAR IN BRYN ATHYN

Toward the very end of the second school year, I was busy in the kitchen when there was a knock on the back (kitchen) door, late one afternoon. There on the doorstep was an older lady I knew only by sight. She'd just come out of the hair shop. I knew because I'd made her hair appointment. She asked me to step outside and talk with her. I was scared and couldn't imagine why she'd come. She cross-questioned me about the day before.

The day before had been the worst day of my life! I'd wondered about what was going to happen in connection with it and almost trembled thinking about it. It turned out to have far-reaching effects, though I didn't have an inkling then.

That day had been a Tuesday, wash day. Besides that, it had been a gym day, which meant I was away for a time in the afternoon. I came home and made lunch, as well as setting up for the wash lady in the kitchen. Then I read the menu for the day, which had been put in the usual place, on a pad by the telephone. There for dessert was a lemon pie. Most often we had an easy dessert like Jell-O on such a busy day. I worried and rushed to get dishes done, kids' clothes changed, and beds made, but too soon it was time for gym.

When I got home, there was still too much to do: towels from the fresh wash to be folded for the shop and the rest of the ironing. There just wasn't enough time to bake the pie. It usually took me about an hour to bake the crust, make the filling, beat the egg whites, and then broil the meringue. I had never before failed to meet the work schedule. There wasn't time to bake the pie, so I didn't. I tried to explain why, as we sat down to supper. They silently looked at each other. I knew they were mad. A few questions were asked, but it was a miserable meal, trying to answer them. "No, I hadn't dawdled over anything," etc. They quietly left the table, and I noticed she'd taken down the menu. I usually tore it off after supper and put it in the wastebasket.

I was afraid of what the punishment was going to be because it was the first time something had gone wrong. They were most cool next day. Then this woman came to the door asking about the incident. What did this mean?

I found out later that the Mrs. had taken the menu downstairs and had discussed it with her patrons, and I was covered with shame. It so happened this woman became interested and had questioned her as to my work schedule. She was flabbergasted at what all I did. She went on to do something about it, after leaving. I, of course, didn't know all this but feared more trouble was at hand. In a few days, another woman came to knock on the back kitchen door. She, I learned, was president of Theta Alpha, the women's organization of the Church. She asked if I'd like to go to the dorm for the next school year. This was something I'd always thought would be fun. When she asked, the only thought that crossed my mind was the fact that I'd been a failure where I was and that there was nothing else for them to do but send me to the dorm!

I said nothing and wondered about it all the rest of the afternoon. Someone must have talked to the Mrs. the same afternoon; I suspect it was that same Theta Alpha president, Mrs. Doris Alden, who wasn't easily intimidated.

We had another grim supper. As we sat down, the Mr. launched right into the fact that other people had been meddling in their private affairs. He then said if I went to the dorm under these circumstances, I'd be a charity case. Did I want to be on charity? "No," I said, and nothing more was mentioned about it.

So I stayed with them for another year – the third.

MRS. HEATH'S

My life was a busy but, in general, happy life, and time flew by. I felt at home in the town and knew everyone, at least by sight and to say "Hello." To me, everyone past school age was old. Some of the older people stayed home, for example, from things like dances. I was "never going to be like that." Older people were in a world of their own; one never suspected that inside they were very much like oneself. They were all wise, knew what they thought about things, where they were going, and how. At least, so it seemed to me.

The best thing about this year's school was the fact that there was no more Latin. We would have French instead.

Everything was very much like the year before. Junior year in high school is something of an in-between year. Freshmen have everything to learn. Sophomores can look back and see their own beginnings. Joining a girl's club helped me belong. I was aware of the big, important seniors. Would I ever be bright enough to be one?

Junior year was a first chance to see how the class fell as to individuals. The more talented had a chance for offices in the clubs and in the class. Who would have thought any individual that kept alert and interested in many things could climb to such heights?

I was too busy doing the necessary things of living. I didn't even have time to hear what others were doing. They seemed way above me as to their doings and their thoughts. I was still at the stage where the smallest things made a difference to me, like passing one more exam. There was so much to learn in every subject. Where were the guidelines to know just what was important to pursue and remember? I greatly enjoyed the doing part of life, rather than the thinking part.

I could be all-absorbed in waking to find a sunny day, hop happily out of bed, and set to work. Each day held little tidbits of something new, and there was always something to look forward to. Perhaps it was a football game and maybe we'd win. Wouldn't that old dress I'd been given look nice if I cut the sleeves out? Even walking down past Mrs. Heath's on the way home from gym was something to think about. Perhaps we'd stop in and a candy bar would be shared.

Mrs. Heath was rather a dainty little old lady who was a widow. Her children were grown and only one remained at home. He had a very bad heart condition, and the slightest exertion turned him even more bluish purple than he normally was.

We were told Mrs. Heath had been an actress, and in those times it wasn't flattering to have made the stage a vocation. However, Mrs. Heath was very much accepted.

She lived in the third house up South Avenue, the swooping road up the hill from Bryn Athyn Station. One pretty daughter was married and lived in a house near the end of Alden Road. That was where Dottie had come to stay at the beginning of her freshman year. Another of her children was married and lived in Canada. Her next one, Binky by name, had collected a fellow, Arnie Larson, who came to school and with a third musician started a dance band. Binky wasn't much on school, but he loved music, especially jazz. He was more and more sought after for his band.

Mrs. Heath was hard up, so she turned her front room into a candy and ice cream shop. She had whole rows of candy for a penny in big glass jars. Walking home from school that way, some of the girls stopped in for treats. After gym, some of them walked down especially to stop in. Up until now my only attempts at independence were to stop in for a few minutes when invited. It meant a lick of an ice cream cone, or once in a long while an entire cone! No one had freezers then or took ice cream home to keep.

Once I kept a nickel out of my allowance to buy a cone for myself on the way home. The D.'s lived down the hill, so close I couldn't get it all eaten in time. Mrs. D. saw me eating the last of it as I came down the hill. I got a lecture: "Don't we feed you enough? That is no way to squander money."

I was too broke to do it often but did manage to sneak in one or two more cones during the year. I gobbled them up before coming in sight of the house. How can anyone say a stolen sweet is doubly enjoyed? I never found it to be true. Not only was it apt to give me a stomach ache, but I felt guilty for some time after, besides.

Those few ice cream cones were an event in my junior year.

MRS. ROSE

Just after my third year of high school ended, the mother of one of my classmates came to the house to see me. She had a large family; her twelfth child was still a baby. She was a most easygoing person as to her house and clothes but most alert as to keeping abreast of things in every field. She was as pleasant as she could be. This was Mrs. Donald Rose.

She asked if I would like to come and live with her over the summer. I was most perturbed, after what had happened the year before. What would I do for a place to stay during my last year of school? I knew I'd never be able to leave the D.'s and then return. However, I was keen to go to the Roses.

She said it would be all right, she'd talked it over and plans were made. I was to go to the dorm for my senior year when school opened again. I could scarce believe my good fortune. Imagine going to the dorm where everyone seemed to have the greatest times, with friends about all the while! I knew that all the "settlement" girls wished they could sometime stay at the dorm.

I very much looked forward to a summer with the Rose family!

But right now there was supper to get. Mrs. D. came upstairs, after Mrs. Rose had gone, and said her sister and husband would be there for supper, so I got busy. The children were to be fed early, as usual, when they had their occasional guests. I was to sit at the table with them. Never before had I sat at table with their guests. Maybe they considered that I had grown up a little, and it would be a good experience. Being used to eating in the kitchen at such times, the idea didn't make me feel too comfortable. However, I usually took things as they came, the way of most young people.

The table was all set and everything cooked, but the guests hadn't arrived yet. Minutes before, the 6 o'clock train had come and gone, so the Mr. was at home. The swinging kitchen door was always kept shut after supper started cooking (a rule). Suddenly it was swung open by a thunderous looking Mr. He was really mad, and his mouth was all puckered up. Mrs. had stayed away from me. I felt that the atmosphere was cool, but I was completely unprepared for what happened next.

His shoulders jutted forward with his face in front of them. He said, "I hear you are leaving." Mrs. must have just heard that afternoon, like I had, and told him the minute he walked in. No time was wasted in the telling because he came out to the kitchen so quickly after getting home. "Yes," I said. "In that case, you can pack up and get out of here tonight," said he. "After supper dishes," he added a bit later. I felt that I'd done nothing wrong. I hated the thought of having to sit out supper now, and with company to boot.

After three years and an accumulation of everything I ever owned, I wondered how long it would take me to pack. Actually, I had less clothes than when I'd left home.

Then we sat down to supper. It was an experience. The brother-in-law had always been pleasant enough when driving me to and from the occasional babysitting at his house. His wife kept rather aloof, but she had given me a necklace the Christmas before. I wore this every time I went to church or got dressed up. I thought it most kind of her and got the idea from the D.'s that it was partly to make up for my getting nothing from home.

So I expected, with company for supper, the nastiness of leaving would be skirted. It was not to be! Right off they took to laughing and joking about where I was going and how dirty the Roses were. I decidedly got the feeling I was asked to sit down to supper especially so they could make fun of me. I had nothing to say and wouldn't have said it if I had. But plenty of thoughts came crowding in. Mrs. Rose had always looked so cheery and kindly, I was glad I was going there. Their house sounded as if it was full of fun and loving besides children.

This was a terrible let-down ending to three years of what had come to seem like home. It wasn't quite the kind of home I felt I'd like some day! But it had been a good feeling to belong in some one place, and I had learned so much.

With the noisy meal over, washing dishes quietly, I was reminded to be extra quiet doing them with company in the house. Then the Mr. pushed the door open enough to stick his head in. He said I could wait till tomorrow morning to pack up. Knowing him, I could see that this was his way of repenting a little, which made me feel better.

Next morning, I phoned the Roses and a couple of them came over to help me get moved. We had fun all the while.

Of all the people in the world, Mrs. Rose was one of two most special people to me (the other one didn't come along until much later). She was a wonderful person. I don't think I could write down all the changes in my life that summer. I wished I could have lived there from the beginning. Surely my life would have been greatly improved if I had never met the D.'s!

The Roses lived in a big white stucco farm house of the early Pennsylvania type. The stone walls were thick, with wide, cozy windowsills everywhere. These were always filled with a child's sweater, an old pillow, or something soft. Any one of them would be found most comfortable to curl up in to look at a magazine or to watch a bit of life go by outside. The whole house had this comfortable flavor. Don Rose wrote a book about his house, *My Own Four Walls*.

That first morning, my trunk was hauled up the narrow winding stairs to the third floor. There, in a big room, were two big beds. I was to share this room with my classmate Tryn. Up the stairs, before and after the trunk, chattered the young ones. My classmate was the oldest in the family. They were eager to see and to hear all about what was happening. I scarcely knew who were family members and who were not, there were so many other children in and out.

Tryn and I settled down that night to talk, long after lights were out, and so we did many times.

The next morning, early, I was startled awake by a squirrel scampering over our bed. Tryn woke to the commotion and assured me it didn't bite. It belonged to her brother Leon, one year younger than she. It soon disappeared out the open window. Leon had raised the little thing, and he carried it around in his pocket. It might be found curled up in some piece of clothing or helping itself to the peanut butter jar that always sat in the middle of the dining room table.

This was a delightful first glimpse of the Rose household. There was always something happening, and if there wasn't, something was being planned. Kids climbed out of the windows and up the tallest trees.

When swimming at the pond, they'd go leap-frogging off the highest dive, a newly acquired attraction. Tryn and I were free to go swimming on the hottest days, or to stay home on others. This was a time when I tried to improve my swimming from mere doggy paddling to something better.

A square wooden raft had been anchored not far off shore at the pond. The second time I got out to it, after a very strenuous swim, a pal of Leon's decided to play King of the Raft. People were being dumped and pushed in all directions, and I had no chance to get away. The water below was over my head and I was scared to death of being pushed off. I attempted to stand and shout to this fellow that I couldn't swim. He heard not a word, nor paid any attention, and I was pushed off, too. As I fell, the end of my backbone hit a corner of the raft. This injury troubled me for several years. For the rest of that summer, I stayed away from the raft!

The Rose children were artists of one sort or another. Leon would get out his watercolors and splash away on some bit of paper. He painted a picture of the bridge at Paper Mill Station, with the creek running below, on a postcard and gave it to me. He and his pals set up a circus on a big lawn. They welcomed any younger boys who wanted to become part of it. This circus was the beginning of the Bryn Athyn Boys Club. Leon spent some time learning to juggle. First it was one or two balls, and then he added lemons, oranges, and perhaps an apple.

The house was filled with books. Mr. Rose wrote a column for the evening paper. He paced the floor, down in his study below the dining room, more times than he wrote. His column was called "Stuff and Nonsense," and he might write about anything from the latest book to how he liked fruit cake. As a result, there was a constant stream of things that came in the mail, hoping he might mention them in his column. His study was filled with books. I even read one or two for fun. They did not *have* to be credit books! Tryn was enthusiastic about books and music, and some of it rubbed off on me. They had summer season tickets to Robin Hood Dell to hear the Philadelphia Orchestra and guest stars. That was where I heard Jeanette MacDonald. She was a favorite movie star who played the heroine and sang in much enjoyed *Maytime* and *Naughty Marietta*.

Going to Robin Hood Dell on a summer's evening was a lark. We drove. If it was just to hear the orchestra playing, we might take a blanket and sit on the grassy hillside under the trees and stars. If there was a guest performer, we took every advantage of the passes and sat as close to the stage as we could get.

A most memorable occasion was a day spent at a big amusement park downtown. It was Woodside Park. The whole family went to spend the day. There were passes for everything. We got on a "Tumble Bug" that went round and round, and when the ride stopped we yelled, "More." So the man put it through another round. There were photographers who took our pictures. The Rose family surely knew how to enjoy life!

The whole day was spent going through mazes, with the mirrors where we laughed to see a dozen selves in strange shapes. There was the "Crazy House" where the rooms were crooked. Outside of every door was a jet of air that blew our skirts way up. After the first door, Tryn and I were careful.

There were so many things to do and see we couldn't get to them all. We broke up in groups, and I'd hate to have been Mrs. Rose trying to collect her brood to get them home for supper.

Seeing a Merry-Go-Round for the first time was sport. We cared not if we weren't very young. We ate hot dogs several times. All things considered, it was a glorious day! We walked and walked besides and came home very ready for sleep.

Having been to the big amusement park in town and enjoyed it so, mother Rose got coupons for the one nearby, in Willow Grove. What a scary ride a Rolly Coaster was! There was a big white structure called "A Trip Through the Clouds," which burned down not too much later. "A Ride Through the Alps" was a canvas mountain which is still there for all to see. Here the cars glided in and out of the tall mountain. It was dark inside, and one expected any minute to be dashed forward, but all rides in there were smooth.

Then there was a ride called the "Baby Scenic."

I didn't like the "Alps" but was glad to have tried it. When they said that there was another ride, I said, "No." "But this one is the lowest of all," they said. It turned out I was most afraid on it. The Baby Scenic ambled around the Park a bit and went only as high as the trees and down again. It was just too fast a way to climb so high!

In those days, everyone tried to visit Willow Grove a time or two during the summer. Lots of B.A. kids went, and it was a nice family place then. When Mrs. Rose was young, they walked the five miles from Bryn Athyn to hear John Philip Sousa's Band. The bandstand where he played was still there. One could take a boat ride on the pond next to it.

Early in June, soon after I moved in, Mrs. Rose said that the wild strawberries were ripe. How about going on a picnic to pick as many as we could? The Roses had a big old clunker of a car that was tall-looking compared with now. The best strawberries grew up on the top of the old Paper Mill stone quarry. We drove over the bumpy dirt road to the shed, which was Paper Mill Station. Instead of leaving the car there and walking, like most did, she drove right on up into the field. We drove here and there to find the best patches. A bumpy ride, but all the more fun.

Then we'd stop and pick. The berries were surprisingly big, and we came home with quite a few. Wild berries are so tender! They were mostly good for jam because of being so easily squashed. We all ate our fill as we picked. Then a blanket was spread and we had a picnic lunch. We walked around the rim at the top of the quarry and down into its depths. It's a most scenic spot and was a favorite for picnics. From the top one could look down on the Pennypack Creek where it curved and ran over a bit of rapids.

A private home stands on top of the quarry today.

Another time, we all packed up to go pick wild cherries. We found many little dusty backroads in the same area. Sometimes we drove over a grassy field to park the car under an especially good tree. We climbed all over the car then, to reach the cherries. It was fun, too, choosing the right spot for the picnic. I loved picnics! It seemed wonderful to be able to take such good things to eat to such lovely places, and I sure got a "bang" out of it.

Mrs. Rose never said anything about work, but I was sure she'd asked me partly to help, as she had so many children. When I asked her what she wished me to do as soon as I arrived, she said, "Oh, help out." This left me a little uncertain as she seemed to be all over the place. She was not very definite about my "duties." I helped to prepare meals and set the table. There were no hard and fast rules about any schedules.

I was quite fascinated with her food buying from the huckster selling vegetables. She bought such small amounts of this and that. She only bought a pound of spinach, for example. One day I asked her why, and she said, "Well, not many children like spinach," so she bought a bit for those who did. These were the first children I had known who were given a choice as to what they wanted to eat.

There were always bananas in abundance, on top of the refrigerator or in the back kitchen. There were also bottles and bottles of milk standing on the cool cement floor. There was so much milk they could never drink it all. In the middle of play, a child might rush in and have a banana or a drink of milk. He might even have a piece of bread, with the ever present peanut butter on the table.

Some of the younger ones didn't stay at the table long at lunch time. One, Stanley, often slid down out of his chair and under the table. He would be off doing his thing, having eaten little or nothing. Figuring his mother hadn't noticed, I sat next to him a few times to see if I couldn't keep him at the table long enough to eat. As soon as Stanley began to slither under the table, I'd hang on to him by his belt. We had several quiet, desperate struggles until he finally squawked one time. His mother said, "Never mind, he eats when he's hungry." So he was freed to do as he pleased! He was a very skinny fellow, but then none of them were plump! Tryn ate circles around me and stayed slim, while I was getting much too plump.

One morning, I decided I'd clean the dining room. The sideboard was piled high and there were other things around. I set to work with a will, trying to decide where to put things and sweeping as I went. By the end of the morning, I had given up! I had bothered Mrs. Rose a number of times. "Where does this belong? Or that"? As soon as I cleared a bare space, some child came in with a treasure to fill it up.

The only other big attempt I made was to try the same procedure on the living room. In the corner by the living room door was a bookcase and below it a radio. In front of this was a big easy chair, sometimes facing out, sometimes turned about facing the corner and the radio. The radio played much of the time; someone or other turned it on. Mr. Rose had said it would help his electric bills if someone remembered to turn the lights off some of the time. I figured that it was the same with the radio. I often asked, and when no one responded, I turned it off. The noise just added to the bustle and rumpus.

In this same radio corner an ironing board stood, most of the time. The big easy chair usually overflowed with clean wash. With such a large family, there were mountainous amounts of wash. Washing went on almost every day of the week. There were no such things as automatic washers. This meant that there were heaps and armfuls of ironing. It was impossible to keep up.

The day I tried to clean the living room, I'd reached over the chair that was facing the radio and turned it off, then went to the kitchen to get a broom. When I came back, the radio was booming again. While reaching over the chair, I said loudly, "Who turned on this radio again?" (I was feeling very much at home.) With that, all six feet of Mr. Rose arose out of the chair. "I did," he said. That ended that! He'd no doubt been there, amidst all the ironing, the first time I'd turned it off.

So, I stopped my well-intentioned attempts to clean up and learned the joy of their happy, easy-going way of doing things.

Mrs. Rose kept an eye out for specials in the department stores. Everyone went to the city to shop; there was nothing in the suburbs then but food stores. After seeing an ad in the paper, she'd be off to town. Every store had marvelous bargain basements where hours could be spent. Then there was always Grants, a glorified five and dime with wonderful bargains.

She came home with her arms loaded and shopping bags bulging, having spent a very few dollars. There might be a couple of pairs of Keds, a blouse or two in whatever size was a good buy, and so on. There was always someone the right size to fit anything she might buy. She usually brought home several pieces of cloth for dresses for the girls. Grants was where she bought the remnants as best buys for the price. She bought me one or two remnants, knowing that I'd need more clothes at the dorm.

She might arrive home at 3 o'clock in the afternoon. Then she would be inspired to get one of the pieces sewed up. Out came the scissors and patterns of sorts, and by nighttime she'd have a dress made. I never saw anyone sew so fast in my life! She only had a little Wilcox & Gibbs chain stitch treadle machine.

Sometimes the dresses turned out fancier than at other times, but her girls were always happy with the outcome.

One day Tryn and I went to town. Since I needed an evening dress, I looked over the materials at Grants. There was some filmy blue rayon fabric (there was no nylon then). Blue was my favorite color. It had darker blue roses printed on it. There were touches of peach color in the centers of the roses. So I bought some peach colored material for trim. Finally, I bought blue satin, at nineteen cents a yard, for a slip.

I came home and set right to work making what was to be a beautiful evening dress. I could just see it! It turned out to involve an untold amount of work. The thin sleazy rayon was no sooner cut out than it frayed so badly that the edges all had to be whipped by hand.

Mrs. Rose willingly offered to help me at every

stage. In fact, this was the only thing that troubled me that summer. I came home one day to find her sewing on my dress. I wanted to make it all myself very carefully but didn't want to hurt her feelings. She was so willing to help, and I appreciated the idea. I ended up hiding the dress when I wasn't at home. When it was finished, I didn't like the way it looked. It did *feel* elegant! The material was so smooth and silky to the touch, and the dress slid so smoothly over the slip.

One thing that impressed me very much with Mrs. Rose was her everyday dealings with her children. She could scold briefly in a firm voice, but this seldom happened. She spent much more time comforting them with a big hug. No matter how busy she was, there was always time to listen to a tale of woe. The children all seemed like such good children. Her method worked! The children were usually happy and didn't waste much of their mother's time when a problem came up. A bruised knee got the same sort of treatment. Maybe a Band Aid was applied, needed or not, and she was always ready with a hug. Even *I* took advantage of that sometimes!

One day, Mr. Rose came home and said that famous movie star Leslie Howard was coming for tea next Sunday. I couldn't believe it. We'd seen him in many movies. Our favorite one was *Smilin' Through* with Norma Shearer. I saw this the following year at the dorm. Several couples went to see it, cried and cried, and thought it was wonderful. It was about a young couple in love, and the girl dies on her wedding day. The hero sat in his garden and she'd appear to him in dreamy form. In the end, he dies an old man and she appears to meet him.

Mr. Howard spoke softly, with an English accent, and looked just like he did in his movies. Mr. Rose had come from England, too. I didn't think Mr. Howard at all good looking in the movies, but he had a charm and seemed *such* a gentleman!

Mr. Rose's hobby was his garden. He had transformed the hillside behind his house with beautiful walks and terraces. There were footprints of his children in cement and all sorts of little odds and ends of family history embedded there. One spot was where the second mortgage on the house was buried. There were many kinds of flowers, with roses predominating. It could have been more beautiful but was always in a state of change. There was even an arbor! The junk left around by the children didn't improve things.

Mr. Rose said the garden must be tidy for the visitor, and everyone was commandeered to help. Tea was to be served there. We managed to keep it pretty tidy for the big day. The house was worked on but didn't fare as well. I know I wondered what a famous person would think, walking in on the turmoil of this carefree household.

The day came, and Mr. Rose was (or seemed) as easy as pie about the whole thing. He let all of us get a good look at the famous man and be there to listen to the talk. He toured him around the garden but had to have tea indoors because of the weather. Tryn and I served tea. I didn't feel it was a most successful occasion, but we young ones were awed.

I met another well-known movie star with the Roses. First we'd seen her movie with Dick Powell, and then Mr. Rose took us backstage to shake hands with Joan Blondell. She had appeared between shows. This was at a theater at about 10th and Market Streets, called the Earle. It screened movies but had acts between them, and quite often a star would appear after one of his own shows.

I was disillusioned.

She didn't fit my idea of beautiful. Up close one saw how all that makeup was used to make her skin seem smooth. She looked sort of brassy. Her blonde hair wasn't really blonde. At the part, you could see a half inch of nondescript brown. Dyed hair then was something one didn't do! Although we did know that some movie stars did.

She shook hands willingly enough and let us pat the Persian cat she held in her arms. It was fun to be able to say we'd met her.

STEEL PIER

One of the most adventurous happenings of the summer at the Roses was a trip to Atlantic City.

Mr. Rose had passes to the Steel Pier there. Atlantic City was a big, noisy summer resort even then, but still possible. There were several Piers on the Boardwalk, but none was as big and exciting as

Steel Pier. I'd heard many stories from others who had been there and all the wonders they saw.

I felt torn every which way, there was so much to see and do. We arrived to see the foaming waves on the beach and all the people on holiday. The salty air and the whole feeling of the place gave one shivers of delight. The buildings seemed to sparkle with white sunlight. It was my second glimpse of the ocean in my life. I'd have been perfectly happy to spend the day on the beach!

In addition to all the regular things that went on, there was one special event booked. The one we went to see was a dance marathon. We'd read about it in the papers. I don't know how many of us went, but a goodly number of the family.

Onto the Pier we went because Mr. Rose wanted to see the marathon right away. Really it was an awful sight. It had been going on for days, and those couples still dancing looked like they hadn't the slightest bit of energy left. In almost every case, one of the two looked to be asleep while the other dragged him about. Their arms were limp and their heads leaned on shoulders, or they just slumped together. Their clothes and hair looked unkempt. Sometimes we'd see one shaking the other awake to take over for a while. Sometimes the one awake hit at the other with a wet cloth. All sorts of things were done to keep going.

After one miserable look, I was not a bit interested. Mr. Rose, being a newspaperman, was. We stopped back a couple of times during the day, and a large number had dropped out even in that short time. The competition was winding down. I think Mr. Rose hoped to see the end.

Tryn and I wanted to see some of the other sights. There were magic shows, all sorts of booths with games of skill, pink fluff spun candy for sale, popcorn stands with their smell that permeates, and dozens of junk things to buy.

On the way down to the shore we'd seen big billboards (many, many lined the roads then) showing the diving white horses at the end of the Pier. A fancy-looking circus lady was pictured on their backs.

Yes, we had passes to that show, too. We sat in the open air with tense, bated breath as each act was announced. After various other activities, the diving horse came last. From way up high, a beautiful white horse plunged into the sea. A circus lady wearing tights was on his back. I wanted to look, and I didn't want to. I felt so sorry for the poor horse and was sure he must be dreadfully frightened each time. After his plunge, it was good to see him swim to shore. I didn't want to see it again but was curious enough to see if it could really happen the first time.

It had certainly been a day full of experiences. I can't say that it was a *perfect* day because the dancers were an unhappy sight. I'd rather have had a swim and seen the crowds and shops.

So, summer came to an end. It had been such a delightful one! I felt that I would cheerfully live the rest of my life as a Rose! To this day, I love Mrs. Rose. She is a most wonderful woman, full of cheeriness and inspiration.

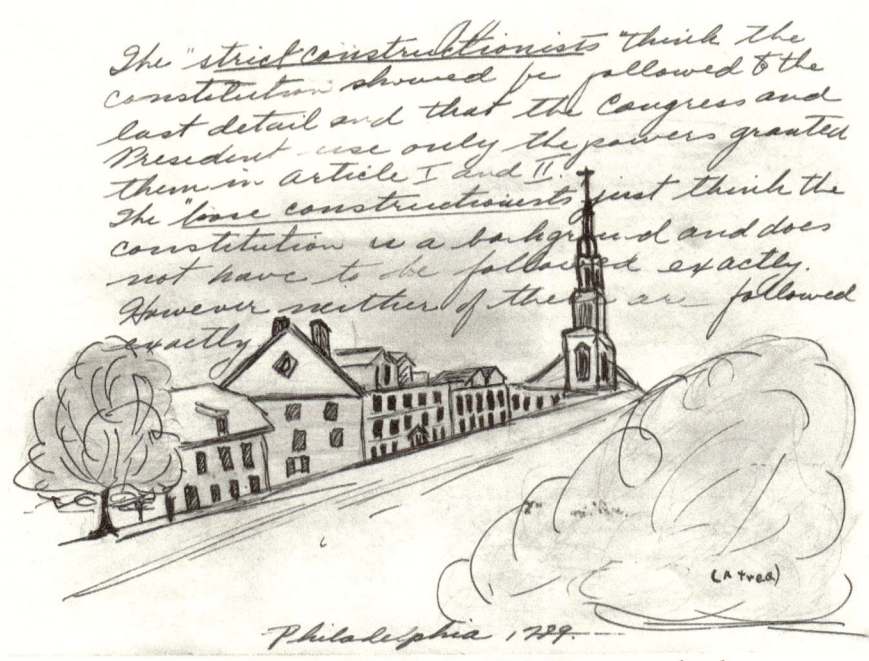

Drawing from Reta's high school U.S. History notebook

Reta with D. kids at the pool. Bryn Athyn Cathedral in the background.

# Chapter 4

SENIOR YEAR IN THE DORM

I was sure I'd never become an exalted senior! When I did, I can assure you I never once felt old and important. While I was a freshman, I'd watched two particular seniors. They seemed to be everywhere! They gave advice, lined others up on the stairs for morning chapel, and sh-shushed everyone. These same two wrote a little booklet with a bright red cover called "A Word to the Wise." In it were many bits of information for a newcomer to high school. They collected groups on the sidelines at football games and led them in the football songs: "Bala Boola," "B.A. Will Shine Tonight," etc. There was a senior class president, and seniors were the presidents of the clubs and of the factores, a liaison group between students and teachers. I held no office.

    The school part of senior year was overshadowed by the fact that I'd moved into the dorm. I had looked forward to this, and I was not disappointed! I enjoyed every bit of it, the whole year. Other kids complained about the rules. I had no trouble with them. These were much easier rules than the ones I had lived with for three years.

    There was only one difficulty that ever arose in connection with the dorm rules. That had to do with invitations from settlement girls to the movies. If we didn't leave early enough, the movie might not be through in time. At least once we had to leave before the end of the show.

Kids had fussed about the food at the Bean Hall. I enjoyed it. I didn't have to cook it! In fact, I got quite plump on it, much too much so to be happy with myself.

It was a crowded, jam-packed year of the best things. My marks weren't very good, but I sure tried hard!

I was given the fullest possible scholarship, which involved waitressing at the Dining Hall. That made me very happy as I considered it the best kind of work. There would be the fun of working with others, though the hours were long. I felt sorry for those who dusted classrooms and cleaned the dorm.

I paid not a cent for school and realized sometime later that some organization or individual had quietly paid. I know not who.

The first things of note about the dorm were the bells. We lived by bells. There was one to awaken, get going, and be there, morning, noon, supper, and bedtime. I'd not be surprised if there were some extras. The same sort of bells rang between classes at school, so their sound was nothing new.

It is hard to write concisely about a year with so many experiences, feelings, thoughts, and reflections. Certainly it was a time when pure happiness hung by a slender thread. Something as small as a glance or a smile would make all the difference. A passing grade on an exam in Human Body, or even money to buy a new pair of silk stockings so another run wouldn't have to be mended in the old ones, mattered very much.

Most of school was over, what lay ahead next year? One remembered seeing the tear or two shed at graduation last year at the parting of friends. When would they see each other again? Life at that age is a very dramatic affair. I never worried about it much but enjoyed the time until that moment came. When it did come, it seemed so sudden.

When I moved into the dorm, I had a roommate from Glenview who was a sophomore. Her name was Aileen King. She had curly black hair, brown eyes, and was a peppy girl. It was her first year in B.A. She had lovely clothes. Among them was a pretty, long pink taffeta evening dress she especially liked.

Most seniors had rooms to themselves, but I roomed with her.

After everyone had arrived, she was moved out, but to all intents and escapades she stayed a roommate. She crept in to sleep and talk after lights out, and she did end up the year back again to stay. She did Bean Hall work, too, as did her brother.

We were up and over to the Bean Hall at 6:30 a.m., setting the table for the rush after seven. Waitresses were the earliest up each day. Breakfast was often skipped by others for a few more minutes of sleep. The minute classes were over at noon, we could be seen hurrying to set up for the noon meal and, of course, again at supper.

In the kitchen, Bert, a black man with a broad smile and big white chef's hat that bloomed up and out over his head, would be busy cooking bacon and making toast. He had cooked for the generation before and did so for the one after us. Everyone liked him. He cheered the ones who were down and whispered little tales about our boyfriends. He was everyone's buddy.

We carried plates to the warming ovens, saw that everything was in order, and waited on table. After a meal, there were dishes to be stacked on carts and pushed to the pantry. There were two boys to scrape and stack the wooden racks for the big steamy dishwasher. Such a clatter. So the week went, but Saturday was a different story. From early morning till noon we six waitresses and the two boys swept, counted linen, polished silver, and even polished the brass doorknobs on the doors into the building.

For breakfast and lunch, big wooden doors were slid shut in the middle of the room. Girls then ate on one side, boys on the other. Before a football game, the team was fed tea and toast early. With the boys eating alone, we'd hear all kinds of racket on their side.

The dining hall mistress was a dear little white-haired lady, Miss Vida Gyllenhaal. We had to be quiet to hear her speak! If the boys would be good for anyone, they would be for her.

At suppertime we all ate together, and the girls primped to look their best with high heels and Sunday best dresses. Miss Vida posted a monthly chart showing who sat at what table. There was always a rush to read it and much discussion.

I liked the two tall fellows who worked scholarship at the Bean Hall. They were buddies.

From the first night on, we roommates had fun doing or planning. My room was the corner front one nearest Alden Road. The window was just above the anchor iron fence that surrounded the yard in back of the dorm. No screen was on the window.

The lights were out and we were talking quietly so the housemother wouldn't hear. Suddenly something came whirring into our room through the window and landed with a thump in the middle of the floor! I let out a frightened squawk. Aileen said, "sh-sh-sh"! Before we knew it, there were footsteps down the hall and our door opened. There stood Miss Dorothy Burnham (the housemother) with her miserable flashlight.

"What's going on here?" she said sternly.

Aileen quickly popped out with, "Oh, Reta was having a nightmare." I'm sure Miss Burnham had expected us to be in the same bed, giggling and laughing. As it was, I was over there in my own bed snuggled down. Aileen had quickly removed the evidence. She was a quick thinker. Miss Burnham saw nothing amiss but looked a bit skeptical and quietly left. She could certainly get around fast, we thought, for one of her age. She was so old, we thought: about forty-five!

After Miss Burnham's footsteps faded away, Aileen and I quietly met in the clothes closet and turned on the light. In her hand she held a nice bouquet of flowers tied in a bunch with a note attached. Some boy had discovered where her room was, and that's how it went for her. She was as popular as could be with both girls and boys. If she went for a walk and some boys tagged along, then I must be included. The boys were always after her.

I had other girlfriends who walked six feet ahead when the boys showed up and "get lost" couldn't have been more evident if it had been said.

One night we found our room in a shambles when we came back from supper. The beds were made up as pie beds, as we discovered later. We got everything squared away, and I remember feeling rather disgusted and wondering who had done such a thing.

There was so little time between getting back from supper and worship. After that there was study hour, which was actually an hour and a half. That left only a half hour for baths, ironing, and anything else that needed doing. I always tried to put my awful straight hair up each night before study hour. On that night, I couldn't find my bobby pins anywhere in the mess! So I was grumbling around and picking up furiously when in came a couple of girls with blindfolds!

They took us down to the sitting rooms and back laundry. This was dorm initiations. I straightened up quickly so's not to be labeled a poor sport! We had to step on peeled grapes in our bare feet and do similar horrifying things. It ended with a friendly chat and welcome before study time.

It took some doing to get our room back in order. We crept about after lights out to do some of it. At the time I felt the whole thing was something we could have done without.

The school year was 1932–33. There were only about nine girls living on the first floor of the dorm, which was the high school area. Some seniors had come back for college, and a number of new people had come to school. Some of these were special students, those who took half senior classes and half college, and all of them lived upstairs. We never went up there.

I had learned how to set waves in a girl's hair, holding it with bobby pins while drying. Several students came to have theirs done once a week. A rich one paid 5 cents, the rest paid nothing; they were as poor as I was.

Everyone on our floor was miserably hard up, except one girl who had everything. She had piles of clothes that had been especially made for her. These, we felt, lacked style. She was the only one who sent her laundry home to get back clean clothes. Along with them came goodies tucked here and there, which she hoarded.

Dorm kids are perpetually starved. If anyone else happened to get cookies from home, they were shared with all. "Miss Everything" liked me enough to share with me once in a while, but I never enjoyed the stuff no matter how good it was. She was the only dorm student who did not do scholarship work. The housemother seemed partial to her. She never seemed to get caught when she stuffed a pillow in her transom and stayed up late to study. We mumbled about how unfair this was when the rest of us had our own washing, ironing, sewing, and scholarship work. We always got caught if we stayed up late. However, we rather pitied her because she was not "one of us."

There was another girl who claimed she had "blue blood" and stayed a bit aloof. When I asked her "How come?" she said there was a Count in her ancestry. She made the mistake of saying this to the group, and no one let her forget it for a while.

Olena was another of my friends. She used to yodel in the bathtub! Her mother was Swiss. Her family had been pioneers, going West in covered wagons all the way to Oregon. We could never persuade Olena to yodel any other place. She, like all of us, was too self conscious, so when we heard her we'd all stop in our tracks to listen.

One of the best feasts we ever had was the day her Aunt Connie Odhner sent a cardboard box as a birthday present to Olena. We all met on the third floor (attic) at midnight sharp. In the box was a whole roasted stuffed chicken and all the trimmings. There were lots of pickles, which everyone seemed to like, especially the dill. I didn't like these. There was even a birthday cake.

One girl from Glenview was really different. She was rather fun, but we didn't know quite what to make of her. She was certainly interesting, even though the housemother found her difficult. She hated to clean her room so had regular punishments. She maintained that "No one, but no one had the right to snoop in her closet." She stuffed everything into it. During inspection this would all come tumbling out. Miss Burnham couldn't even open the door to leave the room without picking some of it up.

The girl fixed up a number of booby traps. One time she used a big box of fine Lux flakes. The box was tied by a string so that opening the closet door would dump the box on the opener. She made the mistake of forgetting about this trap. She had to rush back to her bedroom after breakfast once, and she, herself, got the soap flakes!

This girl never had a bid to a dance in her life, so hated to go. The rule was that everyone went to dances. She climbed into bed the first time, at the last minute, and said she was sick. Miss Burnham didn't have time to investigate, so she got away with it. She might make a big show of going out the front door, only to sneak around and come in the back door to her room. By the time this was discovered, it was too late to make her go.

We all looked around for pictures or something to decorate our rooms. None of us felt we could spend the money. One day this girl asked a couple of us into her room to see what she was going to do. It looked a mess. There were buckets of stuff and newspapers spread around. She was going to make masks of our faces to hang around her room. "Who would volunteer first?"

Someone else spoke up. I didn't want to be first. Olena volunteered and was told to lie on the bed. A handful of gray wet stuff from a bucket was scooped up and patted on the lower part of Olena's face. It was plaster of paris. Of course we were all giggling around, and pretty soon Olena said, "But how am I going to breathe?" So the other gal got a pencil and made two holes for her nostrils. Olena complained a bit about it stinging her face, and much more before she was through.

The procedure went on, Olena shut her eyes, and before long her whole face was covered. The other gal made soothing noises while we all asked questions like, "Are you sure you'll be able to get it off?" At this stage we were sitting around waiting for the plaster to dry enough so it could be taken off. It was a pretty healthy coating of plaster, not a thin layer.

After a while, Olena got a bit impatient and decided she'd lift off one side, although the plaster wasn't dry yet. Soon we saw her kicking her feet in the air and squealing, "My eyelashes are stuck!" With both hands she was pulling at the thing. Thank goodness it wasn't really set! She managed to come through the crisis missing a few eyelashes but with her eyelids still intact! Well, the rest of us were somewhat shaken and not about to volunteer, so that ended that.

That evening, we were asked back to see the finished product. She had dried out the mask, painted the inside with black paint, and poured plaster into that mold. When she finally got the mold broken away, there was Olena's face looking rather mottled and streaked with black paint. It wasn't so easy to tell just whose face it was!

Before long she asked for volunteers again. She said that she had thought of a better method. She bought lots and lots of Vaseline to smear over our faces first. Olena egged me on, saying, "Oh come on," so I timorously volunteered. I only lost one or two eyelashes, and the cast of my face turned out to be white. She had used the Vaseline on the mold, too, instead of the black paint. No one else wanted to try it, so she made one of herself. Thus she had three casts, objects of art, to hang on her wall. She called it her "Gallery."

In the gals' sitting room downstairs was a radio of sorts. We hardly ever spent any time there. For some reason it seemed like a cold room. We did have evening worship there. One or two of us might collect at odd moments, listen to the radio, and try to pick out the words of popular songs. Bing Crosby was becoming a very popular singer. "Night and Day" was a good song, and the new "Star Dust" was chosen by several couples as their theme song.

Of course everyone looked forward to weekends and perhaps a fun date, maybe two. The rules allowed only one date with the same boy on a weekend. Naturally that was easy to get around. On the usual date, the couple went for a walk. The P.'s woods were very pretty; they even had big patches planted, and woods then weren't full of honeysuckle and poison ivy.

Dorm rules were that "three couples could go together." Naturally we tried to arrange a congenial group. The three couple part created problems. So often it was hard to find a third couple wanting to go on the same walk, but we managed. Part of the difficulty was that dorm boys often dated settlement girls, perhaps so they could go to their houses.

Anyhow, all three dates would leave the dorm together, as required. As soon as they were out of sight, they'd shift couples. They often went down the Quarry Road, which is now Harold P.'s driveway. They would walk along the railroad track and up to the Quarry itself where there were all kinds of ledges and views. It was pretty, especially in spring and fall. We had our AKM picnic there.

I always stayed with the date I left the dorm with. I remember one nice date in May with a very special fellow. I had just made a pale green soft fabric suit and had worn it to church that morning. Sunday afternoon was always walking time. I'd been downtown to Philadelphia that Saturday. Because there'd been no time to make a blouse, I had bought a white organdy one in a bargain store on Market Street. I wore it to Church and discovered that it had a number of holes in it, on the folds. This organdy was really cheap material. The blouse had been displayed in a sunny window and was "shop worn." Well, when it came to the walk that afternoon, there was nothing else to wear. It was a warm day, but I couldn't take my jacket off!

I had also bought a pair of white and black saddle shoes because that's what that "special fellow" wore. By the time we reached home there were big blisters on my heels. I bought cheap shoes, which fit abominably. I had to have corns removed every six months.

At Christmastime, a big basket of fruit arrived at the dorm from the P.'s. Theta Alpha gave Aileen and me $5, which was wonderful. Everyone went caroling. We got all our clothes washed and ironed and mended. We skated and visited in town and kids came to the dorm to visit.

Three or four couples went to the movies and saw *Smilin' Through* with Norma Shearer. Such a sad movie. We also went to a movie during spring vacation. I didn't sit with "you-know-who," but I talked with him about the movie afterward. The show was *One Night of Love* with Grace Moore. Anyhow, she sang some classical music, and "he" told me how wonderful it was to know and like such music. I hadn't thought it was anything great, but he'd been thrilled by the way she sang.

He told me he liked a piece called "Schubert's Serenade." I quickly arranged to hear it and decided it had to be a favorite piece. Maybe it's considered only semi-classical but, for me, it was a step in the right direction. He also liked to read and wrote wonderful short stories. He'd been reading Jeffrey Farnol so, as soon as summer came, I read Farnol, too.

SANDWICHES

The year before, two girls had made and sold sandwiches to both boys and girls at recess. The boys had school in the other half of the building. Between the boys' area and the girls' was a very thin frosted glass partition, one section of which turned like a revolving door. This was at the end of the main hall where our book lockers were located. At recess, boys and girls converged on this door to buy sandwiches. The principals kept an eye out to be sure socializing wasn't overdone. Notes were passed back and forth here, too, especially at bid time for dances. Note-passing was frowned on at other times.

Olena and another dorm senior had been smart enough to think of the sandwich business this year, and they got first dibs. Fortunately for me, the other girl's marks started slipping, so the privilege was taken away from her. I was given the chance to share the sandwich concession. Without that income I don't know how I'd ever have managed to get the barest necessities. Once or twice in the year I had a 50 cent baby watching job.

It was lots of work, but only rarely did we chafe under it. The minute the last lunch plate was put away in the cupboards, Olena and I were off to the Valley, come rain or shine, every day of the school year, to buy the sandwich makings at the American store. We started the year off with two loaves of bread, but before long were up to five "because we made them so good." We also varied them from day to day. Every slice was buttered. Each had lettuce and mayonnaise and cheese or meat.

We had deviled eggs, the most work of all, but very popular. We also had lettuce, peanut butter and pickles, as well as other variations. After shopping we stored the food at the Bean Hall. Miss Vida most kindly allowed this, as long as we were tidy and did it without interfering with other routines.

By 6 a.m. at the latest, we were at the Bean Hall hurriedly making sandwiches before getting to our breakfast work. Each one had to be wrapped in wax paper. After a couple of months had gone by, we learned every shortcut and developed a very efficient assembly line for making them.

We sold them for 5 cents apiece. The boys were the worst at paying up, so there was a day of reckoning about every two weeks for charge customers. Rev. Alden, their principal, pinned up pleading notes for us. One time it read, "Pay up, they need shoes," which was a fact, and we were paid in record time.

We cleared as much as $2.50 in a good week. It was glorious to have a little money and to feel independent.

One day a salesman showed up at the dorm. He sold dresses that were like jumpers but were all one piece. The blouse part was plaid and the rest a solid color. All had brass buttons on the front. They were $1.50. That night for supper one girl showed up in green, one in brown, etc. Mine was blue. We felt very tickled with ourselves, but some of the others said, "How could you?"

In the dorm was an old fashioned Wilcox & Gibbs chain stitch, treadle-operated sewing machine I used. With money in my pocket, I went to town and bought cottons for school. I sewed whenever there was a chance. One day I came home with a bargain remnant for 60 cents. There was something like 6 yards of rather flimsy, woven cotton with thin lines of blue criss-crossing and a delicate suggestion of a flower. It was pretty and ended up being a long evening dress with a sash and big bow in back (full flared skirt). The kids loved it. In the end I had others bring gingham and plaids to be made up on the same order. I made at least four more before the next dance.

In the dorm someone suggested one day, not long after we all got acquainted, that we have a "gab fest." Here we were each to tell the other how to improve herself. We must be very frank about faults, which I guess most kids are anyway at that age. That first gab fest started out a little stiffly. Everyone thought it was a good idea. We sat on beds facing each other. Then nobody knew how to get started. Up to that time, I hadn't much noticed the faults of any of them. A messy room didn't seem important enough to mention. I'd been so busy and full of my own interests that I only had time to enjoy the other girls, not to find fault with them.

My first thought was that now maybe I'd find out how to be popular with the boys. After the first time, hope faded, just as it must for the skinny little boy who sends for a set of dumbbells under an ad for Atlas. Only a few things were said, so no one person got a going over, but we each learned a few things to apply in our relations with each other. After a time or two it degenerated into such talk as who was prettiest, who had the best figure, clothes and girl chatter, but all interesting to me.

In looking back, we were most naive. I think today's sixth-grade elementary school children know as much as we did then. Certainly they have as much freedom and wear more sophisticated clothes. We were much more trusting of teachers, grown-ups, and each other, and we worked much, much more. Also, I think we did better on our own because of it. The only planned social life was the monthly school dance, and we greatly looked forward to it. We thought up all kinds of pastimes children today disdain, like making fudge.

All kinds of little odds and ends of fun were forever happening in and out of school. There was one class in school I disliked: history. There was only one good thing about it: I found that it was easy to pass the exams. Our dignified and handsome teacher, Miss Hanlin, gave us one hundred questions the night before. We seniors stuffed the transom, sat in our closets, and stayed up all night most times to find the answers. To memorize these and scribble away the answers next day in class was easy.

The girls in the dorm belonged to a club called the Deka. I was invited to join, but after belonging for two years to the settlement girls' club, the AKM, I decided not to switch my loyalty. The Deka meetings were held promptly after supper, and I was allowed to go visit in the settlement. AKM meetings were in the afternoon.

One spring-like night a fellow in our class happened to drive me home. He had the use of a friend's car. I should have been highly flattered, as he was very popular. Somehow I never aspired to any of these popular fellows, feeling that I'd *never* stand a chance. I think this one was very fond of my roommate, and you know how that is! He was jolly and carefree and never intimidated me, so we had a jolly ride home.

When we turned off of Buck Road into the dorm parking spot, he surprised me. We went right over the lawn, around some big bushes, and down the path with the front wheels up against the big porch of Glenn Hall! It was the first time I'd been involved in such audacity. I tore out of the car without even thanking him for the ride, hoping to avoid Miss Burnham. She was there in a minute to lecture, but she also listened. All she said was, "Don't you go out with that boy again."

On another occasion when he was driving, I was shocked by a remark he made. It was the most shocking thing I heard in all my years of high school!

There were a couple of cars owned by settlement people that were sometimes available to us. One was a station wagon, which was something new. Two boys we knew owned cars of their own, but they were out of school.

My roommate and I were walking home from the settlement when a car came along, filled with some of her lively sophomore friends. I was headed home, but "No, come too," they insisted. (I'll tell you later about those sophomores.)

I was longing to see and hear what the other half did. In today's "mod" language, they were the "in" group. However, I was afraid of scrapes. One could be sent home for misbehaving. They all had lovely homes to go back to; for me it was a lonely western farm. This idea kept me fearfully cautious, besides being a pretty cautious sort anyway.

Dorm kids were not allowed in cars unless they were chaperoned, but on this occasion I went along with my roommate. We had a treat of a ride, all over the local countryside. We speeded up and down a few hills and laughed and sang. Before I knew what happened, the car stopped on the side of the road by a bushy woods, and I heard this voice say, "Does anyone need to go potty?" Someone had disappeared into the woods, and I felt purple with embarrassment. I wasn't so sure I'd like this kind of "wild" life and arrived home thoughtful.

Upstairs lived several fun girls, most all poor, too; in fact, 95% of us were as poor as the proverbial church mice. Right over our room lived the youngest sister of a school professor. At around 9:30 p.m. once a week, a string would appear outside the window with a note and pencil tied on the end. This was during study hour. "Could you please set my hair?" in that half hour before bed. I learned to do this quickly and even took to cutting hair for many of the girls.

Once or twice we got caught for such things as opening windows and giggling. When this happened, we had to take our books and do homework at the long table where the housemother sat on duty. It wasn't so bad when Miss Burnham's helper was the one on duty. She was Aunt Hannah to everyone. She was the perfect picture of a little Swedish peasant, even down to most of the clothes she wore. She was ageless, a face full of fine wrinkles and always smiles for the young. At least I found her so. I often twirled my hair when reading, especially there. She never let me forget it all the years that I knew her.

She had a bit of an apartment downstairs and baked goodies like cinnamon buns, and anyone with "drag" got to sample them. I wasn't one. But her Christmas cookies were different and most delicious. Her date bars were crisp and airy and melted in your mouth, all except the dates.

Another most friendly girl upstairs came from Chicago. No one had known her before school, and no one knew what happened to her afterward. She was well liked. She never mentioned money so we figured she never had to worry. She saw me sewing and asked if I'd make curtains for her room as I'd made ours. I never said no to anyone and often had a furor trying to fit everything in. When the curtains were done, she was most pleased. Then at Christmastime, when her gifts came from home, she came down with a beautiful pair of shoe skates. Would I like them because she'd never go skating? I wondered because she enjoyed hockey and sports so much at gym.

Anyhow, I was now the proud owner of skates and could go along with the group who skated on the Pennypack. It was holiday time.

When on the ice, I spent most of the time walking on my ankles or leaning far forward making wobbly slides. I did a pretty good job of keeping the ice dusted! Sometimes I was on two feet, sometimes four! I finally managed some tiny short glides. This worked if no one was in the way so I could go straight ahead. There were bonfires on the bank to warm up, and some of the boys played hockey. On the way home we might have cocoa at someone's house and get rid of chilblains, which I always got.

Kids didn't go home for holidays. Maybe one or two who lived near did for Christmas. Halloween time was fun at the dorm. The Bean Hall was cleared for a party. A nephew of Miss Vida's was forever playing the upright piano that resided at the girls' end of the room. So along with a theolog who played the banjo, we had music. We watched them play, sat around, or danced.

There were way more girls than boys, so a broom dance was instigated. It was fun and lively, but you had to be careful not to pass it to some girl whose fellow might "hate" you for taking his pet girl away and having to dance with you.

It didn't seem as hard a year at school as the previous ones. I didn't get any better marks, but they came easier, probably partly due to a bit more time for study. The biggest change was long paper assignments with a fair amount of warning. Credit books were a struggle to fit in, but I came to enjoy the papers and wished there was more time to pursue some of the references further.

The only school-planned activity was the monthly dance and little else. We hunted up our own relaxation and social life. Booked activities for a whole weekend were never handed to us. Dorm girls were especially busy, washing, mending, cleaning, and goodness knows what.

I snatched an odd bit of time some afternoons to walk to a friend's house in the town, but this mostly happened on weekends. I felt very lucky to know so many settlement girls, having lived there.

THOSE AWFUL SOPHOMORES OF 1932

All good things must come to an end. That was the sad feeling some of us older ones felt in senior year. Perhaps the teachers had some of the same feelings.

A large girls' class had hit high school as freshmen the year before. They were the most noisy, lively bunch, with barely an exception. The one or two quiet ones were badgered into following suit. This class added zest and pep to the halls between classes and raised the noise level above average. This fact was accepted, but their full impact was not felt until their sophomore year. Now they were full of ideas of how things should be done, mostly what shouldn't be done, and felt very free about voicing their ideas. We'd seen this one and that retained in the principal's room, only to come out steaming about "that Miss Buell."

We noticed all this and found it interesting but were unconcerned until it came time to take them into the AKM, when we were hit full force. Someone was always objecting to something, but this class had a new wrinkle. They organized as one voice. Girls wore long silk (really rayon) stockings to school and what a chore to keep supplied. They got runs every other day and holes in the toes with a few wearings. We were always at them mending, mending, mending. Darning baskets with smooth polished "eggs" to drop into the toes were forever filled at everyone's house with the mama's, papa's, and children's socks.

Everyone arrived at school one morning, found a bustle in the hall, and Miss Buell calling all sophomores into her principal's room. They had all shown up in their little white gym ankle socks! What an idea. We all liked it, wouldn't have dared ourselves, but hoped for the best.

Loud voices came from Miss Buell's room. The few ringleaders weren't easily intimidated and were well versed in arguing. They'd had much practice with each other. There were a large majority almost about as vociferous and plenty willing to follow. The couple of very good girls couldn't be "poor sports." Miss Buell tried to send them home to change. They refused. Being such a big class, it made up about a third of the high school, and she couldn't expel that many. Besides, several came from very influential parents.

They continued to come in ankle socks and the teachers tried to "sit on them" individually as much as possible. Gradually, more and more girls slipped on a pair. Some of us more timorous ones waited until the subject was an old one and Miss Buell seemed to have given up her battle before we happily donned them.

We were quite in favor of sophomore ideas.

Then came AKM initiations, and we found ourselves sympathetic with Miss Buell. They would double our numbers in the club, and we needed them. We could scarce believe that it seemed to matter so little to them whether they joined or not. They refused to do some things we asked them to do. When it came to the big night and each one was handled individually, we managed quite well to have them knuckle under. One or two of the most imaginative ones were roughest, so we closed our eyes to some of their refusals. They could be good members and their bright ideas and talents a help. One young artist sort came under this listing.

So we took them all in.

Up came the first meeting. We all held hands in a circle to repeat the club's motto. "We won't do that," they chanted. "Silly, old fashioned, and sentimental." Here we were seniors never having questioned any of the ins and outs of customs, and it was a blow. The meeting was less than successful and seemed to put each one of us "on our mettle." We older ones had almost a lonely feeling; some sort of unity had disappeared. With the time-worn feeling that all good things must come to an end, we accepted the fact but felt it was a loss. However, the club did have more vitality, and some clever ideas were presented for the dance, etc. We liked that, even though the club didn't seem ours anymore.

Soon these girls pulled another sit down strike. Labor unions were just getting under way doing the same thing. They came to school with makeup on. All of them again, even though some preferred not to wear it. Before then, if Miss Buell had so much as suspected she saw any rouge or lipstick on anyone, they were sent downstairs to wash it off.

Now Miss Buell spoke hesitatingly, never charging into anything, even a question asked. To see her come out into the hall and face a number of red-lipsticked lips and ask them questions, one saw the English bulldog tenacity. Her face was a study. She did not approve, but disapproval was not so evident as a feeling of helplessness. She was short and had to look up when talking to most all of them, a beseeching look. The flush on her usually pale face could almost be construed as "makeup."

She lost that battle, too.

While lined up for chapel, she talked and threatened to ban them from it, but it did no good. Next day, little makeup was worn, but those who wished to did wear it. Everyone had put a little on for dances but not so's you'd notice.

There was another episode with Miss Buell that reverberated home to parents and back again. It was really quite funny, looking back, but at the time all done so seriously. It had upset some.

In an English class which she taught, the subject of fairies came up. After mentioning elves and such, Miss Buell made some remark, in what seemed an off-hand way about there really being fairies. A couple of girls picked it up. Was Miss Buell so "way out" as to believe in such things? She did have an unusual personality and never seemed to speak her own opinions, just facts from books about a subject. Outside of class this was talked up, then taken home. "Yes, there are," said some of the girls' mothers. "Of course there aren't," said others. Others of us who didn't have parents around, wondered.

Finally, one of those sophomore girls whispered only that real fairies were "an awful kind of men," no more. Could you tell by seeing them? and other such questions came to mind with no answers. It was sad to think of fairies in such a connection, and Miss Buell? Had she wanted to open our eyes to a few things without being in the uncomfortable position of telling all?

Grown-ups were very secretive about life. The chums of mine weren't told even the facts of life when they'd reached high school. We touched only on the subject among ourselves. Each knew a little bit to whisper about to one another, one at a time. Girls were too reticent to embarrass their mothers. Mothers usually passed off any touching upon the subject with a remark such as, "You'll find out when you've grown up." It was a little scary. How much was there to find out?

BOYS

Why is it that the boys that like you to begin with are the ones you never like? I figured it came from trying to be nice to everyone, like we were told to do. Then all the awkward ones don't feel so awkward with you. And then you're stuck because you're just like them.

From the first few months of school anyone could see what categories others fell into. All, of course, were interested in what the most popular did, and some yearned to be with them. To me that was time wasted. You were either "there" or had to work at it gradually, and even then know you'd maybe never make it. When you have no clothes, looks, money, and especially know how, you didn't even want to.

I was certainly glad to have come as a freshman to learn as much as possible. In those first years there was a chance to make some good girlfriends before boys became so important to social life. Of course, having no bid to a dance was a blow to any girl's ego. That's all I wished for the first year or two. Freshman year, I had three out of the nine, and there were more the next year. I aimed to go with boys with some popularity and finally made it.

Everyone went to the dances, with the exception of a few rebellious boys (when they couldn't take their favorite dates). Even then they showed up for a dance or two. Girls had programs the boys who brought them to the dance filled out. The steadies filled in as few names as possible, of course. Then there were others who couldn't fill them. There were circle dances every so often, and that was one time I wasn't backward. Some girls refused to join in, but I figured they'd never learn to be good dancers or get to know the boys. Only once in a while a fellow would show how stuck he was because they changed every few minutes, and anyone could put up with that!

Once I got really nervy. I was a sophomore then and there was a pompous senior who liked a first-rate girl, but she laughed at him. In a circle dance, he stepped on my feet and looked for a likely chance of someone better. In fact, he hardly danced but was waiting for the whistle to blow again. He intimidated many (he had money). I stood still and said, "I'd rather sit down" and startled him into thinking I was a person.

By junior year, two girls in our class were going steady and having lots of dates, but, of course, I couldn't even if I'd had the chance because of where I was living and working.

I did have one date in the summer of sophomore year. The D.'s were going to the movies; in fact, they had gone when he called. He was that nuisancy fellow who had always trailed along on the way home from dancing classes. Then this telephone call when I hadn't even seen him since the start of the year. Dancing class had only lasted the first six weeks.

I said, "Yes," and he came down. He was older by two years so interesting to chance it if for no other reason. I scarce knew what to do or talk about on a date and hoped he wouldn't be bored. He had no money, so there was no problem there. I turned on the radio, and then we made fudge I hoped would turn out. Then we sat on the couch sampling it and trying to talk. He said, "Why not try dancing?" So we turned back the corner of the rug and had danced only a few minutes when the D.'s arrived home. He soon left, and I didn't see him again till the following summer.

His name was Keneth Simons, and I promptly forgot all about him.

Now that I was at the dorm, there seemed a chance with the boys. While at the Roses, Tryn's oldest brother asked me to the first dance, and I was pleased. It was a nice way to start off the new school year. It was easy to feel lonelier at the first and last dances because there were so many more people.

The next and second dance, a fellow in our class asked me. He was big and sort of slow but always ready with a wide grin. He was not considered a catch. He was called "Worlds." That stood for "world's ugliest." Each dance that came along I had at least one bid till the last one senior year. Then I had three most exciting ones and had to go with a fellow who asked me six months before. He was nice enough, but I had no time for him. He made me furious. He was foxy, too, and said if I turned him down he'd tell, and I'd get no one else. When he asked me, I was uncertain enough about status with the boys not to refuse. It didn't seem polite either.

There was an outstandingly pretty girl in the class who became a friend this last year. She didn't date a lot of boys at once but was the steady sort. There were exclusive small parties at her house that everyone loved to go to. Lights were dimmed, it was cozy, good refreshments, and her mother disappeared after shaking hands. Her brother (she had several) was sort of my partner. They were all sociable. Steadies were invited, or rather most collected there on Saturday night, and they were all the "fun" ones. A few other couples they wished to have were invited individually. They were dancing evenings with refreshments before going home. The school had few students at this time, and private parties were very much noticed.

By this time I'd about forgotten my first crush. He'd gone away to college, and I would have forgotten him completely, but he asked me to my junior dance and arrived with a little bouquet of Lily of the Valley, which he'd picked from his mother's garden. They were my first flowers from a boy, and I managed to pin them on my shoulder. Fellows back then were allowed to bring girls a flower to be worn as a corsage at the dances. The biggest thrill was a gardenia, "the" flower.

Later, when senior year came along, he again asked me to my class dance, which was a surprise. I recall his standing at the foot of the stairs in the downstairs hall of the girls' dorm while I hurriedly sewed the last tab on our banner. I felt he could have liked me very much if I'd been comfortable with him and could chat as I did with fellows I didn't give a toot about. He was not at ease socially either. Why was I always tongue and brain-tied with favorite boys? However, in senior year while having the time of my life at the dorm, boys were only a part-time preoccupation.

My senior dorm year had been underway only a short time when I was first asked to a party at my friend's home. I'd known her well in school since freshman year, but this was a new status. Toward the end of the evening someone suggested, "Let's shift partners for one dance." I found myself with a tall, dark, well-built fellow, curly hair and nice, nice brown eyes. I knew little about him but his name, which was Cedric King. He'd been at school the year before. Later, I remembered Tryn talking so much about him.

There was just something immensely appealing about him. We danced a minute or two, and then he asked where I came from. When I said, "the West," he stopped still, looked at me from arm's length, and said, "So did I." Then he pulled me close and hugged me good.

'Twas the most romantic moment in my life. I was thrilled!

Cedric King

Betty and Reta in June 1933

Left to right: Patsy, Reta and Catherine H. lying on stomachs in May 1933

Reta on right with Bean Hall crew

AKM 1933? Standing: Betty Cronlund, Tryn Rose, Joyce Cooper, Reta Evens
Middle row: Claire Heaton, Ann Walter, Gay P., Francie Bostock
Front row: Eleanor Cranch on left

Reta's brothers Ted and Bill back home on the farm

Reta's sisters Margaret and Beatrice on the farm in 1933

Chapter 5

THE SENIOR CLASS

There were four fellows from California in our class, and they pretty well set the pace. Most of the time they were bored with the whole thing. One who did much of the talking, though held no office, was blond, cleverly sassy, and good looking. He later became a columnist on the west coast. One was a dark, rather short he-man fellow, the Clark Gable sort. He even looked like Gable. He had a large crush on my friend who gave that "neat" party early in the year. The other two Californians were the Davis brothers. The one named Rudy did more work for the class than anyone else. He carved the bar for mounting the class banner.

No one could say of our class that there was much whole hearted unity, nor overwhelming class or school spirit. The boys were a drag. But a banner had to be prepared. Seniors put on their own dances in those days, so that had to be done. It was lucky the dance came in May. The flowering branches of trees were easy decorating material to obtain. That was the extent of senior class activities.

During senior year, I first became aware of something that goes on, best called "social under-currents." I've been learning about them ever since. My very special person was sought out to attend some of the other little parties. Many girls were keen on him. After I was seen out with him a time or two, I was also invited. At one house, I knew it wasn't because they wanted me.

At that time the Assembly Hall was built, and the town's social life took place there. We had rattled around at first in the Assembly Hall and found it almost too big to decorate. We beefed about it but had pretty well adjusted to the idea. Then we were told that it must be shut down, due to lack of funds. We, along with the town, were unhappy about going back to the old auditorium.

There was a tall, bashful, and very awkward fellow in the class. No girls looked at him. This boy, Curtis Glen, wrote a poem about the situation, and my special friend popularized it with music. It was sung in school hallways and at dances, long after we left, and made quite a hit. Also, it roused more spirit for our class than ever before.

(Sung to the tune of an inter-frat song.)

The Assembly Hall is clos-ed
It's a tough break for all
But social life must be carried on
We must not admit defeat
For the class of thirty three-e
Must ever ready be
To carry on, establish the same old school spirit

My popular friend also had another sidekick who was willing to follow him around almost like a pup. He was a special student, short and blonde, and the son of a convention minister. He knew no one. They became, and still are, friends. The little fellow grew to be six feet tall and very successful but, sad to say, out of touch with B.A. He became a real estate broker and builder in Colorado Springs.

But back to the class...

There were twelve boys and eight girls, as well as four special students. These four were girls who would graduate with us. Having an even number of boys and girls was quite unusual. This equality may not have been the cause, but we were given some unusually wonderful parties during the last half of the year. One was at the Jeffrey Childs' home. Having money, they were able to hire an orchestra with all the trimmings. Their daughter, in the class below me, was my friend.

Another party was given by Tryn Rose's father, Don. I believe it was at a place downtown called the 49th Street Playhouse. What a big outing that was! Everything took place in one building. Dinner was served on white tablecloths. A play was performed in a little theater on another floor. Finally, upstairs, there was dancing where the roof opened to the stars. Never had a class been treated to so many good things! In fact, there were so many at the end of the year, it left us breathless!

Every year, Mrs. Harold P. gave a wonderful garden party for the school. Her home, Cairncrest, was such a fabulous, beautiful place! It had a huge tiled hall for dancing, a pretty living room for talking, and then a lovely terrace for strolling between dances and having refreshments with a favorite date.

The senior dance had to be organized and the banner had to be made. The class could not agree on the colors for the banner. At one desperate meeting a popular girl said, "Let's have two greens." This was accepted, although some of us felt we had been railroaded. The girl's brother drew our symbol, the Unicorn, and over it our motto "Strength Through Good."

I was given the job of sewing the banner. For weeks I canvassed Philadelphia for the right kind of embroidery materials. I had no money and didn't do too well. To this day I consider it a pretty sad banner. When I got the materials, I stitched and sewed every spare moment to make the banner. I even held up my date to the dance for the last few stitches!

The bid had been a surprise. Out of the past came my old crush to take me; made me feel kind of strange!

THE SEASHORE

Miss Buell, the school principal, had a summer cottage at Seaside Park, New Jersey. Professor Howard had a cottage almost across the street. His daughters were friends of mine. The senior girls were invited down for a long weekend, probably on Memorial Day, to share both cottages. What a scrumptious holiday that was!

Miss Buell's was next to the bay, and she had a rowboat. None of us could row. You wouldn't believe how wild and pretty the shore was then! There were so few people compared with now. We filled the boat to overflowing and took turns walking up to our middles to push it around for a ride. The water was clear as clear, and when we spied a crab or two we gave up. Miss Buell took us to visit the author of *The Slipper Point Mystery*, Augusta Huiell Seaman, who served us tea, which was interesting.

But the very best fun was the Beach Bug. Mary, one of the professor's daughters, a year younger than I, had come down with us. The Howards owned an old Model T Ford without a top and without doors. With Mary at the wheel, we'd toot down the beach following the tide in and out so's to keep on the hard sand. We had a hilarious time and the going was tricky. Sometimes we drove for miles to find the right spot wide enough for turning around. Then one time we missed. With each oncoming wave the jalopy sank further. Water sloshed through the open doorways. Meanwhile a couple of girls tore off for the Coast Guard Station which, thank goodness, was nearby. In those days, some girls wore beach robes over knitted bathing suits when not in the water. Others wore long, floppy beach pajamas. We all were a drippy lot trying to rescue the Bug.

Then four handsome fellows came running to the rescue. They wore navy blue uniforms, gold buttons, and white hats. They hoisted up the Beach Bug and carried it to higher ground. They turned it around to head home. Their pretty suits got all wet. The suits looked pretty sad, but they laughed.

In the melee of pushing and shoving and trying to hold up the wheels on the ocean side, one girl, Joyce Cooper, said, "My ring, I've lost my good pearl ring." It was an heirloom. For fun, I said, "Oh I'll get it," and scooped down in the water to bring up a double handful of sand. There, gleaming in the sand, was her lost ring!

Our chaperons, Miss Buell and Mrs. Howard, were very old (about forty-five!). They didn't ask us why we'd been gone so long, so we kept very quiet about it all. They had been sitting rocking at home on the Howards' porch as one expected of such old people!

There were lovely big sand dunes to explore, with valleys between, filled with treasures from the ocean. Several girls found pretty, old glass bottles and driftwood among some of the tall grasses. We were sunburned and happy.

Such a fun trip! For most of us, it was an outstanding event just to be on such an outing. People didn't have vacation spots like they do now. Many didn't even have vacations. Only the rich and a few school teachers were so lucky.

When the warm weather came we took another enjoyable trip. The school hired a large bus for a drive to Washington, with all the seniors aboard. We certainly saw a lot of sights, including Congress, where we were shocked to see the members loafing around in their chairs. Some of them were talking in little groups, paying no attention to the speaker. We knew nothing about world affairs, and many adults weren't any better.

At the Bureau of Printing & Engraving, we saw many bills of money banging off the presses, even full wastebaskets stuffed with rejects. At the White House, President Hoover was just behind one of the doors in a conference. We saw the Library of Congress and the original Constitution. We walked around the newish Lincoln Memorial; the Jefferson Memorial hadn't been built yet. Some of the students walked up the Washington Monument.

This city was different, alien looking; we felt it must be something like Athens. It was so white and sparkling with majesty in the sun. We thought it was beautiful. The Smithsonian Institute was especially interesting. Colonel Lindberg's plane was there, the one in which he had just crossed the Atlantic. Airplanes in those days were quite small. They were very exciting to see. If one ever flew over during school, we were allowed to rush to the nearest window and watch it fly over.

No one in our group could afford a class ring so, for $1.50, we had little gold chains attached to our sorority pins with "33" fastened to them. I thought class rings weren't attractive anyway. The biggest excuse for them was for the steadies who might exchange rings.

She Stoops to Conquer was chosen to be the senior play, partly because no royalties had to be paid. Gifted or not, every one of the girls was keen for a good part, preferably the heroine. Boys, as usual, had to be prodded. The ones we'd expected to get the leads, did. That special fellow was the hero, and how I wished I could play opposite him! I'd have loved every minute of it. More than one romance blossomed or was enhanced by a situation like this. I was at least glad he didn't care for his heroine! My acting ability was zilch to say nothing of fright in front of an audience, be it ever so small.

K.R. Alden, who was an English teacher as well as boys' principal, was the producer. During tryouts, I still wanted that big part. You know how you think you could somehow do it? The costumes were to be old-fashioned, long, full-skirted southern belle types, which I loved. Costumes with so much to them would surely make it easier to play the part and forget one's bashfulness. After others were chosen for the lead parts, K.R. asked me to come up on the stage where they'd been practicing tryouts. Said he, "You are going to be the announcer. What is more, you will come out before the curtain goes up and recite a poem I am going to write."

This seemed almost worse than a part, and I balked inwardly, but how can one act like a sissy in front of the whole class? Besides, he stated this as a fact and did not even ask me how I felt about doing it!

This was the poem I was to read:

> In this year of depression
> When gloom fills the land
> When incomes are shrinking
> And dollars won't stand
> To think of a play
> That won't cost a cent
> Oh – that was the thing
> Upon which we were bent.

It went on for something like 35 lines. Then there was the announcing between scenes and acts. I went to many play practices, and one day near deadline K.R. gave me a workout all alone on the stage. First a bow and a finger lifted when the "ah" part came. In other words, a little life was to be put into it. But boy, was I mechanical about it, and constantly he said, "Speak up"!

Came the night of the play, and we were all backstage, costumed, waiting for the audience to collect and settle. Somehow there was a radio playing the popular "I've Told Every Little Star." While standing slightly apart, tensely reciting my lines to myself and trying to think, "I'm not afraid, I'm not afraid," a pair of strong arms were around my waist, and we waltzed away to the music until curtain time.

"He" was like that. Know what a thrill that can be?

A SPECIAL PICNIC

Having never grown up with picnics, they were something quite special. The D.'s never went on them. My first experience was an AKM one in sophomore year when we went to the cliffs of the old stone quarry at Paper Mill Station. It was early on a Sunday morning, and the D.'s let me go and be back in time for breakfast. It was such fun cooking hot dogs and marshmallows over a fire. Also, it was the first time I'd eaten the toasted, gooey, sweet white things. Having them for breakfast was unusual, I felt, but I loved sweet stuff.

A horrid old man followed us up the tracks and later took a naked swim in the creek below. The chaperone told us not to look, so of course we all did in two's or singly.

Then there were the sandwich picnics at the Roses, while gathering berries.

Sometime in May of senior year, with only a short spell of school days left, my roommate Aileen said, "Let's cook up a picnic." I was game for anything provided it was safe and OK. She got a look in her eyes that meant discretion wasn't involved. "We'll ask about 6 girls and 6 boys. I'll ask the boys. Who shall we invite?" It was settled for an early Sunday morning, very early, before daylight. We'd all climb out our window. It would really have to be a quiet, sneaky exit or we'd find ourselves out of school and no finishing the year. This kind of thing bothered me to pieces, but I sure didn't want to miss it.

Aileen had told the boys where to meet us and had given them money for all the food. We'd each donated.

We ended up approximately in what is now Cranch's woods at the end of Sycamore Road. That whole section was completely wild. There was a fenced field from Cherry Lane up to about Orchard Lane that young steers roamed in.

Down the road, out of sight of the dorm, we met the boys, all our favorites, and talked low. Girls always want to giggle, and we had a terrible time getting out and being quiet. Everything is *so* funny under such circumstances.

We built a fire and cooked our hot dogs. It was damp, so wood was hard to keep going, and we got more smoke than fire. But everything was delicious.

I don't think any of us had too good a time for worrying how we'd get back in. Getting out was so much easier. Aileen didn't seem to worry.

We made it back OK, and I could relax. Whew. Everyone else seemed to have a much less precarious setup than I did. They'd be sent to towns and friends, and I guessed I'd try and find a job, but who in B.A. would take such a culprit? So we survived to grin about it from time to time. We didn't take the chance of talking about it to others till school was behind us. By that time it was stale.

STAN'S WEDDING

Now it happened that the big, handsome football coach, Stan Ebert, had fallen in love during the year. Nancy was a tall, blonde, sophisticated senior when I was a freshman, and her aloofness progressed. She didn't mix, and she didn't talk to just anyone. But Stan sparkled, and the boys all kidded him. He handed it right back.

Everyone in school enjoyed watching the romance. At a big garden party at Theo P.'s, Stan arrived with an armful of red roses for her (because he was late). We scurried to see him present them. We lived every minute of it and ate it up.

My dark-haired and most lively, popular roommate had come to school with a pale pink taffeta evening dress she much favored. Her

Aunt Vivian had given it to her, and it was above the usual cut of evening dresses the rest of us wore. "It came from Hollywood," she said, and it was worn only once or twice for her most special dance dates. She had another one or two of homemade vintage.

This roommate was often late home on a Saturday afternoon. With a dance that night, I promised to press her pretty pink dress when I did my own. No such fabrics as now. I first touched the cloth where one sits down and up came the iron, a syrupy, gooey mess, leaving a perfect hole of its shape behind! A pair of scissors could not have left a more clean-cut, gaping hole. She was pretty nice about the sad affair and said not a word of reproof.

With weeks' worth of hoarded sandwich money, I took a train to town and bought yards and yards of white organdy and enough for a red sash. As a senior with graduation looming, I was very busy. I had to snatch odd moments to sew this big undertaking. When finished, ruffles cascaded from below the hips to the floor, after the fashion of flamenco dancers. School days were ending when, at last, it was finished.

The senior boys were the ones who kidded Stan the most. He vowed he'd have the whole football team as ushers. He also promised a big dance in the Assembly Hall so's we could "dance at his wedding." He was true to his word and set the date for the weekend of school closing. This was an extra goody because we could go with special dates, and the school would have nothing to say. The school rule was: only two dances a year with the same boy.

Guess who asked me?

The Hall was beautifully decorated as a garden, and a wonderful orchestra played waltzes. My roommate wore the long white dress I'd made her for the first and last time, was happy with it, and certainly looked pretty on the arm of her hero, who, in the course of time, she married.

It was a much-anticipated evening, floating on cloud nine, but somehow when it came there wasn't the anticipated carefree pleasure. We were weighed down by the feeling of vague numbness that this was the end of things

Two weeks went by, and now I was living again in the town. One afternoon one of my good friends gave me shocking news. When Stan was driving home from his honeymoon there had been a bad car accident. His bride had been killed. In stunned sadness, we attended the funeral. At the grave, we watched Stan place three white gardenias on her coffin. He was overcome with grief. We each added our floral tribute. It was like being an eyewitness to a fairy story with a sad, sad ending.

A letter came for me from my special someone. My plans were underway for a long-awaited visit home as soon as enough money was earned. We'd planned a date to dance to Wayne King's waltzes at the World's Fair in Chicago, but I couldn't make it.

Letters stopped between us, and time went on.

GRADUATION

All too soon it was June and finals. Final exams were the only thing marks stood on; no papers ahead of time or anything changed that. We practiced marching to the Assembly Hall (opened again) and sang forlorn songs. Kipling's "Recessional" was rather stirring.

I think we all felt it was more a sad day than a glad day. None of us were going on to college, so graduation seemed like the end. Gold and silver awards were handed out.

I hadn't thought much about what I would do next. It wouldn't have done any good anyway. The thing everyone else did was to go home, but I had no money for the rail fare. I must have caused a wrinkle or two on the brows of the teachers, now that I think about it, kind people that they were. On the other hand, I guess it is lucky youth can be as matter of fact as it is. I didn't worry much about the future but figured I'd find my way somehow.

At the last minute, Dear Miss Vida asked if I'd like to move over to the Bean Hall with her for a week to help tidy up. I was delighted, but did it ever seem bleak with everyone gone. The older girl from Washington, Emily Boatman, who'd been her assistant, stayed too.

There was such a sudden end to life as we had known it. Life had been school. Now the yawning chasm of "the future" faced all of us. I wonder where I thought to go when the dorm closed.

I spent most of the time mending tablecloths and making big white aprons for next year's crew. When the time was up, Miss Vida presented me with a gift: a nice suitcase and $7 earnings. She was such a sweet little person and so feminine. She had taught us Human Body, whispering the "difficult" parts. The kids rather made fun of her, but they liked her too.

Next, Miss Buell offered to have me stay with her to work. She would pay me $7 a week. I was pleased and a bit awed. She lived in a beautiful stone house on Alnwick Road and was a different sort of person. No one felt as though they knew her very well, even though she'd been our principal for four years. Some didn't like her and constantly made fun of her fuddy-duddy ways, and we all laughed heartily. I didn't know what to make of her at all but didn't hesitate a moment to go live with her.

There was a fellow, Alex Iungerich, who had graduated the year I was a freshman. His father was the one who'd visited us out West as a minister and who started me on my way to B.A. Miss Buell rather mothered this fellow, or shall I say befriended him. She wasn't exactly the motherly sort, at least in appearance. Miss Buell was always a good listener.

I moved into Miss Buell's and was shown to a pretty room on the second floor, with a little iron balcony looking over Alnwick Road. I wasn't too sure how I felt about the house. It was so different. It didn't quite seem like a home.

Mr. Raymond P. was interested in architecture and had built her house to try out some of his ideas, I gathered. He'd then presented it to her and she, in turn, said she'd willed it to the school for the girls' principals in future. Its entrance hall was attractive, tasteful and cozy. It wasn't big.

The living room had a handsome, odd-shaped terra cotta floor, polished and waxed, with little rugs here and there. The ceiling was way up high. The windows were small, with leaded glass. There was a row of them on the end, with a long, very narrow, antique sort of table under them. They overlooked a garden. There was a fancy fireplace, which was nice and cozy to sit in front of.

The kitchen had a wide wooden floor and a bit of an alcove for a table overlooking the same garden. The kitchen didn't seem very much like a kitchen, perhaps because of the beautiful floor.

The garden was lovely! It was a beautifully walled garden with walks laid out. The flowers somehow always looked weedy. I felt it needed the sort of flowers you could see and wished it was mine to plant. It was planted with wildflowers. At the end of the garden was a kind of open pagoda with a sandy-colored stone walk leading up to it. There was a roof over it, held up by lovely round pillars. The view across the green grass to the church was beautiful. It was so cool to sit there in summer. This was an outstandingly beautiful setup.

All of my friends felt Miss Buell had idiosyncrasies, and maybe she did. Our meals were rather stilted affairs; conversation was stilted. That was about the one time we sat and faced each other for any period of time. I couldn't forget she had been the very important head of the girls' school.

One thing she kept in her refrigerator tray at all times was orange ice. This was for any guest who might stop in. If no one came, we ate it so's there'd always be fresh. She had a recipe for it, and I think she told me at least six times how to make it. I had a hard time not giggling because this was the sort of thing kids had told me about.

Her cooking was simple, cleaning wasn't hard and was mostly dusting. Then there was sewing. She wished to have dresses for school next year. She wore nondescript dresses, dark prints with all-over, blurry sort of patterns. Never stylish-looking nor fitted. We looked over her materials and cut and sewed. I had a fidgety time trying to decide just how to fit her. I don't think we got all the sewing done she had expected. She didn't say straightforwardly, "I'd like this one done this way out of that cloth."

Two girls who lived nearby, Nancy Pendleton and Muriel Childs, came to visit a number of times. They had belonged to that "awful sophomore class" and were lots of fun. They laughed at the dresses I was making, and that didn't help at all.

We visited in my room a number of evenings amid much lively talk and giggling. I don't think Miss Buell was fond of them. She made all sorts of rules about them. Once they stayed after 10 p.m., and next day she was pacing the floor, a habit of hers when something was on her mind. I'd noticed that in class. Finally, she came out with it.

Miss Buell was basically most kind, and I think she found it very difficult to scold anyone. Yet you knew she felt firmly about things. She tried to be tactful, too.

An example:

She must have heard about someone "necking." As a result, when we collected for English class one day, she was pacing the side of the room, not up front at her desk as usual. We knew something was in the wind. After we were seated, she said, "Girls get out a fresh, clean piece of paper and your pens. Now write down, 'A bunch of grapes is beautiful, but when it is handled the grapes lose their luster.' "

That was all.

After a bit she came around to her desk, and we went on with our English class. We sort of didn't know what to do with the piece of paper but took it with us when we left. Some kids giggled and laughed and tossed it into the wastebasket. I thought it very clever of her and was much impressed.

I never let boys get the slightest bit familiar. On a date with a rather nice fellow once, we were relegated to the rumble seat of the car. It was dark, and I think we were coming home from the movies. He put his arm around me tight, and I said, "None of that." He wasn't the slightest bit friendly after that. I heard that some girls "got around" socially this way. I often wondered where to draw the line. I didn't want to be prissy, but I had standards. I chose to be firm and keep my conscience because I'd rather be liked for other reasons. Also, I remembered Mom's advice: "Trust no man"!

Over a month was spent at Miss Buell's house. I never got to feeling at all close to her; I don't think anyone did. She had a most varied bunch of friends. She liked to talk gardening, and lots of would-be writers came to leave their masterpieces for her to read. She liked artists and antiques. She had a small collection of antique silver and gave me my choice of teaspoons. At my stage and spot in life it was a big treasure! I still love and treasure it.

That fellow, Alex Iungerich, came to visit a time or two, and Miss Buell carefully chaperoned us and beamed on the relationship. He was a big, handsome fellow but outside of a fun ride or a friendly chat for something to do – "No."

Then one evening the telephone rang. It was a long distance call for me!

GLEN TONCHE

The call came from the Catskills up in New York state. There the Raymond P.'s had a summer home, and it was known as Glen Tonche. The "Glen" came from Mrs. P.'s maiden name, and it was built on the mountain called Tonche. There were two adjacent mountains which were originally called "Big Tonche" and "Little Tonche." Big Tonche became Glen Tonche.

They asked if I would like to come up there to work. One of the girls was on vacation, and they needed someone to fill in.

"Sure," I said.

When I hung up the phone, I noticed that Miss Buell looked a little upset. She said right away, "How is it that you didn't ask me?" Whereupon I said, "Couldn't I call them back?" "No, it's all right," was her answer. I don't know whether she'd really counted on me or not. She had never had full-time help before. I think she was giving me a lesson in manners, which I didn't know enough about. Also, I muddled through pretty well not knowing the answers but knowing how to ask the right questions.

A day or so later, a big black chauffeur-driven car stopped to pick me up. The drive to Glen Tonche took five or six hours in those days. We rode and rode and finally saw, in the distance, some soft green mountains. They were not at all like pictures of the Rockies I had seen. Those were *real* mountains!

Soon the car went back and forth up the side of one of the green mountains. There was a sharp curve, like the number eight, when almost at the top. There were glimpses through clearings of a valley with a beautiful lake. This was the Ashokan reservoir, the source of water for New York City. No swimming or motor boats were allowed.

All of a sudden, we arrived at a white clapboard house on top of the mountain. We drove through an arch with a bell hung above. This led into a big stone courtyard surrounded by the various wings of the house.

My bags were taken from the car, and we went straight ahead into an enormous kitchen. Here we found two black cooks bustling about. The walls were just clean boards with the two-by-fours showing. This was the case most everywhere, though some places were painted. It added simplicity.

Down a hall leading from the kitchen, we came to a covered semi-circular walk attached to another section of the house. There was an enormously big living room with windows providing a view of the valley and the mountains ringing the horizon. Along this was another hall with bedrooms on one side and a sleeping balcony on the other. On the second floor above this were the children's bedrooms.

Our journey ended at the very end of the hall and slightly to the right. It was a nice big room with two beds and a dresser. It had a large walk-in closet and a lovely bath. I later found out that Mr. and Mrs. P.'s bedrooms were directly above that room.

My roommate was a whimsical girl named Ann Walter. She wore her long black hair parted in the middle with a soft knot in the back. She had been Gay P.'s classmate and friend. Her parents were Austrian. I started to unpack and in came the children's nursemaid, Bea, to see how things were. My roommate, Ann, was her helper.

At that time, I was plagued with some nasty boils on my arm. Bea noticed them right away. She had much to say. I gathered from what she said that I was to stay away from the children. It made me feel like an outcast. I didn't know what work there was going to be. I sat alone on the bed and felt kind of lonely. Maybe I shouldn't have come. It was a big, bare place and yet nice, but I had to get used to it. Bea came back shortly with bandages and salves and fixed up my arm.

Then it was time to set tables, so back outside and over to the kitchen, on into another big room known as the pantry. There the walls were lined with dish cupboards, with sinks on two walls, and a big table in the middle. The room seemed full of people. There were about six girls like myself. Everyone pitched in at mealtimes.

Across the hall from the pantry was the dining room, a big high-ceilinged room ringed by windows. Next to this was a big screened porch. The ground was far below. Standing there, I felt perched on an aerie overlooking the world. Everywhere around was beautiful scenery.

A big fireplace occupied much of the side wall in the dining room. Just inside the door was a small table with the coffee percolator. Such a lot of time was spent fussing over this. I swear no one knew how to make good coffee. Not much was used really, as the family did not drink coffee. It was there chiefly for guests and the "girls." The white help were always called "the girls." That was us. White ones were "girls," black ones were "maids".

Near the door there was a big white scale. This was for weighing people, and it was much used. There always seemed to be someone seeing how much they had gained or lost and talking about diets. With all that good food, weight was a problem! I gained thirteen pounds that summer and felt *so* fat and quite unhappy about it.

In the middle of the room sat a huge square table that could seat, I would guess, about thirty-five people. There was a smaller table for the help and another for serving vegetables and the like.

We were dressed and on deck by seven o'clock. We set tables and cut up big yummy melons. How I remember those big juicy honeydews with a slice of lemon! There were dozens of fresh oranges to squeeze, the biggest early morning job, so everyone could have a tumbler full. Bacon, eggs, and toast were made to order by the cook in the kitchen. Breakfast was *so* delicious!

All the young people loved working there. The people were nice, the scenery was magnificent, and the food was out of this world!

It took a while to learn where everything was, but there was always a more experienced companion to work with, which made learning easier. Two girls together made beds while others dusted. All work was finished by about ten, then we were free to do as we pleased.

There were tennis courts where I learned to play, but not too well. The family went riding and skeet shooting.

There was a wooden tower on the very peak of the mountain. This looked out over the valley, the mountains, and the reservoir below. There were a couple of boys doing heavy work up there. They helped to clear the woods of dead trees.

In the afternoons we most often went down the back of the mountain to the swimming pool. This was fed by a mountain stream, and it was cold! We often walked down and were driven back up.

In the evenings there was music, jigsaw puzzles, many books to read, and a snack before bed. The snack was an occasion! Everyone collected about eight-thirty over in the kitchen. There was a whirr of blenders making milkshakes, amid much merriment. The ice cream was usually homemade, utterly delicious, and rich. I noticed black spots, which I tried to pick out. Then I was told this was the real vanilla bean it had been flavored with, after much work of chopping it up preparing it.

I think that those milkshakes that could stand alone, with extras like malted milk if we wished, were mostly responsible for the poundage I gained that month. Of course there were big fat sticky buns on Saturdays, steak two inches thick, butterscotch pies oozing butter and whipped cream, to say nothing of the most delicious little cakes (petit fours) and cookies. The refrigerators were bulging with leftover drumsticks and such for snacks.

I hated gaining weight. When the daughters of the house saw they had gained even half a pound, they would go on a diet. There was nearly always a lineup before lunch for the scales in the dining room. Those who gained, groaned. Mr. P. noticed when anyone gained.

Bedtime was nine o'clock. Everyone beefed. We stayed up in the kitchen. Often the phone rang with a message to be quiet and get to bed. Then we reluctantly scattered. Ann often went into our big closet with a book and a pillow. She read till quite late with no light showing to disturb the P.'s. I often joined her. Most of our letters were written in that closet.

We had to be up and over to the other side by 7 a.m. This caused more beefing. I really came to love it and always considered the early morning hours as the most beautiful. The mountains were often seen all covered with mist, with big fluffy clouds floating in the valleys below. Everything was so still, and the sun sparkled on the dewy grass in the semi-circle of cut lawn. The mountains being so high, the sun shone through them. The beautiful flower beds under the bedroom wings were so fragrant with lilies, roses, and other flowers. I particularly remember the little heliotrope trees with the hummingbirds fluttering and darting after their breakfasts.

By August it was right brisk when we got up, and we dashed about to keep warm. The kitchen was forever cozy. Bed was so cozy, too.

We wore what we called "bloomers." They were pretty much like gym suits, and the legs must be worn modestly long. I made myself  some blue-checked gingham ones with white rickrack. They were wonderfully comfortable. For supper the young people were allowed to wear slacks, baggy things with bell bottoms. Like most in their generation, the P.'s didn't really approve of girls in slacks. But their own daughters insisted, so it was allowed. It was a first for many of us.

I had an accident that summer. Everyone seemed very quiet about it. It took a couple of weeks to repair, so I had all that time to feel uncomfortable about it. Only a few remarks were made. It happened this way:

All bathroom facilities were cleaned and polished frequently. The cleaner used was ammonia, which came in one-quart glass bottles. These were broad and flat, with very narrow tops. It was almost impossible to carry a bottle with one hand. We carried them around to each of the numerous bathrooms. A little was poured onto a cloth for cleaning. It made my eyes sting.

One morning I was working in the bathroom shared by two of the daughters. I picked up the bottle from the floor and started to clean the sink. Just as I was about to pour, the bottle slipped from my hands. To my horror, I saw it go right through the bottom of the pale yellow sink! It crashed on the tile floor beneath. Such a pretty sink! Who would ever guess that some sinks are made of china!

Usually the housekeeper was very pleasant. At this time she was grim! That sink didn't come from just any old plumber; it was special. My! Was I happy when the man finally came with a new one!

I seemed to be in trouble in several ways but didn't know why. I hurried to finish all my work and often got left with jobs when everyone else was free. I wasn't happy, although I loved everything about the place.

Several times a week, huge wicker hampers arrived by train. In them were sheets, towels, and laundry, which had been cleaned in Bryn Athyn. The male workers hauled them upstairs to the sewing room. The girls then unloaded the sheets and towels and carried them to all the bathroom closets. All the dresses, blouses, and shirts were hung in the sewing room for me. I spent hours by myself pressing out all the folds and hanging each item in the closet where it belonged. Then there was mending and buttons to sew on. Sometimes there were visiting aunties or relatives whose hems needed turning up. I even did some fine sewing, like making a very fine-stitched blouse for Mrs. P.

I set the hair of each daughter and of some of the girls.

The whole family was there that year, but the oldest daughter, Gay, was engaged to Willard Pendleton and looking forward to her wedding. The oldest son, Nathan, was lots of fun and kidded me about coming from the "far West." The third one in the family, Karen, was nearest my age, and she was nice and friendly.

Around 10:30 every morning, everyone looked forward to the arrival of the mail. The chauffeur went down the mountain to get it with his locked leather bag. It came again around 3:30 in the afternoon.

The chauffeur did odd jobs, too, so mail came sometimes earlier, sometimes later.

After I had been there for about a week, I went over to the kitchen one morning and asked if the mail had come yet. Everyone had finished work by then. The chauffeur was lounging on a kitchen stool talking to the cook, and Nathan came in. He said he'd take his car and go for the mail. Then he asked, "Would you care to go with me?" I figured anything the family suggested was OK. We took orders from all of them.

I was most anxious to see if that special fellow from school days, Ceddy King, had learned of my new address. In fact, all we gals collected in the kitchen around this time to ask if the mail was in.

To Nathan's invitation I answered, "Well, sure." It was a glorious morning, the air sparkled, the sun shone through the trees as we rode down the side of the mountain. He had a nice convertible, and we were young and gay. He was the first fellow I really felt easy with. We had a good time together.

After getting to the station, a wee bit of a one, he picked up the mail, got back in his car, and away we went. Somehow it didn't seem that we were headed toward home. When I asked about this he said, "Wouldn't you like to go for a little ride?" "Well, sure, but..." It was a change to see something new. The unspoken rule was "Never go off the mountain." We seldom did. There was an exception a time or two, and that was fine. It was easy to understand the need for rules with so many young people there. Actually, there was lots to keep anyone happy right there on top.

We talked and kidded as we rode down the mountain. We saw the beautiful Ashokan reservoir I'd been told about (or heard about). The fountains were beautiful. One big section looked like dozens of fountains, and the grounds around it were handsome too. We rode for perhaps a half an hour and then headed home.

The word about this expedition got around promptly. When I walked back into the kitchen, there were a couple of members of the family whispering. They kept right on. It made me slightly uneasy at the moment, and I didn't forget it. I became very pally with my roommate, Ann. She was whimsical and different than anyone I'd been with before or since. She was a great friend of the family. In our free time we walked up the mountain to sit on the rocks at the tippy-top and talk. She smoked (a very wicked thing) and felt happier to do that away from the house. At night we went to the big porch off the dining room, away from all the living quarters. She liked company, and I was happy to go along. Everyone was supposed to be in bed at nine o'clock, but she was pretty much a night owl.

After snack time, we were often called on the kitchen phone and told it was time to retire. Then I often sneaked to the porch with her. Later we'd have a long, slow process getting back to our room and into bed. We'd take a few steps, listen, often giggle, but honestly without a sound or we'd have been scolded. Finally we'd make it.

Most evenings everyone stayed together, often playing games in the living room.

One evening Nathan came looking for fun, found Ann and me, and asked if we'd like to go to a play in Woodstock. They had a summer theater there. I'd never been to a play and was thrilled with the idea. There again I figured it was perfectly all right if he asked, and I never questioned the fact! He was a perfect gentleman, too. I said, "Oh, if you'll take Ann, too." She demurred, and we didn't go. Later she did go one night when we went for a short jaunt to get french fries.

He fooled around when we went swimming, and I thought he was lots of fun. One day I couldn't go swimming and knew he'd be around looking for me. So I went out to Mrs. P.'s porch, off the living room, with a book. We girls never went there, but I knew Mrs. P. wouldn't be there at that hour. But she was! In banged the young man hollering for me. It was a most awkward moment!

I quietly said I was going to read, and he left. So did I, as fast as possible. Well, the family cooled toward me, and I wondered why. I had been completely above board in everything I had done. I guess I just didn't understand them. Perhaps they felt above me socially and didn't make friends with such lowly people. Of course there were exceptions, such as the need for someone to play along in their orchestra.

I never once got a "case" on Nathan. I knew that he was just looking for something to do. There were books to read and puzzles to do, but young men aren't too interested in them!

A letter or two did come from that very special person. These were hoarded in a dresser drawer to be read and re-read. His picture sat on my dresser. Mrs. P. disliked this; she felt that young people shouldn't exchange pictures unless they were engaged. His first letter told of his working on road building, hard work and long hours. On the middle page there was an ink blot, and he'd circled it and written "a blue tear."

When fall came and it was time to go home, it was sad to leave those beautiful mountains. We young people talked nostalgically of summer, what we'd done and seen. The air had become crisp, it was September, and time to start another year's routine.

Nathan asked me to ride down in the car with him. Three or four big cars drove home in a cavalcade, with six or eight people in each car. He drove one.

When we arrived at the porte-cochere at Cairnwood, I had the feeling of arriving at the seat of government or its equivalent and was awed. How did one behave? There must be procedures I'd known nothing about. The mountain house had been a rambling, informal setup.

We rang the doorbell at Cairnwood, and it was opened by two older girls. When I stepped out of the car, they said, "Oh, we've heard about you," as if it were something shocking.

Questioning did no good.

It was sometime later that I cornered Ann alone and asked her what it was all about. She told me only that it was because Nathan had been paying me attention. Since she had been my confidant, I wanted to know more and asked why she hadn't told me how feelings ran. "Because you did nothing wrong," was her flat statement. She also knew how I dog-eared all the letters from that very special person.

AN INTERIM

This time was an awkward spell. I know I felt rather up in the air. The housekeeper asked my plans, and I told her I'd be going home as soon as I'd earned enough money for a round trip ticket to the West. I'd had a taste of too much good life to want to be stuck out on the prairies. I thought I had to go back to find out about staying in the U.S. As it turned out, I wouldn't have had to. It was the other way round. I was allowed six months at home if I wished to keep my chance to stay in the U.S.

I decided to stay at Cairnwood until I'd saved the required eighty to one hundred dollars. This I did, but it wasn't easy. I had earned about sixty dollars over the summer. I got the feeling that they invented things for me to do. There seemed to be scads of people, and it wasn't easy sorting things out as to all the setups I might help with.

Nathan lived in an apartment across the pike, and he sometimes phoned in the evenings to ask me out. I talked to him but always said, "No." I thought he was nice and didn't want to hurt his feelings, but, in this regard, the family's attitude was chilly. I didn't know what to do and was anxious to get on home.

Those weeks dragged, and I remember little about them. Finally, the day came. My suitcase was packed and ready to go. My trunk was packed, too, with school pictures and all my belongings, to be shown at home.

HOME AT 18

Again I suffered through the long train ride back. I wore the thin brown suit I'd made out of an old one at Miss Buell's and a yellow blouse I'd also made. It was the one decent thing I owned.

I took the coach at Philadelphia on to Duluth where there was an eleven hour wait for the train to Winnipeg. By the time I got there, I was more than tired of trains. At Winnipeg there was another wait, thirteen hours this time. I decided to do something better than just sit in the boring station. I found the nearest movie theater and saw a movie, my one treat on the way home.

Back on the train, I ate a sandwich each time they carried them through the car. This was breakfast, lunch, and supper. It was the same when we stopped at the stations. Regular food cost too much money.

It took something like four days and five nights to arrive home. The air was crisp when I left the East, and by the time I reached the Northwest it was winter. I could scarcely keep warm and thought about my winter woollies, even though none of them had been stylish back East.

There was only one good thing about the long, dirty train ride home. It gave me time to think and become somewhat adjusted to this change in my lifestyle.

The cities disappeared, also the scenery with lush growth and trees and broad rivers. As the plains rushed by outside, I began feeling bleak, remembering the poorness and the loneliness at home. There were two feelings set aside. One had to do with the return ticket and the uncertainty as to how to get work on my return. Just show up and ask from door to door? The other was to have lots and lots of things to tell the family about. I could already see Mom's face light up when I told her about the good times I'd had. She would also be sad because she often yearned for a change like that for herself.

The train stations seemed to get smaller and less noticeable. When the conductor asked me which one was mine, I said, "Benton," and was sure it "would be better than any of those." We talked about it and he said, "It is smaller than that," as we stopped at one just up the line from home.

It was dark when the hissing, steaming noise came to a halt. There was Dad at the bottom of the steps. I was the only one who got off the train. We got into the car and it was so quiet. There was snow on the ground. Not much. We talked a bit. One of Dad's first comments was, "Your voice is so quiet." I felt pleased; mom had always wanted us to act like ladies, and this must be a first sign some change had come about.

I hardly knew what all to say to Dad. He was very quiet, and I was sorry it was the middle of the night. I'd have liked to have seen everything as we drove home.

We came to the house, and there was Mom with a big hug. Everything was strangely familiar. I crawled into bed with sister Mabel. She snuggled up close with arms tight around me and said, "Don't ever go away again." She would never get away from home. She found studies impossible. It made me feel lonely for her. She was left at home to work with the same outlook each year and no social life to speak of. She never did learn to go out with other people.

The next sister, Irene, was sick. In the morning, I sat on the side of her bed and talked. She was miserable but had passed the worst of it. She cried a good deal. There had been an epidemic of infantile paralysis, and it sounded very much as if she had caught it. Her right side was in trouble, and she had to use her left hand to pick up her right one. Thank goodness she was fourteen and fully grown!

For about two weeks I completely devoted myself to nursing her, giving her baths, cooking, and carrying trays. The hardest part was trying to cheer her. She had been a very active person and lashed out often at her fate. It meant learning to write again. She tried her left hand and came to using her right one, but the left had to push it along across the paper. Her fingers worked fine.

When she became strong again and was up and about, her only problem was a limp right arm, which was bad enough. I had been afraid much worse things might result.

Irene had always been such a wide-awake, capable person, it was very hard for her to accept the disability. However, as soon as she recovered, she stopped crying and went to work on the problem. From then on, she learned to compromise and did not let the bad arm slow her down in any way.

Dad was in touch with the doctor; they hadn't the slightest idea of what to do with polio then. The doctor didn't come to the house after I got there. The polio vaccine had not been invented yet. The doctor did have a plan. He suggested that Irene be sent to the University Hospital. This was in Edmonton, five hundred miles to the north. It was the northernmost city in Alberta. Beyond it was wilderness. It was the capital of the Province.

In about two months, I dressed Irene in the warmest and best of what I could find in my trunk. I particularly remember a brand new white woolen toque I'd bought for skating. I was so pleased to know that I could do something by giving it to her. It all was such bad luck for her. She took the train alone and spent two years stranded in that hospital.

I thought that it was remarkable that Dad and Mom reached this decision so promptly. It was a hard one, too, because in letting her go they had to sign a paper allowing the hospital to "experiment" as they saw fit.

The stay at the hospital helped Irene in more ways than one. She saw many children worse off than herself. She seemed to absorb learning into her pores and learned to help the others. She had quite a major operation on her shoulder and spent something like six months in an awkward cast. After they took it off, she was around the hospital, learning and doing.

Brother Leslie was growing up. He was 12. Brother Bill was 10. They were inseparable and full of activity. The rest seemed very young still but much changed since I last saw them.

FUN AT HOME

I'd been home about a week when the teacher sent word she'd like me to give a talk at school. The idea startled me; I realized how much they thought I had learned back East. After giving a history report or two in class at the Academy in Bryn Athyn, I decided that public speaking was not for me. I hoped I would never have to do it again. I thought hard about this invitation.

Anything at all different was a treat for these people. Mom hadn't helped by telling me that everyone was interested in seeing how I behaved and how I'd changed. "Don't do anything that might make them think you've become snooty." It was the furthest thought from my mind! I did feel they would consider me grown up and should know how to act in all situations. The truth of it was that I was still quite unsure of myself.

In the end, I accepted, pressed the brown suit I'd worn home, and walked to school. The schoolteacher had light brown hair and freckles. She was a nice, wholesome-looking girl. She was a revelation to me. She seemed to be just about my age. And she was accomplished enough to teach a whole room full of children of assorted ages. I felt outclassed.

I had no clear idea as to what to talk about, so I asked her. She said, "Oh anything you feel like." Knowing how I would have liked to hear about the fun things, I didn't mention school much. Instead, I spent most of the time telling about life in the dormitory. It was not easy. I talked to the faces I knew, which helped. I was relieved when

I finished but felt it had been rather stilted. The kids asked for more, and the teacher was full of questions.

I went down to Benton to get the mail with Dad. I was anxious to see and do everything and tried to feel that I was at home again. It didn't work. The fact that I chose the coldest part of the year didn't help. I wasn't able to walk outside. I couldn't see the old familiar sights, like the buffalo wallows.

The first trip to town set the pace with the town people. I walked into the little post office that had a few canned things at one end. There were several people collected there, leaning against the window sills and walls, chatting as usual. When I walked in, there was dead silence! Dad tried to make things more comfortable with introductions all around. After the "How do ya do's", more silence. I tried to think of things to say. Some were strangers. Knowing where I had been, they were interested, yet reticent. They were also putting "The East" on its mettle.

I finally ended up getting to the cozy corner where the canned goods were, with our old postman behind the tiny counter. When I said that the town hadn't changed much, he said, "No," and there the conversation ended. We left as soon as I could get Dad away. He was not thinking of things to say either.

While I was at home I did get re-acquainted with a few old friends and met a few new ones. That part was real fun and ended up with a couple of special social events. I went to a couple of dances and, something new in our district, a skating party.

One of the first dances was held at our school, Wavy Plains. It was still hard to get used to the fact they'd changed the building around inside and out.

It was crowded. My old classmate Richard was most in evidence. He tried to pick up where he had left off when I had been sent away to school. There weren't any other young men more exciting than Richard, but he was hard to discourage.

It was an experience to find myself "belle of the ball," and I wished I could have handled it better. It's hard to stay composed when everyone is looking at you. Anyway, poise was never my greatest accomplishment. Besides, I didn't know how to square dance or polka, which was quite a large handicap. But when we were young a dance was a dance! Great fun, and no one worried about steps. I did get to dance with a big, quiet blonde farm boy. He was just about my age, and he was most appealing.

There was a three-piece orchestra. The fellow who played the guitar asked a violin player to take his place in the band. Then he asked to dance with me. My, I was flattered but not "easy." He was a tall, handsome thing and sure of himself. I thought about him the rest of the time at home. He was wide awake to everything. In later years he went on to become a very successful farmer, with clothes tailored in England, no less.

Then there was Dan Breitenbach. He was the oldest of that German family that used to fight with the Moores when we were in school together. He was, perhaps, a class behind me and rather quiet. His brother was the fighting one and forever at it.

At the first dance, Dan very shyly asked me to have supper with him. Richard had already asked, so he sat on the other side. Richard was most annoyed. Dan had grown into a very nice fellow, and I enjoyed his company.

Some of the older men asked to me to dance. At those affairs everyone dances all evening, regardless of age.

In the next school district, Glenada, a family invited me to a skating party. They had a slough right outside the kitchen door of their house, down a ten-foot bank. I knew their names but that was all. The oldest girl was a pretty thing and my age. We nearly froze going there in the sled so got toasty in the house before donning our skates. The young people were clamoring, "Put on your skates and come," but I didn't know how to skate.

Bent double, I could manage a slide here and there. That didn't matter; I got plenty of help. They formed long lines and cracked the whip. Couples skated for a while, Richard helping me, and back to more group antics. Whenever anyone got too cold, they clambered up the bank and into the kitchen for a spell. After a hearty feed around midnight that went on at length, we took ourselves home.

Then came a big dance at Benton Hall. Richard came to our

house to see what I would wear. He'd asked everything about down East and knew we wore long dresses, so he must see what I had.

For the end of school, I'd made a blue organdy with a double ruffle around the neck and ruffles on the end of the sash. He insisted I wear it. "But nobody else has a dress like that." That didn't matter, "Everyone would love to see it," etc. The night came and we were ready to go when Mom said, "You're not going out in this cold with a dress like that!" We argued, and we argued some more.

I'd vowed to be good when I went back home, not to be argumentative with Dad, no matter what! This resolution lasted just one day! He just couldn't leave people alone, and I was caught more times just trying to answer what seemingly started out to be a simple question. If he didn't see something, he wasn't likely to believe it. This went for ideas as well as things. I was surprised to run up against a stone wall with Mom, also. Not having ever been directly disobedient, I let her talk me into going to that dance with long winter underwear and only silk stockings to cover my legs! And I had on high heels!

Well, I'll tell you, this gave me a bad time all evening, and sometimes I didn't dance. With people watching from the sidelines, I couldn't swish through the fun of the all-the-men-left's as the others did. If I did, that awful bump at the ankles would show. When it came to the very lively foursomes of "Sally-in-the-Sugar-Bowl", it wasn't so bad. I made sure we were in the middle of the floor and, with so much activity, no one would notice.

Not knowing all the square dance routines was awkward. The dancers wouldn't let me sit one out. They pulled me out onto the floor willy-nilly.

Richard at once asked for the supper dance. When Dan asked later, I told him about Richard and thought no more about it. When it was time for supper, I didn't see either of them. I asked someone near the door if they knew what happened, and they said they were outside fighting over me!

What was I to do? I knew Richard hated anything physically unpleasant. I knew that Dan would quietly do what he had to do to protect himself when cornered but wasn't apt to fight otherwise. What would happen? After hesitating only a minute, I ran out to find them. I was able to stop the fight before it got bad. I still couldn't tell you who I ate supper with.

When I again got back East and was telling a friend about everything, I didn't leave out this story. To my chagrin, she thought it was awful. How could I let such a thing happen? So I said no more. I didn't like to see them fighting, but I couldn't help feeling flattered! How in the world did my friend think I could stop the fight before I even knew about it? That was a typical Easterner for you!

My next adventure involved a redheaded freckle-faced boy. He had been the first boy I'd ever noticed and liked. His family was Methodist, so he wasn't allowed to indulge in worldly pleasures like dancing.

East of his farm was a long wide slough connecting to the one that ran through our south pasture. It was frozen beautifully smooth, so he gave a skating party for me. It was a dark night, and I don't know who all came, but it was a goodly crowd. He kept a bonfire going on the bank for quite a time. This was a feat in that lumber scarce country. It was too far from his house to go back and forth for warmth, and we sure got cold. We'd take off our skates to rub our feet when they got impossibly numb.

There were two men with mouth organs, and we skated to the music in couples. For the life of me, I couldn't see the difference between that and dancing. We also strung out in long lines to follow the leader and crack the whip. Above it all, we heard the far away booming sound of the ice cracking, even though it was frozen solid. It was a delightful evening.

During these six months at home I tried to cook new things, though I didn't have much to work with. There was lots of work to be done, and I pitched in.

When fall came, and then early winter, Dad decided that there wasn't enough forage around home for the horses. As he did each year, he drove them all further north to more open spaces. He was gone several days. There were several inches of snow on the ground and it was cold. We women hoped the horses would be able to find shelter of some sort through the winter storms, poor things.

While dad was gone, Mom woke Mabel and me in our beds one night. She was sure she'd seen a man come over the hill from the west, carrying a lantern. We felt helpless and scared. I'm sure we saw the man open the tool house, hold the lantern over his head a moment, and then go in with his light. Whether anything was taken, we never found out, but it was so lonely out there anyway we were glad not to have it turn out any worse.

Times were not good; people seemed to be barely making enough to live.

Dad and Mabel had been doing the milking when I got home. With Dad away, I felt guilty about Mabel doing it all. So, with the lantern lit, I went out to help her. It seemed such a long time since hanging the lantern on the cross beam of the stable, where it shed its circle of light, and seeing the cows in the evening standing quietly chewing their cuds.

I got the little milking stool and very tentatively sat down. Cows seem to know if you're anxious, and Bessie looked around a number of times.

It was slow going, and I forgot how tired your hands can get. So I haltingly milked and found it a job. Mabel seemed to think little of people who couldn't even milk a cow properly! I let Dad take over the job when he came back home.

I did all sorts of mending because sewing was now something I could do easily. The biggest thing I tackled was to cut down almost everything I owned to make into dresses for the younger sisters. There were no patterns. It was fun. Before I left, I lined them up and took pictures of them with a small box camera. I wanted the pictures to keep, wondering when I'd see my sisters again. The camera was one Mom had persuaded Dad to get when I left for school. They got precious few pictures from school because there was no money for film.

In spite of being busy, time dragged at home. After so many activities to attend, there was nothing to keep one inspired and no raw materials to work with. I wrote letters to all my friends in Bryn Athyn and watercolored Christmas cards for them on scraps of paper.

I spent a good bit of time talking with the family and told them all and everything of the past years in school. The younger ones were most anxious to have their chance to see the same things.

Mom was very surprised to hear how things had *really* been those first three years.

Reta at Tonche. Maybe taken by Keneth?

Reta with Richard, at the dance

On the back of this photo Reta wrote: "Some of the Senior girls at the seashore. See me?" (Reta with headband in black top and patterned pants)

Chapter 6

THINGS NOT TO BE FORGOTTEN

After greeting the family, Mom brought old Purp in for me to see. He'd been such a pleasant companion on all our walks, hunting up the cows night after night for all the years I could remember. Now he was a sorry sight. Thin, head down, fur so piecey, and looking very tired of living. Mom said they'd kept him so I might see him again, even though he was blind and miserable. Truly, I was sorry they had done that. Within a day or two he disappeared, and I scarcely noticed. Dad, no doubt, had "seen to him" and never mentioned him again.

Maybe seeing Purp struck me as extra sad because everything was sad. Crops had been poor and getting worse. The Dust Bowl era had begun. Kitchen chairs were wired together, the linoleum had lost all its color and holes were wearing through.

I'd not been home too long when Aunt Kate phoned. She was not to be left out of all the excitement. I was to come to tea. Relations between our family and theirs never did become smooth; most of the time it was an armed truce! We might visit each other a time or two, and then no more speaking for a year or more. I knew our family reputation was at stake, so there was no choice but to go.

Aunt Kate greeted us at the door wearing white gloves! When tea was served I said, "Thank you," and sat very straight on the hard-backed chair. Conversation didn't flow easily. Soon I realized Aunt Kate wanted me to realize that *she* knew how to do things as well as they did them down East. For example, she pointed out the fact the tea was made with tea bags instead of the loose handful that "some people" throw in the big teapot. Dear, dear, I hadn't noticed!

During the winter, the big prairie jackrabbits turn pure white, except for the black tips on their ears. Evening jackets made of rabbit fur were being worn by lucky girls. Velvet ones had at least a collar of white. When I saw the first rabbit change color that winter, I asked Dad if he could get me one. Somehow he managed to kill one but left it for me to skin. The fur was spread out flat to dry. I knew if it became too dry there'd be no chance of getting it soft again, so I "bent it around" each day. As it became dryer, it was rubbed as one would scrub out a washcloth, which kept it pliable enough.

When I got back to Bryn Athyn, I bought some bright pink crepe at W.T. Grants basement in Philadelphia, where everyone shopped, and made an evening dress. Also, a little cape was made to go over my shoulders. The white fur was to go around the edge of the cape. One rabbit does not supply enough to do that much properly, and I found that cutting strips left raw edges. The answer was snipping and tearing it into little tufts. With these sewn fairly close together around the edge, the effect was most attractive. All the girls admired it, and I felt very dressed up. The boys needn't know I'd been so practical!

The other wild animal that turned white in winter was the weasel. I saw only one before the snow became deep, when they seemed to disappear. I vowed I'd have him and, after tracking him to a gopher hole, carried buckets of water to drown him out. When he showed his head, I had a stick handy. Dad helped me skin him, saving paws and ears and even whiskers. He was "peeled" and left like a hollow tube. The skin was tanned like that of the rabbit. His bit of fur never did get used for anything but was kept as a memento for "show and tell."

MARCH

We had a radio, run from a wet cell battery for power. When the battery ran down, which it did during that winter, Dad had to have it recharged somewhere.

The redheaded freckled boy who gave the skating party offered to do this for me as a favor. I left the battery with him. They had a windmill and thus a wind charger.

No one had been to Benton for the mail in some time, so I decided I'd go and pick up the battery on the way home. We'd been without the radio for some time. There wasn't much snow on the ground and I'd take the cart. Dad had acquired this or made it while I was away. It was a foreshortened sort of small wagon with a spring seat that sat up in the air. The sides of the box part of it were very low.

Mabel and I hitched up the team. I'd almost forgotten how. She'd never take the initiative, so I was to drive. It was a chore, as I hadn't driven for years and was unfamiliar with the ways of these particular horses. We managed to get to Benton, up and down all the hills and grades. We bought a box of groceries and put them in behind the seat. The horses took much prodding to keep them going. They were the heavy workhorses. When we got back to the neighbor's farm, within sight of home, and turned into their dirt driveway, we felt almost home and glad.

I pulled up and turned around by their kitchen door, almost under the clothesline. The young fellow came out with the battery. He had just put the battery on the floor of the cart when a gust of wind flipped the towels on the line.

I was sitting with the reins in my hand and my head turned round watching him. Those poky horses took off like a shot! Reflex made me hold tight to the lines and call for a "Whoa" while pulling them back hard.

Everything happened so fast then. The next thing I realized was that I was lying on the ground. I tried to sit up and felt smothered by my own skirts! The young fellow and his brother were fussing about. I finally got my skirts down from over my head and could sit up. Such a sight I saw! Those horses were tearing for the row of trees planted as a windbreak. First one horse jerked ahead and then the other. Out of the cart bounced the battery and landed very near. Groceries were bouncing up in the air and landing here and there, and I laughed. Then I realized Mabel was still sitting on the seat. She soon jumped free, to the side, and after a rough landing she was all right.

The horses crashed into the trees and stopped. Suddenly I felt that I hurt, but I couldn't tell where. My clothes were still all twisted about, and I couldn't move without hurting. But move I did, enough to pull my skirts under me. I thought how lucky it was that Mom made me wear that long-legged fleece underwear. Those boys managed to carry me into the house and phone Dad. I got home in a wagon, I don't know whose, nor do I know who untangled the mess of horses and harness from the trees.

This is Mabel's version of what she saw happen: After the horses bolted, I was yanked forward because of holding so tight to the lines. I landed in front of the cart at the horses' heels. My clothes caught on the whiffletree of the harness and were wedged there when the first horse pulled ahead. She said, "I watched you being dragged with those big hoofs coming so close to your back." Then the other horse pulled ahead see-saw fashion, and thus I was freed. This was to one side, and after this the cart wheels on that side ran over me. Thank goodness it wasn't the heavy wagon we often used. She then said to herself, "I'm in a runaway, I'd better get out," and she jumped.

I was laid on the couch in the sitting room, there to stay for a week. After first getting there and taking inspection, I found an enormous hole in the underwear on my right hip and a big patch of flesh rubbed off. It was very painful. My whole left leg was black and blue and swollen. Mom got a basin of water to wash out dust and pebbles.

As the week wore on, my hurts felt worse and worse. The big hurt on the hip was a sight of open soreness and proud flesh and didn't seem to be healing at all. I asked Dad if there wasn't a doctor somewhere. He located one in the town of Alsask, on the border of Saskatchewan, about twenty miles away.

I can't remember getting there.

Alsask, like many towns, had a one-room hospital. The doctor went from one to another on a sort of circuit. After looking at the sore, the doctor sent someone for very hot water and a couple of towels. After dropping a towel in the bucket of water, he wrung it out, still piping hot, and covered the sore. It was blissful and stopped the worst of the pain.

Upon feeling everything and looking over all bruises, he said that a bone in my leg was broken just above the ankle. No wonder that leg hurt so much! Mabel had said I'd been caught and held by my ankle. Next, he covered the leg in a heavy plaster cast, leaving just my toes free, and covering up to my knee. It was such a thick, heavy weight, and how was I to keep toes warm??

I went home to some peace for the first time in a week. The doctor said to come back in six weeks to have the cast removed. He said also to keep on with the hot towels a few times a day, until all was healed. He had cut away the bumpy edges.

I only had a month. Early in April I'd have to be back across the border or lose my chance at U.S. citizenship. Goodness knew what trouble it would be to start all over again. I'd be an immigrant this time, with no funds.

I hadn't the foggiest notion of what I would do after I did get back to Pennsylvania. During this month, I got a letter from the D. family I'd stayed with when I first went to Bryn Athyn. The beauty shop was still going strong, and she needed help very much. She would pay me seven dollars a week, and I could have every Sunday after dinner off. I wasn't thrilled by this but was very glad to have a destination, so I accepted.

I packed the few things left to take back in the suitcase Miss Vida had given me. Mom was sad to see me go and so was Mabel. I had tried to do as much for her as I could by way of telling her things and showing her about sewing.

Then I went to work on the cast. I wouldn't go near the doctor for fear he'd say, "NO." With the hammer and butcher knife (I wouldn't trust any help) I spent hours taking it off in bits and pieces. The parents made no objections. Dad said he'd take me to the train along with the carefully saved money for the ticket I'd brought with me. As I remember, it was around forty-five dollars. I was careful not to put my weight on the sore leg and got along well enough.

I was glad to be going back to all the things and people back East. That now meant home to me more than the place where I grew up. I sure felt sorry for those I left behind. Such contrasts are hard to handle when one is young. All I felt was gratitude that I'd been rescued from a life like my mother's. I did sometimes feel that I belonged nowhere.

After another long, disjointed train ride of sitting up and sandwiches, I arrived back at Bryn Athyn Station.

BACK TO BRYN ATHYN

It was nice to be back in that familiar place! After being in school for so many years, I felt adrift. It had stopped so suddenly, and all the young people's social life died with it. All the graduation speeches talked of going out into the world, but we were *so* green in our outlook and experience compared with children today. The thought of "going out" wasn't anticipated with pleasure. Being in familiar surroundings helped to tide over the change from childhood to adult responsibility. It took a long time to become accustomed to the idea.

We were too young to join the Civic and Social Club, which didn't do much anyway. Mrs. Heath, the lady with the candy and ice cream store, had turned her basement into a sort of Beer Parlor. Many growled about it, but she felt there should be some spot to socialize other than just the formal affairs. Usually a few men stopped there for beer, and we young people thought it was a den of iniquity!

That first social center grew more popular, so a larger and better place was found, a rather pretty stucco and brown trim house on Alden Road, directly below Mrs. Heath's. The Club couldn't afford the whole building, so they used the second floor. The first floor was rented as a grocery store.

Knowing all the ropes at the D.'s this time made it rather easy and satisfying to clean and cook. With the children older and no school or studies for me, the work was easier. However, I was casting around in my mind as to some more challenging occupation. A girl had the choice between being a teacher or a nurse. I knew I was never cut out to be a teacher. After a number of weeks, I decided "maybe" on the nursing. I liked helping the sick. One day I took a tour of Abington Hospital but had gone no further when my plans changed, and I was offered a job by the P.'s. I had been at the D.'s for only a matter of months. Things were worse and worse and worse at home because of the dust storms, so, while at the D.'s, I sent five of my seven dollars home each week.

It was the summer before this when I lived here and there taking any job to earn money for the round-trip ticket home that a classmate asked me to come visit her. K.R. Alden, the boys' principal who raised his family in Stuart Hall for several years, had pitched a tent in Theo P.'s woods for a goodly part of the summer. After living alone awhile, Thoreau-like, his family joined him for their vacation. It was quite a piece up the railroad tracks. This friend of mine was staying with them to help cook over the campfire and mind the children.

One evening, a few young people, including her, were at the Don Roses' when she asked me to settle on a date to visit her. It was to be on a Saturday or Sunday night. Keneth Simons happened to be there, and he overheard the arrangements. He didn't like the idea of my walking up to the camp alone at night. (I'd probably have gone while it was still daylight and had a ride home.) He offered to walk me up there, saying that K.R. was his uncle, and he'd like to visit him anyway. I accepted. So that was one more isolated incident of seeing Keneth Simons!

I wondered from time to time what the future would bring, mostly by way of likely boys. Outside of seeing a girlfriend or two at their house on a Sunday off, there was not one place to get together with a mixed group of young people. The girls felt most self conscious about having parties. It would look like they were trying too hard. The one or two with a steady didn't give parties any more at their homes. I accepted any invitation I got, but they were few. I was still very unsure about boys. How did one talk to them interestingly? What could be done to encourage them to plan something? There were so few likely ones, and they were just as timid as we.

After a week or two of settling in at the D.'s, the telephone rang for me. It was Nathan. His calling me had Mrs. D. "all of a dither." He asked for a date, and I accepted. After getting into his nice little convertible, he suggested Willow Grove Amusement Park, and it was a fun place for a date.

We rode the scooter cars with rubber bumpers and banged into each other all over the circular pen. Then we decided to be "kiddy" and enjoyed the merry-go-round. After that he said, "Why not the Alps?" This was a roller coaster which ran in and out of dark, fake mountains. I wasn't enthusiastic about that strange-looking contraption. In fact, I was scared of it.

As we were about to enter a tunnel, he asked if he could put his arm around me. I said, "Oh, if you have to," thinking we must be about to take a nasty dip. When we came out into the open again, I felt foolish; it had been perfectly flat in there!

On the way home, he pulled off to the side of the road and stopped the car. I became slightly alarmed and asked, "Aren't you going to take me home?" He at once started up the car and home we came. It didn't even occur to me he might like to talk a bit. He was as awkward with girls as I was with boys. There was no place to visit alone at his house or at the D.'s and, since I was only nineteen, we'd never have considered a night spot. I felt the evening had fallen flat, but I was still dreaming of someone else anyway.

Charter Day was coming up. Nathan invited me to the dance. It was held later in the year then. Now it is celebrated earlier, so there is better weather for marching and football games.

Mrs. D. had a patron who brought her a lovely, used evening dress for me. It was one of her friend's from out of town. I suspected that Mrs. D. told her who I was going out with, and she was wondering about what I'd wear. At least she'd never handed over anything so pretty before, nor after. It was of lovely white net, as full-skirted as a Southern belle, with fingers of fine white taffeta running down onto the skirt. In back was a large soft bow of the same, lined with red.

I was surprised Nathan had asked me to go to the Charter Day dance, and I was delighted to accept. The evening was pleasant, not outstanding, but it turned out to be the last date I ever had with him.

CAIRNWOOD

One day I got a letter asking if I'd like to come and work at Cairnwood. I didn't hesitate to say, "Yes" to the job, and the D.'s were mighty put out. Mrs. P. had asked if the D.'s had paid my fare back. When she found they hadn't, she saw no reason why I couldn't do as I chose. January 5, 1935, I moved to Cairnwood.

Even though I'd spent several weeks there the year before, it was not all that familiar. This time there was a regular routine and a whole group of us working together.

John P.'s oldest granddaughter, Gay, had been married the year before at the Cathedral, which he had built. The wedding was a very elegant affair. The reception took place in the Assembly Hall, which was decorated to be a beautiful garden, even including fountains.

I have to say something about Cairnwood, the family's home at that time. Cairnwood was a lovely old mansion, also built by John P. It was constructed of soft, sandy colored orange-tinted brick. It was surrounded by an expanse of well-groomed grass bordered by trees. It came from a time of gracious living, the turn of the century. Carriages drove through tall iron gates to the porte cochere. While I lived there, two liveried chauffeurs drove big, black, comfortable cars. One was used by Mr. P., the other by the family. The front door at Cairnwood was opened by one of the girls. She would hear the bell in the back hall and could see by the "box" with its clock-like hands which door had to be answered. Someone was constantly on duty to listen for this.

Inside was a red-carpeted hall, bearing slightly to the right. This careful curve prevented those entering the door from seeing directly into the living area. This was a clever means of ensuring privacy without being inefficient. Almost directly across from the entry, but a little way up the hall, was the doorway to the dining room. Directly across at the other end were windows looking out at the lawn.

Overhead, in the dining room, the ceilings were supported by lovely, dark old beams decorated with gold leaf. To one side was a large fireplace. I never saw it used. On the other wall was a big sideboard holding silver candlesticks and such. The table was long and covered with white linen. There was an open corner cupboard containing more silver. On one of its shelves, of special importance, sat a large silver wine cooler just presented to Mr. P. He had helped to repeal the Eighteenth Amendment on prohibition, and the cooler was inscribed with the names of famous people who were grateful for his help. This was used each Sunday at dinnertime.

Under the dining table, at Mrs. P.'s place, was an electric button. When she pushed it, the "girls" rushed in from their dining room to wait on table. In our own dining room, we dined quite formally. One of the black cooks waited on us, and we ate the same food as the family.

Their dining room was never light but was comfortable looking and gave one a rather hushed feeling. It wasn't gloomy, though in passing one might wonder. Here Mrs. P. presided at the head of the table. Under the table, on a long cord, was a button that sounded a buzzer in the pantry.

Two white girls waited on table in very stiff, starched, white nurse-like uniforms. We girls also dined quite formally, and when the housekeeper rang our bell one of the black kitchen cooks waited on us. Our roasts, steaks, and desserts were the same as those served to the family up front.

Two black cooks worked in the kitchen. Their personalities were vastly different. One was Lena, the other was Jenny. Both were old.

Lena was heavily built. It seemed surprising that her thin legs could carry all that weight! We speculated as to how so much heft and such big bosoms developed above such spindly legs! Her hair was thin and straight, and she wore it all messed up with a bit of a bun on top.

Lena considered herself high class, and she was. She spoke excellent English, had good manners, and ruled the kitchen with "a rod of iron." When she was nervous or excited, she spoke in a very high-pitched voice and then, look out! Never did she take a day off unless forced into it, which rarely happened. She didn't seem to have any family and wasn't about to tell you very much about herself. She cooked very special things for Mrs. P., like plunkets, which were like very soft, light sponge cupcakes. For the rest of us, she made big, fat, superb sticky buns covered with nuts, butterscotch pies dripping with butter, chocolate marshmallow and lady finger pudding that was out of this world! Everything she cooked was a gourmet's treat.

Jenny was very different. She was cook's helper, and when Lena did take a day off, the housekeeper picked an easy menu. Jenny was a reprobate. I wonder how she ever kept the job. Lena never liked her, but Lena probably wouldn't have liked anyone sharing her kitchen. We'd hear them quarreling hotly sometimes, and the housekeeper would have to step in. We girls, the white help, all enjoyed Jenny's humor and swapped tales about her. She was quiet in general but muttered when she was angry. At those times she became almost frightening, glancing sideways with only the whites of her eyes showing. She was pretty old, and her bones seemed to have sagged. She shuffled when she walked.

Jenny was untidy about her person, and we sometimes came upon the housekeeper speaking to her about this. Her hair was short and seldom brushed. It stuck out in pieces from her head. Sometimes she smelled awful from the mange cure she'd put on her hair. She was jolly to talk with most of the time and always took her day off. When I asked her once what she did with her day off, she told me she had visited her relatives in jail! When I looked a bit shocked she said, "Why, haven't you ever visited anyone in jail?"

There were six other girls working there at that time. They ranged in age from nineteen to forty. I was the youngest. There was also a housekeeper.

Our dining room was beyond the kitchen, the last room at the end of the hall. Jenny waited on us when the housekeeper rang her little bell under the table. Such wonderful luxury, and we had exactly the same goodies as up front. Across the hall from our dining room was a big room with wooden refrigerators lining one wall and food storage cupboards along the other. All this back hall was very dark and musty.

Above this part, on the second floor, were five bedrooms and a bath for us girls. The housekeeper had a little room to herself. Across the hall was the room of the head nursemaid, who worked with the children. Next to her was another, older woman who did a lot of secretarial work. She often made beds with me. The two rooms on the end, with the bath between, were shared with two in each room.

I did substitute waitressing two days a week, for lunch and supper, when each of these girls had a day off. The housekeeper, Teddy, let us choose at the beginning of the year which day of the week we wished to take off. Mine was Tuesday. She was a most kind, pleasant woman. She was very active and set a good example. She made it known that anyone could talk to her any time.

On the other side of the bath lived the other waitress, my friend and former roommate, Ann, from the mountains. Ann was assistant nursemaid and helper with the children. She was wonderful at telling them stories while helping them to bed.

She and I most always made all the beds together and had lots of ideas to exchange. We came to make beds in record time. We worked together so often that we knew the next move and didn't have to think about it. Then we dusted and mopped the upstairs. There was a house man to do all the vacuuming and scrubbing of floors. On Saturdays, we polished all the brass doorknobs on the second floor, and there were dozens. The big third floor was used as a bedroom, too, so we worked up there. This did not take up our whole day.

I felt that I had the best job of any. It had so much variety. I made beds and dusted every morning, which took a couple of hours. I waitressed two days a week, didn't enjoy that and would never have liked it as a steady job, though it did allow lots of free time. When regular waitress girls were on duty answering the doorbell in the afternoon and often part of the morning, they were free to write letters, iron, and sew. When I was on duty, on the days I waitressed, I spent every bit of my free time sewing fine hems on new table napkins and the like.

A little old lady was brought each morning by the chauffeur to sit in the sewing room and go over the laundry as it came up. Sheets and tablecloths were hauled up on a dumbwaiter. Ann and I went down to the laundry in the basement, where a couple did the wash, to carry up all the clothes and put them away in various closets and dressers.

I spent much time pressing. In those days, cotton dresses were starched and became wrinkled if one sat down in them. So, after a girl in the family wore a dress to school, I would press it for next day.

The nursemaid washed the children's hair. When the family's daughters saw me doing my own hair, they asked if I would set theirs. So, each week I set hair for two of the daughters of the house and for the older married sister when she visited. From this beginning, the girl my age in the family became a friend. Her name was Karen, and her younger sister was Beth.

Mrs. P. sometimes asked me to do her hair, and I was awed and so anxious to have it turn out well. I also did hair for the housekeeper. I very much liked doing this. It was a wonderful way to get to know people.

The fun part of finger-waving the two girls' hair was when there was a dance or a party. After they were all ready in their party dresses, I went up to their room to comb out their hair, tie sashes, or any little last minute thing. Sometimes they would sneak a little makeup on but most often took it with them to put on when they got to the dance. Their papa and mama disapproved. Karen was a very good girl, and I think that putting on makeup was the only disobedient thing she ever did.

These girls were still in school, but many times I went to the same dances as they did. After "doing" them, I'd pop back to my room to finish my own dressing. Boys were allowed to bring corsages to girls then, but I didn't have that kind of boyfriend.

After the dance, I'd often get a message from Karen to come to her room and we'd have lots of fun talking over what sort of times we had. These were most enjoyable times! We talked about life in general, about books, and many other things.

I did other sewing. We would look at all the French fashion magazines they had and Karen would find a sleeve she liked in one, a blouse in another, and I would put it all together. I spent many long hours on a cream-colored georgette blouse with a finely-tucked yoke and a hand-rolled ruffled edge.

I was sending home all the money I could, so I still made cheap cotton dresses for myself. These I whipped up in no time, in the evenings. More than once, the family and the housekeeper gave me the feeling that they wondered why their jobs took so long to make, and mine were done so quickly. This made me feel a little guilty. Their work had to be made so perfectly and had to have all the inside seams bound or carefully whipped by hand. They loved hand work and tiny stitches.

Each girl had half the afternoon off. This was either from lunch until four, which was longer, or from four till five-thirty. I had lots of friends in the town, so I nearly always took a walk to see them. No one said anything about this but always in that house, you knew. When given a choice, I would choose the early break because it gave me more time for the walk. When I found they weren't too happy about this, I chose the later short break. I was determined not to give up my outing. After all, it was my free time!

Rarely did anyone else go out. In fact, I was kidded about working there forever and becoming an old maid. At least three of the girls were over forty, and I was the youngest. Keeping in touch with my friends outside seemed like good insurance against this old maid business.

Cairnwood was like a whole little world to itself, and much that went on there was very interesting and very nice. I noticed, however, that the working girls who didn't go out became moody.

Anyhow, I was always out to enjoy anything there was to enjoy and to try to do the right and decorous thing as well. I gradually became aware of some of the taboos. These weren't spelled out, but I think it would have been fairer to us girls if they had been. Some of us grew up so differently!

One day Karen came home to say she had been chosen as the heroine in a play. She picked out a pretty, old-fashioned costume made of blue silk and soft white organdy. Between us we sketched out the way it was to be made. It was quite intricate. I enjoyed so much working on it. I had to make several attempts before I found out how to set in the smooth-fitting sleeves at the shoulder. They had to have enough stretch to allow freedom of movement. The sewing room was equipped with Wilcox and Gibbs sewing machines. I didn't know then how simple a Singer machine was, by comparison.

Right at this time, Mrs. P.'s dressmaker came from New York to make her a dress. I was invited into the sewing room to hand the woman pins. This was arranged so that I could watch what she did. She was a fabulous seamstress.

Standing for hours can be impossible. Mrs. P. used an antique Persian prayer stool. She sat on it while this lady snipped and cut unbleached muslin into a wonder of perfection. The pins were used so carefully and in such a way as to almost make seams. It was so thoughtful of Mrs. P. to let me watch. This happened a number of times after that.

I finished Karen's dress for the play, and they were well pleased with it. It was most carefully done. Then I was called into Mrs. P.'s boudoir one morning and given a ten dollar raise. Now I got sixty dollars every month!

I'd felt a little bitter about my pay. I was lowest paid in the group, and yet felt I did more than some. I felt it was an old hangover from the summer I'd first been there. In fact, when I was first asked back again, it seemed most surprising. I was sure they did not like me. Even the housekeeper kept herself aloof.

After I had been there six months, the housekeeper told me that they were quite satisfied with my work. She was much more friendly, too. So, I asked her how it was that they had asked me to live and work there? She said it was "so they could keep an eye on me." Besides, I could sew. There must have been a little more to it than that. I knew that they never hired anyone that they disliked!

Here is more about the house. The sewing room was in the back hall beside the bedrooms, at the top of the stairs. This was where a woman called Mrs. D. sat and did her mending, often in a rocking chair. She had a habit of tapping her foot on the floor as she worked. This would greatly annoy me when I was doing long stints of hand stitching.

There were two sewing machines. She used the newer one. There were cupboards along one wall and an ironing board. I used this for pressing.

A wide doorway connected the sewing room to the girls' sitting room. This was quite small, with a couch and a couple of chairs. It had a nice little fireplace, sometimes lit on winter evenings. All the woodwork in this back hall was varnished dark wood. The rugs were dark, too. Nothing about any of it was light.

I was the only one who dated any boys there. Ann had dates, but she lived only ten miles away, so that is where she went. It seemed like an imposition on the other girls to bring a boy up to the girls' sitting room. I only did it a couple of times. There really was no privacy, and with a roommate like mine, no feeling of an "own" place to go to. There were all kinds of sticky wickets in connection with dates. They really didn't seem to like us to have dates. But I charged merrily ahead with my own life and did some worrying on the side.

They were always fussing about the hours Ann and I kept. "Everyone should be in bed very early." If I waited on table and had a date to go to the movies, it would be after eight before the dishes were done. In this case we would go to the second show. With a snack somewhere after, it could be midnight by the time I got home. Thank goodness for Ann. We'd sneak in together. This worked as long as she lived there. The difficulty was that the last person in had to set the burglar alarm. The nuisancy thing *would* have to be in the front part of the house, at the end of the long second floor hall. The sneaking part came when Ann would insist I go with her (often I just did it alone), and we'd creep softly along on the rug, hesitating and listening for any stirrings, and then move on. If there was a sound, we'd fly back to our hall and wait a while.

Occasionally the alarm would show that some door was unlocked, and we'd have to wander around in the dark to shut it. The housekeeper had to be avoided if possible, too. She'd no doubt report our hours. "They" always seemed to know a lot what we did, and how else did they find out? Children slept all along that hall, and they might have awakened sometimes, but I doubt it. They were behind big closed doors, on offset halls.

I always felt that the front part of the house, on the first floor, was oddly arranged. There was a large room that was pretty much a central hall, but it was used as a bare sort of living room. The family spent quite a bit of time there. Most outstanding about it was a wide and beautiful stairway that turned and came down from the floor above. It was a picture to see the daughters come along the balcony and down this stairway in their long, lovely evening gowns.

I hardly knew the downstairs, outside of this hall, and in the years I lived there was never in some of the first-floor rooms.

One room on the way to this hall from the porte-cochere was the music room. It looked just right for a music room, all done with dainty French chairs. The children played all their various instruments there, and many a teacher we ushered in. Some were from the Philadelphia Orchestra.

Each of the family bedrooms on the second floor opened on a lovely, white-railed balcony. This part of the house was home ground to me. These rooms were light and white. Most noteworthy was a big room to the left at the end of the hall. It had French doors to let in light from a little balcony, a fireplace, a big couch, and a nice chaise lounge. I loved the idea of that chaise lounge. When children or their parents were recuperating and trays were brought up, that's where they sat.

This big room was Mrs. P.'s boudoir. When she wanted to see all of us together to tell us something, this was where we went. It was where I went to see her fittings. It was a much-used room and ever so nice.

We were all given one round-trip ticket to town each week if we wished to shop. We usually did. We each had our own key to the back door.

Cairnwood had a tall, skinny black man who went the rounds at night. His name was George Belt. He carried a policeman's stick and wore a uniform of sorts. His face was full of kindly wrinkles. Sometimes we would walk home in the dark, up the path along the Pike. When we came in through the big gates, he would step out from behind a bush so quietly we'd be startled out of our wits. We were relieved to see it was only George, who seemed pleased to see someone to chat with. He was such a kindly old gentleman, I don't know how he would ever have hurt any prowler if he had to. Fortunately, in those times, we in B.A. were way out in the country where life was rural and safe.

Down in the woods was a little stone house Mr. P. had built, more than a tea house, but not for sleeping. This was Mrs. P.'s hideaway. Beside it was a little stream with a pool filled with water lilies at one end and with myriads of goldfish of all sizes. There were smaller rocky ponds, waterfalls and beautiful flowers along the bank with a place to sit.

Ann and I went down to dust the little house perhaps once in two weeks. We had such a good time talking on the way and taking a quick look at the pool and flowers. Once or twice I walked down with a date late in the evening, on a moonlit night. I have most fond recollections of the place.

The apartment across the road where Nathan lived was over the car garages. On the other end of the building was an apartment where the caretaker of the grounds lived. Behind all of it were several long greenhouses, next to a big garden patch where the most delicious vegetables were grown. The prize ones were peas, and later lima beans, to say nothing of big fat red strawberries.

On the Cairnwood side of the road, next to the big iron gates, was another sandy brick building. It housed beautiful, old-fashioned carriages from grandfather's time. There was an apartment there, too. In it lived the family who did the laundry.

To the left of the gates were shrubs and another greenhouse. Behind this was an enchanted place known as the "pergola." A high brick wall hid the road. Over the top were big beams, open and covered with climbing wisteria, lovely to behold and smell in the spring. Under the pergola, at one end, was a wishing well. The open front looked out on a flower garden. Here was another nice place to walk with a date at night.

Nathan's apartment had to be dusted once a week, which was another job for Ann and me. It was a beautiful studio sort of place with a high ceiling of dark beams and a fireplace. Ann used to be very whimsical and would imagine what it would be like to live there, almost like a princess.

When Karen and Beth went to town to shop, I went to keep them company, or to watch out for them, I'm not quite sure which. We'd be driven to town, which was delightful compared with riding the train. I loved every minute of it. When they looked for pretty dresses I looked, too, to help and often got ideas to use in sewing my own clothes. I loved to sew.

Pretty soon I had another job of the same sort, that I loved very much. Granny Glenn, Mrs. P.'s mother, went to a bank in the city to "clip coupons," whatever *they* were! Something like once a month she'd be driven in, and I went along with her. My, it was scary in that big bank vault! The doors were so thick. The back was covered with glass and what looked like the innards of huge clocks. Granny was the best company, so alert and caring for others. She was a storehouse of practical knowledge. All in all, I felt I had any number of useful jobs which made work there a pleasure.

Not long after getting the job at Cairnwood, I was invited to quite a big party. The hostess had been in school with me, but I didn't know her very well. Also, I didn't know a lot of the young people there. Some were older brothers and sisters of kids I had gone to school with. Early in the evening, while standing in a group, someone said, "We hear you are having the best time anyone ever had at that job?"

It was said as a question and dampened the party for me. I didn't know what to say. Before they were through, I felt somewhat defensive but knew I did have a good time and felt most grateful and happy to have the job. It made me a bit wary. Life sometimes seemed hard to figure out, and I wished for some older confidant. Young people needed parents sometimes, too, I decided; they weren't just for when one was a baby.

Soon I heard other people say they'd heard I was enjoying it there and in such a way as to say, "How could you?" My feeling was, how could I help but not! Then I wondered whether I was doing all the right things. It was hard to be sure. But I trusted people and felt the housekeeper would tell me, at least anything that was important.

By this time, I was fairly used to the routine. I was sorry Tuesday was my day off because that was steak night. I even gave up and came home from a friend's for supper periodically to have the treat. After a while, it didn't matter. There were so many good things. I always had a safe and comfortable feeling there because there was no want.

THE MOUNTAINS

When May came there began to be talk of the mountains and wondering when we'd leave. There was nothing that wasn't thoroughly discussed as a general rule. Would we go by the Storm King Highway? Should I take this or that?

When school closed there was an impatience to be off. We girls liked going, and the sooner the better. To me, one part was awfully boring and that was the packing. Great wicker hampers covered with canvas about three by four feet wide and three and a half feet tall were carried to various rooms and set along the upstairs hall. With them were reams of tissue paper. For days, any spare time was spent packing. Nothing was done in a hurry and finished with, for sure. After packing as much as had been decided upon up to that time, we'd wait till handed, say, a sweater. After a couple of days maybe something packed would be wanted, and such a chore to find it and restore all to order. My, I disliked the job!

The chosen day arrived, and a cavalcade of cars set off. Maybe one of the school boys would drive one of the trucks up. A couple of very nice boys were chosen each summer to go and work around the place. They were always friends of the family.

Those lovely mountains! Whoever would have thought I'd see them again! I had my same room back, and with Ann. All the years I worked there it was my room, though roommates varied due to vacations of the girls when substitutes came. I think it the best room still, even though one had to be so quiet not to disturb the P.'s overhead. Certainly they could keep very good track of anyone in that room!

Again the early rising with the sun, books, music, and swimming. A hike "up top" when work was done, and a smoke for Ann. By this time, I was getting pretty heavy and someone said, "Instead of dessert, why don't you try a cigarette?" I loved to eat but was most unhappy about how my clothes fit. In fact, I'd have to shorten the waistline on anything I bought, which was a big nuisance. And to be seen in a bathing suit!

The P.'s liked "nice sized" persons and abhorred seeing fat people.

I weighed myself when no one was around, instead of being in line like the others. At lunchtime, when someone might say, "Let's get weighed," I didn't.

We still wore rompers most of the time and were very comfortable in them. Outsiders called them our uniforms.

Down the back of the mountain was a little town called Woodstock. We girls always loved to go there, but it only happened a couple of times in a summer.

Most every day was spent on the mountain, but after supper we might go down to Kingston, as often as three times in a summer, to see a movie. A few evenings we might have all the young people in two big cars and just go for an hour's ride to see the reservoir or down a country road.

All the cars were named by the kids. "Sail Boat" was the favorite. It was a big old-fashioned touring car, and the top could be put down. All the cars had two little seats that pulled down from the front seats so that as many as eight people could ride comfortably.

Once one of the P. boys was driving "Sail Boat." On the road we passed a funny old man with an accordion. Even though we all had shivers of doing wrong, we stopped and picked him up. He'd play us some music as we drove and we'd sing. We were always singing. He said he knew lots of songs. We asked him to sing "The Prisoner's Song," and he launched into "Turkey in the Straw." We laughed. No matter what we asked him to play, he still played "Turkey in the Straw." Pretty soon we began to wonder how would we get rid of him. He was quite a disappointment. We whispered and giggled and worried, "What if we couldn't get rid of him?" Along another road we stopped the car and said, "Thank you, we'd better leave now." He wobbled out.

We giggled and laughed about it and promised we'd never tell we'd picked him up.

But best of all to me were the trips to Woodstock. It was a quaint place with crooked streets and little shops. It was an artists' colony. Nearby was the little stock company playhouse. It was such fun to look through all the shops, even though I rarely bought anything.

One shop sold bright but nice print dresses, long and with rows of bias tape above the hems. A visiting aunt of the family bought one. She wore it to supper and we all thought it so pretty. It became a regular thing.

After I looked the dress over, I was asked if I could copy it. So I got busy and made I don't know how many. Most everyone dressed in them for supper from then on, and it added something to the fun of the summer. If we played dance music after supper in the big living room, they were such fun to dance in. We all danced. Being short of boys, I took a boy's part many times. I made myself one of these "Woodstock dresses" in a lovely blue print (rather like an Indian bedspread).

Something very nice happened as a result of my making these dresses. A shop in Woodstock carried Indian turquoise jewelry. I had looked at it often, but it cost too much for me. After I'd finished Karen's Woodstock dress, she came one day with one of those pretty little turquoise pendants as a gift. She was like that.

There were very often guests at the mountains, some staying only a day or two, but some much longer. A maiden aunt who taught singing, Miss Creda, always spent part of her summer there. I used to sometimes set her hair, so she decided she'd give me a singing lesson. I balked. I felt that it needed more than a singing lesson to help *my* voice. One day I succumbed, and it was remarkable what all she did accomplish, but you should have heard! She was quite a gifted woman. Karen took some singing lessons from her, and I loved hearing them do the Kashmiri Songs. A

schoolteacher or two came for a couple of weeks at a time, often the Bishop and his wife.

One person who came and was prevailed upon to stay was Mrs. P.'s mother, Mrs. Glenn. She was Granny Glenn to everyone. She had been a widow since before her last baby was born but took it in her stride. She was so trim, even though at this time she was slightly bent and pretty old (seventy two, I believe). She got up early to help us set the breakfast table. We all tried to stop her, but she said she would rather "wear out than rust out." She took time to know everyone and befriend them. I got to know her quite well and sure liked her. She asked about my family and was partly responsible for arranging to bring more of them down to school.

One time, all the young folks were going to the movies. We needed a chaperon. Granny Glenn decided she'd go because it was a Clark Gable movie. She'd heard so much about him and wanted to see for herself. She reported back that she couldn't see his appeal, saying "He looked like a thug." We all protested and could scarce believe it! He was such a go-getting, appealing he-man, and that smile! How could anyone feel that way?

Being at the mountains this time for the whole summer, except for a week's holiday, gave me a complete feeling about the family. Gradually over the years, I saw the places I had heard talked about. Mr. P. liked very much to hike and went back to his old haunts and favorite places with perhaps a year in between. These were the summer's highlights. Everyone was invited to go. Mrs. P. and the nursemaid, Bea, usually stayed home.

Right after work was finished in the morning, we'd make and pack up dozens of sandwiches and lemonade. Then, in another of our cavalcades, we'd start out for Lookout Mountain. Mr. P., with an old stick in his right hand, led the way up whatever trail he chose, and sometimes there wasn't much of one. We panted and puffed after him. He rarely stopped unless he came to an outcropping of rock where he could see a view. He seemed to be *so* fond of views.

Sometimes they were nice, but I most often liked the brooks and ferny dells which abound in that area. Perhaps he'd decide to take a picture. It seemed to us he took hours to get one to suit him. Some were of the group. Then we'd each ask for a copy. I never thought, until much later, how cheeky this must have seemed to him, but he never intimated as much or said a word. He was rather quiet with us and said very little. I used to wish very much I could talk intelligently with him when he did say something. I think it was because I was so much in awe of him that it made me act even dumber than I was. In his very pleasant way, he seemed a man very sure of himself.

Finally, we'd get to the top. By this time, Mr. P. had his sweater tied around his middle, by the sleeves, and so would all the rest. On the very top was a great big hotel, half built and abandoned. We newcomers had fun looking it over. I wonder what is there today?

Nearby we'd look for a good picnic spot and hugely enjoy lunch and chatter before the more pleasant trip down again.

Perhaps that would be it for that summer. Or we might also go to Lake Mohonk. I thought that one of the nicer trips. The car would be driven halfway up, then we'd walk. There were horses and buggies to be hired, and once we did that, but we at least walked back down. Lake Mohonk looks to be a bottomless lake and is right on top of a mountain. Tucked in one corner was an unusual hotel with several types of architecture. It looked as if each addition was done by a man determined to do it *his* way. A road wound around the side of the water and up to a higher spot. Along the sides were attractive, rustic roofed stands, to sit a spell out of the sun. On the highest cliffside was a beautiful view, and we could see Tonche Mountain across the valley with the white house of Glen Tonche tucked on the side. It would have to be a clear day, but we always chose a clear day.

The treat of this trip would be eating lunch on the way back at the little half-way restaurant. No sandwiches to make! We girls seldom ate in restaurants, so this was a big treat.

The mountains had such very nice names, like "Peekamoose" and "Sugar Loaf." I think Peekamoose was where we took my favorite trip. There was quite a climb up an almost dry creek bed. The rocks were sometimes like flat stepping stones and the greenery all around was so perfect and unspoiled. The underbrush was ferns, laurels, and rhododendrons; no untidiness, such as honeysuckle and poison ivy. The clean, clean water trickled over little ledges and into clear pools.

At last one came to a pretty little lake. Around it were the cutest birchbark cabins. We went into one and even the bookcases were rustic and made of birchbark.

Glen Tonche was built on a mountain originally called Tonche. Next to it was a smaller round-topped mountain known as Little Tonche. Out that same side was one called "Look Out," and when out for a shorter trip we climbed it. Below was the beautiful, clear Ashokan reservoir. It looked like a big sprawling lake with fingers disappearing around other mountains. Some evenings we'd go down to its edge and out in rowboats to see the sun set.

The Fourth of July came soon after we arrived at the mountains. We often celebrated with a picnic on the banks of the reservoir. We shot off fireworks, to be reflected in its waters. We'd had our own little parade with flags and music in the courtyard in the morning.

As summer wore on, the peace of those beautiful views all around Glen Tonche seeped in. There were times when we sat on a grassy patch under the trees, below the balcony or way off to the back side of the house, and felt the hazy, lazy summer day go by. The fluff of white clouds in the valley had risen to stand and billow above the encircling mountains. Crickets chirped in the grass, and we lay in the sun a bit to tan the back of our legs, and perhaps there'd be a bit of friendly talk.

Just below us were two enormous, tall, artistic-shaped white pine trees we looked through to see the valley. Many times later, when things weren't so good, I recalled that view and the feeling under those pines. It was restorative.

The *Jalna* books were read and discussed, and the characters in them were almost like people we knew.

Sometimes Bishop Willard, who was just a minister then, would visit and read aloud to all. It might be Wodehouse, which he enjoyed, or it might be a mystery which set all to speculating as to "Who did it?" We sprawled on the lawn sunning or embroidering as he sat just in the shade of the walkway.

Down the mountains and in the woods was the little summer theater of Woodstock. When an auntie came to visit, it might turn out she'd like to see a play. Off again would go the cavalcade. It was the greatest.

One time we went in such a hurry we left our long Woodstock dresses on.

As I was walking out of the playhouse after the show, a fellow tapped me on the arm. "Please, can I paint your picture?" he said. The place is full of artists. The girls nearby giggled and pushed to get out faster. I was asked what I said or did to encourage him to speak to me. I was insulted to have them say that. I guessed it was because they figured I "liked the boys" and dated, but I felt defensive about it all the same. Secretly, I was a bit flattered and would have liked to have seen what he'd painted. Then someone said it was probably because I was plump!

One summer we were told all who wished could go on a drive to West Point. I'd never heard where it was. Everyone packed cameras along with all the sandwiches. Such a beautiful drive down the Hudson! Someday I'd like to explore more of that river and up into its hills.

At a breathtaking point, there was the Cadet Academy before us. We arrived to see those handsome fellows, all decked out, come marching into their dining halls. We were most surprised to hear the band playing some of the most popular jazz tunes as they marched! We'd expected something like the "Stars and Stripes Forever." But we didn't waste time, out came the cameras to snap as they marched by, and guess what? My camera jammed on the second picture.

DI, LIB, AND GWEN

I must tell something of these three girls. They were classmates, a year behind me, and often got together in twos or threes for outings to the movies, etc. They lived very near each other in town.

In the course of their senior year, I'd gone home for six months, back to the D.'s to work, and finally up to Cairnwood to work, there to stay for five years. I'd gradually become acquainted with these girls. When I was a senior myself, I'd been invited to Di's house for Thanksgiving dinner. Bryn Athyn folk were very kind about adding a few dorm students to Sunday dinners or holiday meals. That Thanksgiving dinner was fun. After the big meal, we crowd of invited young folk, as well as their daughters, went for a long walk afterwards to Theo P.'s beautiful woods. The nip in the air added zest. Best of all, that special boy was also invited.

I'd also been invited to the Cooper house, which was Gwen's family. Lib was a special friend of Gwen's. Peggy, Tryn, and Eleanor were still about, but the other girls seemed to have such a good time together and often cooked up things to do as a group. Lib liked plays and was the moving force in getting tickets. Gwen liked picnics. Di mostly went along with whatever was planned.

Both Lib and Gwen got some sort of secretarial jobs, and Di went off to Ambler and horticultural school. She visited home on weekends for a year, or was it two?

Gwen's father, whom we all called Uncle Will, loved to read aloud. He was a tall man, most neat and proper in manners, but pleasant. Gwen invited us to bring embroidery or sewing one night a week and listen to Uncle Will read aloud. The first book read was one by Dickens, his favorite author. This went on for years, and it was a most pleasant evening, ending with refreshments.

MY FIRST VACATION

After having a job, the next big thing was to look around for social doings. Outside of a Charter Day Dance, and later the New Year's Dance if girls got bids, there was literally nothing in town for the young people. Under 21 you couldn't go to the Clubhouse, and there was nothing doing there anyway. All the houses that had parties while we were in school seemed to have stopped. So odd girls looked each other up here and there to go to the movies and maybe shop in town. I used to go down to visit the Roses and talk.

Several of us would get together to have gabs about what we were doing, wishing, and wearing.

In the course of events, about four of us gravitated into a group. We planned picnics in the woods with roasted hot dogs on sticks and toasted marshmallows. Three of us were working, the other going to horticultural school not too far away (the latter had no money). One gal loved to go to plays, so each winter we decided on one. The first I remember was *Porgy and Bess*. Another was *Our Town*. Both thrilling experiences.

But our big talk for months was that each was going to get a vacation. Was I? As a very special favor, I'd been allowed three days in April to go to Chicago and be a bridesmaid in my dorm roommate's wedding. The housekeeper didn't like my asking such a favor so soon after taking the job and took quite some time giving permission. So I didn't dare ask her if I got a vacation in summer. Most everyone worked a year before getting any, and only six months had passed.

In the meantime, the girls all talked and planned and Ocean City was chosen as the spot. It was considered our first vacation in our lives, and it was for me. It was the most exciting event since school. Next, we wrote to a number of likely-looking places, one girl having secured the names from somewhere. We got together to pore over the folders and prices. No one had much money to spend. I knew nothing about the procedures so just felt like an onlooker. They all had been there before so were somewhat familiar with the town.

The Brighton Hotel was chosen, I want to say around 9th Street. It was $9 apiece for the week, and I think we had just one room.

I was told in time for reservations that I would have a week's vacation. Two weeks was the regular amount.

Next we went on a shopping trip to buy a pair of shorts, bathing suits, caps, and a beach robe. The beach robe was the thing we took time over. We wanted as nice as we could find for our meager money. Beach robes were mostly a thing of modesty, but a rule. Three of us were going, so we ended up with 3 royal blue floor-length robes made of firm plissé (like seersucker) with short sleeves and belted about the middle. Today they would be looked upon as long housecoats that never belonged on the beach!

Then we felt like we were really set up.

The big day came when, with packed suitcases, we caught the train to town and then to the bus terminal to ride the big Greyhound bus.

My, it was exciting.

From the time we got on the bus we were on holiday, giggled over everything, anticipated what everything would be like, and enjoyed the feeling we were on our own to do absolutely anything that came along by way of fun. And such a fun time we had. None of us had ever felt so free.

That old hotel was something out of Currier & Ives. Not many years later it was torn down or we'd surely have gone back to see it again. It was a big, square, *old* wooden structure, three floors high with white balconies and rocking chairs across its three sides. Long narrow halls that sagged with baths of ancient vintage at the end. I don't remember how many rooms shared the same bath, but we soon planned their use early, before each mealtime, so we'd not have to wait in line. Out the front door was its big sandy parking lot and a nice view of the ocean. Its roar could be heard at night. Imagine sleeping to the sound of the surf! No vacation was ever more of a thrill.

We were up bright and early every morning to walk on the edge of the sea and hunt up different open-air eating spots for pancakes on the boardwalk.

Our first day, we hunted for hats and found three big Chinese coolie hats along with Gaby's suntan lotion.

After trying several spots, we most often chose the beach by the Lifeguard station. It was so sparkling white, and its pretty, bright colored pennants constantly flapped in the breeze. With lifesavers around its deck, we could imagine it as a boat. All along was a beautiful beach and not too crowded. (I can scarce believe how within perhaps 10 years the beach was gone.)

We swam and swam, sunned, admired the handsome lifeguards, and read magazines on our tummies.

Walking back down the boardwalk, all dressed alike, we had lots of whistles and a number of pictures taken. We shivered a bit with doubt when a fellow whistled, and we hurried faster to our room.

Suppertime found us all dressed up, comparing our tans, and discussing what spot we'd try for supper. Then we'd study menus for the cheapest and best meals. Watson's had by far the most delicious food, and even early a double line formed down the street.

After supper we walked the boardwalk, and our hair got fuzzy (no sprays of lacquer then!) from the moist air. It was so deliciously cool. We saw each shop and looked at the least thing. I bought two books for 50 cents apiece. One was *Alice in Wonderland*, the other *Green Forest*, lovely stories. Both were done in white pigskin covers. A real bargain. We fell into bed each night dead tired and happy.

Reta wrote on the back: These 2 kids came to see me one Sunday at home so – Lib Walter in my house dress – Gwen Cooper in my gymsuit & we're about to pick cherries. We got lots! You can see a few branches of the tree above us. I'm in navy pants! (Branches are mostly cropped out here. Taken at the pergola)

Reta and Dianne at the seashore.

Reta (third from left) with some of the daughters in Woodstock dresses she made

Cairnwood in Bryn Athyn

Reta wrote on the back: This is we 3 waitresses at Cairnwood. Me in the middle.
I only wait for dinner & supper when these girls get a day off.
Eunice is shortest, Marge is the other.

Chapter 7

SOME YOUNG MEN

One night I was walking up the path along the Pike on the way home when a little black flivver of a Ford stopped and the driver asked if I'd like a ride? It was that Keneth Simons fellow, coming in the opposite direction from a Sons' Picnic in Coffins' Woods. It was early still, close to 10 p.m., so I thought, "Why not?" In those days few young people had cars, so a ride was a lark. I'd expected to just be taken down the road to turn around and then back home.

It was a funny, ramshackle little roadster with a rumble seat. He had just bought it from Norbert Rogers for $15. The top was up, but the isinglass windows on the sides had worn out, so there was no protection at all from the weather. I felt like I was in a buggy, sitting up pretty high. It was very breezy driving. We went for a short ride up Buck Road and back down the Pike. It was a pleasant episode to end an evening.

Going out for walks and planning events with three or four other girls had its drawbacks. I'd decided that if asked by a boy to go to the movies, even on the spur of the moment, I would go. Of course, I'd let the girls know, but they didn't give up easily. By and by they began dating themselves, and all got married. Each one turned out to have a quite unusual romance, all but me; mine was usual.

This was the stage in my life when I was plump. I wouldn't let anyone say I was big and fat. Plump sounded better!

I bought size 18 dresses. Cheap dresses always have to be bought in a bigger size. They'd have to be taken up at the waist and the zipper put back in. I sure wished I had a good figure, but the food was *so* good.

One night I was asked out on a date by a fellow who had once taken me to a school dance. He didn't appeal to me at all, but it was a date. He was visiting from Chicago. A classmate who had lived at the dorm, Peggy, made a foursome with her date. They had tickets to a theater downtown.

Those were the days of big bands. The band was the thing! The singer, usually a girl, was hardly noticed by comparison. The orchestras did some showy bits and often there was a star musician. Mal Hallett was one example. His bass violin player put on a show of spinning it like a top between notes, slapping it with his big hands, etc. At that time Benny Goodman was coming into his own with his clarinet, and Gene Krupa could really rattle his drums. Paul Whiteman had been a big timer and still was. Wayne King was known as the Waltz King and was my favorite. Such smooth, smooth music. I didn't like the rowdy, noisy sort. They played in the Blue Room, the Pump Room, the Steel Pier, and other exotic places. Anyone who got a chance crowded in to dance to them and many watched. Artie Shaw was another one.

It turned out that our tickets were to a show Cab Calloway's orchestra was putting on. Cab's wife, Blanche, was the singer, and the orchestra was all black. We drove and drove and ended up at a dark, run-down theater. Almost the entire audience was black. The rhythm never "got to me," and I felt most alien. The others seemed to enjoy it. I was glad when it was over and chalked it up to experience. Peggy always did like the unusual!

Also in the offing once in a while was that fellow who asked so far ahead for my graduation dance. He was kind of nice, most kindly. I liked him as a friend to talk to. But how do you keep fellows just friends and no more?

The one at Miss Buell's, Alex Iungerich, had joined the Navy and showed up once in a while. He got more serious all the time and wrote long, long letters which read as travel logs. It's nice to get letters. He was a rather interesting friend, too, but gave me the same kind of problem. Later, when I was going steady, he came back and was most serious. The answer was, "No," and thereby hangs a small tale.

He once sent me a beautiful gold pin with a sapphire in it. I gave it back to him like a hot potato! It was a lovely thing, and to this day I have nothing like it. But a girl can't accept such a gift unless she's engaged! Then he shipped out to Hawaii and sent back another beautiful pin, exquisitely made. A jeweler friend told me that it was a very valuable piece. Red lacquer under smooth, rounded glass (sort of crisscrosses). Lustrous little pearls. Gold edges. A diamond!

Anyway, I sent it back to him again. Back it came, with a letter saying I was to keep it as a remembrance of friendship! It had been bought for me! What could he do with it?

I kept it until I saw him and again tried to give it back, but he wouldn't hear of it. He said it was for all our pleasant walks, talks, etc. So I did keep it and treasured it. Sad to say, years later I lost it one night at the Keswick Theater while watching a movie. The nasty manager wouldn't let us look for it. He said he'd find it and call us in the morning. Of course, he never did.

So I worked and took time off and wondered about the future. Several years went by and I still wondered. Maybe I'd end up an old maid, perish the thought. I'd been a bridesmaid in another friend's wedding. We all wore white; flowers were, too. That one was in the Cathedral. It was a big day and an elegant wedding.

NEW YORK

Sometime in November, one of the girls who was a full-time waitress at Cairnwood said, "Let's arrange for a day off together and go to New York."

She'd come from a small suburb of Chicago, the then unknown Glenview. She'd never been anywhere on her own but only to school as I had.

We had both bought new winter coats and black hats. I think that was what inspired her. The daring black derby hat she'd chosen made her feel very chic. The housekeeper OK'd the adventure, and I think drove us to Jenkintown, for we caught the Crusader from there. It was a delightfully new, shining silver train, an express.

As we neared New York, populated areas piled up on top of one another; there was no country-like atmosphere such as the miles of wooded land around B.A. It was a new, exciting feeling of approaching a very cosmopolitan world. New York was the center of glamour in a more classy way than Hollywood. Both were at their peaks compared to now. And we'd never looked so good to ourselves before. The new coats were the best ever owned, with fur collars to boot. After feeling like a rag-a-muffin all one's life, better clothes do help self assurance.

The train pulled into Jersey City, a dirty, dusty place, and there we caught a ferry to Manhattan Island. The ferry itself looked used and old, but the panoramic view of that beautiful city seen from its deck had to be the most exciting sight in the world! The wind and spray with seagulls swooping beside us, wondrous skyscrapers in the background, was a blood-tingling bit of anticipation.

A feeling of letdown met us when first setting foot aground, until further exploration revived all the enchantment.

We rode on two-storied buses and climbed up the Empire State Building, where a kindly person snapped a picture on our box camera for us to send to less fortunate souls. We stopped in Times Square to read the twinkling lights of the latest news as they scampered across the building. Wall Street was gazed up upon; truly it looked a canyon of walls, but gloomy. We lunched at Stouffer's and stopped at Saks

5th Avenue with gowns in the window for wondrous prices. Inside, we looked for a hankie to take home as a souvenir (everyone carried them then) and were stupefied to find you could pay over $50 for one.

We saved the best till last. Radio City Music Hall was new and shining. All of Rockefeller Center was the cream of New York. On stage, between movie runs, were the famous Rockettes, a male chorus in costume, and a wonderful ballet act. In huge fluffy skirts they floated down to congregate on the stage for their twirls and rompings.

A pipe organ played here and there with its vibrant sounds encircling us.

I had a funny experience at the Music Hall. I asked for the Ladies' room and was told to go down certain stairs and to turn to the right. When I did this, all light seemed to stop. Below was an enormous black and white room with a carpeted floor. It had a very high ceiling, lost in darkness. All about were square glass pillars of mirrors with small lights way up there. The general effect was one of a room in ultra-violet light, which turned the large area into a maze with four-sided glass pillars reflecting people walking to and fro. It was a busy place.

I wove my way across the room, stopping to let people pass and going on until I came up short with someone smack in front of me. I muttered, "Excuse me," and stepped aside into a glass pillar and my own image. Nonplussed for a moment, I then had to glance about to see if anyone was witness before starting out again. If I could find someone standing still, perhaps directions could be asked?

It took some time wandering about to even locate a wall to follow. Walls were bound to lead to doors!

IRENE

As soon as I went to work for the P.'s with a salary of $15 a week, I sent more money home. My family was then living on relief, getting $1 a month from the Canadian government. In addition, they received some scroungy, rubbery turnips, carrots, potatoes, and beets shipped in by the government to the small town. This was the time of the Dust Bowl.

At the same time, I was saving money to bring sister Irene down to school and making arrangements to get her across the border. Over six months had gone by since my visit home, and she was to start school in September. It seemed unbelievable. I would have a relative in B.A.! I could hardly wait! She would have to go to the dorm, which cost a lot of money, because I could think of no place where she'd be "taken in." My school friends' families already had enough children. As the time drew near, I knew that I was short of money for her railway fare. Granny Glenn found this out and told Mrs. P., who then offered to pay the fare.

I met the train, and a bouncing dark-haired girl got off. She was a bedraggled sight and looked quite alien. She had really grown up. I hated to see that bad arm. An operation had made it solid at the shoulder, sticking out at an angle from her body. She didn't let it bother her in any way. By overlooking it, she made others do so, too.

I took her back home to Cairnwood, where we scrubbed her up with lots of warm water and fat towels and something of mine to wear. Soon she was in the dorm and a handful. She was like Dad, who had his own ideas as to what he'd say and do. I was constantly torn between being so glad to see her and wondering how in the world to handle situations. How could I tell her what the teachers had called me about? She refused to listen to *them*. A time or two I tried to pass on to her suggestions her teachers made. It was no good. She said she didn't "want to be told anything" but would "find things out" for herself.

In the meantime, I sewed away on bargain remnants to get her some clothes. She was not one to take care of anything. She complained about them not being nice enough. From then on, when I bought a cheap dress for myself, I bought one for her. It was awfully disappointing to have so much difficulty, but that's the way it was. We had pleasant times when sharing letters from home, and I had her up often for meals.

She'd argue with anyone and sometimes left the other girls miffed, which was very awkward for me. It was nice to have her up for Christmas dinner when everyone thought of family. We had no Christmas dinners at home; Christmas was the same as any other day.

Every year thereafter, for many years, we two girls always had our Christmas dinner together.

CHRISTMAS AT CAIRNWOOD

I still love to think of Christmastime at Cairnwood. It was right out of a storybook. If someone asked what part to pick out as a highlight, it would be hard to say. It was all a mixture of happiness, pretty things, secret bustlings, and delectable goodies.

My Christmas preparations started way ahead of time, collecting all sorts of things for the big box to be sent home. It had to be sure and arrive on time, and no one knew how long it would take to cross the border or if it would be held up by customs. It was such fun coming home from town each week with a new thing for the box. I shopped long for bargains to stretch my few dollars. The most fun of all was hunting for dolls for the younger sisters. I just loved them myself. Sometimes I made clothes for them, too.

Besides sending playthings, I tried to send the kids something useful to wear. After the box was filled, I sprinkled candies through the package for the kids to hunt as they took out packages. On the top was a branch of pine tied with a nice red ribbon bow. It probably got squashed in shipment, but it would smell good. The P.'s often sent stacks of books for the children, piled in groups according to age. Most of these had been read and passed on during the summer at the mountains. *Babar* was new then.

In preparing for her Christmas, Mrs. P. had lists of small relatives, and others, and would read off their names. Certain piles grew, for this family and that, as we stacked them. Then they would be tied and tagged. All sorts of boxes would pile up in the "package room" to be tied as the housekeeper shopped in town. Trucks delivered them. Stores sent other things ordered to be looked over by Mrs. P.; some were returned.

In the playroom there were beautiful papers and ribbons. Any spare time was used wrapping Christmas presents. Such fun to have a free choice of choosing this paper and that ribbon. Often there were two girls at a time tying presents, which was more fun.

Good things collected all over the house. We girls allowed previews of what we were giving each other. The last week before the big day was a busy time indeed.

Nice-smelling wooden market baskets would line the long back hall one morning. Along with them would be branches of pine and ribbon. We twined the pine around the handles and tied a nice big bow on the top. There were certain baskets set aside as turkey baskets and others for fruit. Mrs. P. had a list of how many of each. They went to teachers and older people, relatives and friends. I could imagine what fun they would be to receive.

This was my favorite Christmas job. We were free to fill the baskets and at the end chose strings of chocolate candies in the shape of animals, covered in colored tinfoil, strung together with ribbon, to add a touch.

The turkey baskets were very straightforward. In each was a nice fat turkey, an extra perfect bunch of celery, cranberries, and things for stuffing. The fruit baskets were more fun because things had to be arranged. Most impressive of all were boxes in the refrigerator room, wooden boxes that needed the house man to open. They were filled with sawdust, and each held big perfect bunches of grapes shipped from South Africa. A bunch was carefully put on the top of each basket. The oranges were so big and fat you could scarce believe it.

Another big job was sending the flowers. Early morning found all of us on the long glassed-in west porch, amid dozens of flower boxes to be folded and ribbon and cards. Tubs and containers of flowers, with more to come, lined the walls.

Mrs. P. sat with her lists, and after we'd put in fine waxed paper and filled a box with a selection of flowers and ferns, we took it to her. She might suggest we add a few more roses and then tell us to whom to send it. Next it was tied and stacked for the busy chauffeurs to deliver.

The flowers were beautiful to see, but we got damp, nippy noses and toes before we were through. The flowers stood in water until we boxed them. Water was dripped on the floor, and there was no heat in the glassed-in porch.

From Sautters in town came unbelievable goodies. I think petit fours were at the top of my list. They were beautiful looking, and the tiny layers melted in your mouth. If you ever tasted one, you'd be spoiled for life on any other goodie. Running a close second was the very special, once-a-year, Nesselrode Pudding for Christmas dessert. It is a creamy yellow ice cream with marrons (chestnuts) and a whipped cream rum sauce. Nowhere can you find anything like it now.

Sautters shipped ice cream from Philadelphia in dry ice for Sunday dinners, too. It is too bad that they went out of business because tasting their things was an experience. True, some people felt their ice cream too rich. It could leave the mouth coated. But there were other things, I know not the names. One dessert came in a mold and looked like half a watermelon. It was clear red raspberry ice with two-inch thick frozen white whipped cream on the outside. Sometimes it was served on spun sugar nests, so fine and extra tasty. Called Bon Glace.

Christmas Eve found everyone decorating the big Christmas tree in the hall; no one did that job ahead of time. In would come all the carolers, happy to be in out of the cold and to see the sights as they sang. We helped pass out apples and those BIG oranges. Each one would make a whole breakfast.

Early Christmas morning, we girls had our Christmas time exchanging gifts with each other. We'd even filled stockings and hung them on the chimney in the girls' sitting room. In each stocking was an envelope from Mrs. P. with a $25 check.

Our first year, we youngest treated ourselves by spending it on long black velvet evening wraps with little white fur collars. They were so elegant feeling and lasted years and years. Every banquet, wedding, and dance found B.A. ladies in long evening clothes, so they were very useful. Some years there were wonderful tickets to Gilbert & Sullivan performances of our choice.

After breakfast was served to the family, there was worship, and we were on hand to help with their packages. After they were untied, we collected all the pretty paper and carefully folded it. This was taken to the girls' sitting room where we took turns "choosing." None of us had money to buy Hallmark wrapping paper then, so this was saved and wrapped nearly all our gifts the next Christmas. We saved the ribbon, too. We hurried to attend church and came home to the big turkey dinner.

In the afternoon, all the family's relatives showed up to exchange gifts, and there were dozens of them. They all had to be served ice cream, those tiny petit fours, and cookies.

So by suppertime most of the excitement was over, and we could put up our feet and visit with one another.

YOUNG PEOPLE

We usually dated on weekends. Most any kind of dating Ann and I did was overshadowed by some guilt because we never got home early enough. It wouldn't have been so noticed if we didn't have to contend with setting that awful burglar alarm. Every night the last one in had to set it. Being situated at the other end of that long hall, in plain view of the boudoir and all bedrooms around, was bad. I didn't think they had the right to control our hours unless we were *very* late because we were on our own, especially after reaching twenty one. The alarm part I could understand, but no one made any to-do over that.

I still did almost all of my own sewing to save money. It so happened I'd bought a piece of plissé (soft seersucker) and made a straight-skirted nightgown. The material came very narrow, so I made it do.

One night Ann and I came in about one in the morning. We had a cigarette (she was a fond smoker), and I could see that she wanted me to set the alarm. I didn't usually even think about it but went ahead and did it. It was like pulling teeth for her to do it. I guess she had more of a conscience about her guilt than I did.

This night we were so late, we sat and talked about it. She suggested we get undressed first and creep over in bare feet. She'd stay at the end of the hall on the lookout while I braved the attempt. By this time, it was about two.

We opened the door into the front hall. The boudoir light was on. We quickly shut the door and discussed it. We walked down the hall again for a bit and listened. All was quiet. She stood still and I went on.

When I got level with the boudoir door, I could see Mr. P. sitting there absorbed in writing something. I gave him no chance to look up but pulled that tight-skirted nightgown up and walked on for the safety of the dark back hall. Ann had disappeared, but the door was open wide for my exit. This door was usually kept closed.

Next day I waitressed at lunch and, when I started out serving Mrs. P., she turned and said, "Why didn't you send my husband to bed?"

So he had seen me! He must have heard the sound of running and gone to look down the hall. And in my nightgown! I almost expected to get fired. Ann steamed about it, and we decided we'd have even more trouble getting out for a good time now.

Later, Mrs. P. said a few words when she called everyone together to talk about late hours. Years later she told me how she didn't like it, and the most she could say was it hurt our work. She did not believe in hurting the freedom of others so tried gentle hints when wanting us to change our ways.

It took me time to look for her meanings. I liked and admired her more all the time but did not want to give up going out.

Ann finally decided to solve her problem in relation to it. Her home was within ten miles, so she moved back there to live and rode the bus each day. So I was mighty glad when later a girl from Illinois, Shirley, came to work, and I again had company with my escapades of setting the alarm.

MY TWENTY-FIRST BIRTHDAY

While I was living at Cairnwood, my twenty-first birthday came along. I couldn't have enjoyed it more if I'd been a debutante! I guess girls are supposed to have a special celebration on their eighteenth birthday, but I can't remember mine. I guess I was at the dorm busy being a senior. So the twenty-first made up for it. Actually, it was happenstance but nonetheless enjoyable. Three things happened I know, but only two are remembered.

The P.'s gave a dancing party in the front hall with an orchestra. They'd never done anything like that before, and it was most exciting with such a gracious setting.

Girls then always wore long dresses to dances, and boys were allowed to send flowers. That went for school dances, too. Everyone at the house was invited, but only a couple of the youngest like myself showed up at all. Ann had a date, her steady, and I think stayed most of the evening. She was reticent though and kept to the sidelines. Not I!

I had a date. His name was Guy Alden, and he was very nice to me, almost too nice. We'd gone on a couple of walks, and he was most gentlemanly. I could have gone steady with him and wasn't quite sure how to handle it. I liked him as a friend very much. When he asked to take me to the party, I was tickled because I for sure had a date and liked the way he danced. He liked to waltz, too.

Just at this time I'd been to a movie of Ginger Rogers and Fred Astaire's. They were a a wonderful dancing team and in delightful movies. Ginger wore a beautiful dress of fluff and ruffles (movies then were only black and white). This one, I believe, was *Flying Down to Rio*. Anyhow, I bought a movie magazine with a picture of her in it so that I could copy that lovely dress.

It turned out to be all I'd hoped for. It was made of pale blue organdy with cascaded ruffles at the bottom. I was a bit bothered with style to hide my plumpness, but the skirt was bias cut so fell gracefully, with the ruffles holding it out in billows at the bottom. A circle of rhinestones, three wide, made a belt. The belt was a chore to make; that kind of thing was only used in theatrical productions. When evening slippers came out in silver and gold kid, everyone bought a pair as soon as soon. They were hard to keep looking decent.

I loved the dress and had dozens of compliments on it. It was a lovely pale but bright blue. So I wore it to the party.

Just before I went downstairs, Guy arrived with a white box tied in ribbon. Pink carnations were arranged in a professional corsage. To have a first corsage was all part of it, and I felt all ready to step into a wonderful evening.

Naturally, I danced all night. The P.'s daughters liked waltzes, too, and this dress was perfect for that. The only problem I had was it seemed that Mrs. P. was not overly warm towards me. She always gave me the feeling I was not demure enough, and I cared very much how she felt.

During the evening, they broke up the dancing by having little favors to change partners. Charlie Cole asked me for a dance. At the end, pencils and papers were handed out to each boy to write a squib about his partner. Charlie wrote a long page that was fun, all about a cloud of blue and a smile. Everyone thought it well done until another fellow's remarks were read. All he said about his girl was "She's a pip."

He won the prize.

I saved all such moments and later made a fat illustrated scrapbook to show my children someday. When I went home on that long visit, it was an accomplished fact of school days and only special things were added after that. It burned up later when our house was destroyed.

The other thing I remembered as a celebration was something Mrs. P. did that was special. She gave me six tickets to a Philadelphia Orchestra Concert. Four of them were box seats, right on the front row of the balcony. She had season tickets for Friday afternoons and there was always a stir in the house when they planned what people were picked up and plans made. It seemed the height of culture.

I was astounded when she gave the tickets to me. Of course I was thrilled with the idea, though concerts weren't something I ever missed. They were for the "dignified" people!

I went to some of the Youth Concerts to be with other young people and felt it was an area that something should be known about. It was a rare piece of music that I had any feeling for, but I was told that the taste grew on you. Right now I can say it takes some doing, along with an affirmative attitude. Unless you grow up with an understanding of classical music, it does not come readily.

Along with the tickets came the gift of the chauffeur and the big black car to drive us there and back.

Finally, five friends were chosen and away we went. The most fun was the coming and going, besides the idea of such a wonderful gift. The concert was secondary.

BOYS AND PROBLEMS

I must tell you about one special friend I made at this time. Every girl should have one like him. Probably many did but some, I'm sure, never. My closest girlfriends didn't, but then all of us had been tongue-tied with boys. That's what was so nice about this fellow. He just waltzed along, there was no self-consciousness.

Children now are taught to public speak from first grade on and by college age are running the world so perhaps would never notice such small things. As a matter of fact, I think that is what is partially the matter with them. Quiet, individual growth, each in his own way, to add to the whole, is missing. It took the "hippies" to come along later and have some idea of this.

A woman who had lived in South Africa moved to B.A. with her children when her husband died. This young acquaintance came to the States to study and looked her up. She knew his family very well. When he asked her to suggest someone for a date, she gave him my name. I couldn't have been more surprised because I scarcely knew her outside of her name. She called me, told me about him, and he phoned. "Would I like an evening of dinner downtown and perhaps dancing afterward?"

"Sure!" No one had ever invited me on such an outing, and it was an elegant idea. Our boys had no money and, if some did, I had never heard of it happening. Outside of a hot dog or hamburger, I'd never been faced across a table to dine as a couple. I hoped he was nice, and safe too; downtown was a long way to go with someone you didn't know.

Working with a bunch of girls was fun in that they shared your ups and downs; at least the ones around the same age did. All girls that age like to share each other's experiences and talk things over anyway. So when the night came, they said, "Yes, your hair looks nice" or "Have a good time" and thought up ways of getting a peek at him.

The doorbell rang and one of them answered it. I came down the back hall and there he was, a nice-looking, smiling fellow, as easy as could be to meet. He took my arm outside, where he had a car.

We drove downtown! We chit-chatted all the way, getting acquainted, and he asked me about places to eat in Philadelphia. Of course I didn't know any! But having often shopped along Chestnut Street, I'd seen a sign on a second-story window which said, "Chinese Tea Gardens," and under it "Dancing." It sounded picturesque. I hadn't the slightest idea of what kind of food the Chinese served outside of rice! Anytime I'd walked along under the sign, I'd thought how nice it would be to see such a place, so I told him about it and that's where we went.

It decidedly was not a first-rate place, but I didn't know it then and so enjoyed it thoroughly. The whole idea was now to enjoy.

There were arbors of sorts around the room with bits of artificial flowers (then they really looked fake, not any of the realistic plastic ones we have now). Tables lined the room between the arbor effects, and a nice big middle section was free for dancing. The room was dimly lit.

After being seated and studying the menu (Don't order the most expensive. I was told a poor boy might not have all that much money to spend), the first surprise came along. He was a vegetarian and asked if I wouldn't like eggs cooked in some way. "No," and I must say I never hesitated when asked. Manners of any subtle sort were something I knew nothing about, and I still wonder about how much I don't know!

He said money was no problem, and I happily ordered beef. Before I was through we'd talked about it, and I saw it did not make him happy, but then I just felt he was foolish and supposed he'd change some day. We were having such a good time anyway it didn't matter, at least to me. We danced before, after, and between courses and strung out the evening. It was all lots of fun.

After getting home, we stood by the back door and talked for a while. After thanking him and turning to unlock the door, he quickly reached down and kissed me on top of the head. By the time I looked around he was gone.

A few days later, I got the nicest, fun letter. He'd gone out to Minneapolis to look over a school and would be back for the weekend and another date. He came back for other holidays, too, and this stretched out the times of seeing him.

Very soon he got quite serious, and I was sorry. The first inkling I had of it was one Saturday afternoon when six of us decided to drive in his car to the Steel Pier and the boardwalk in Atlantic City. After a laughing ride, we broke up in couples to walk the boardwalk, have our fortunes told, etc. Halfway through the evening, we passed a fur shop window. He was quite insistent he buy me a little fur cape, and we stood sometime with my insisting "No"! Finally, I laughingly said, "How would I explain it?" and walked on. The idea was surely a pleasant one, but I wanted no gifts from anyone unless I was engaged. I'd had enough qualms over the one I had accepted, and it was the only thing I'd ever been talked into.

I took to thinking about how all the fun letters had been part of the way we got to know each other. There weren't many, and it all happened in a matter of less than six months. South Africa wasn't for me and neither were vegetarians, and I never once felt serious about him.

During a moonlight ride along Creek Road, he stopped the car and I turned him down flat. He was very talkative and at first refused to listen. I'd intimated before that we hardly knew each other. So that was that, and I had no more dates with him.

Something like fifteen years later, a couple returned from South Africa. They knew him and, while at a party celebrating their return, they mentioned something I considered very much a compliment, though embarrassing to me. While their boat was still in port with the gangplank about to be removed, he rushed up to them and said, "Give my love to Reta. She was cute!"

I heard he'd taken out a number of other girls and was now happily married to a most attractive girl and had a family. His acquaintance had been a delightful experience.

While on the subject of boys, which then was the most interesting subject in the world, another thing happened the last Christmas at Cairnwood.

One of the friends that I saw most often was Dianne. Now she had started having dates. Her date was an older fellow who had an open two-seated touring car with a top that went up and down like a convertible. His name was Ros. He loved his dark red car with its black cloth top, and on sunny days we'd see him pass on his way to the mail, etc. He was bouncy and smiling. He fell very hard for Dianne, but she was hesitant.

At this time she had gone off to live about twenty miles away in Ambler to attend the Pennsylvania School of Horticulture for Women, so I didn't see her as often. She came home sometimes on weekends and we visited. She told me how Ros was pressing his case and what she did to slow him down, but she never stopped him.

He loved airplanes and knew how to fly a Piper Cub. He spent much of his free time at a small nearby airport fussing with them. One day he bought her a box of Whitman's Samplers and flew it over her school. With a note attached, he parachuted it down in front of her on the school grounds.

One thing Dianne did was to persuade Ros she'd go on some dates with him if someone else was along, a double date. At this same time, Ros got to be good friends with Dianne's first cousin, who had once in a while taken her to dances and such. This was the same boy, Keneth Simons, I had met before.

Keneth had been something of a "fair-haired boy." While in school he worked to pay his tuition because his mother was a widow with eight children, the youngest only a few years old. He became interested in ham radio, which took the rest of his time. Ros and Keneth became an unlikely pair of friends. From then on they saw quite a bit of each other. Keneth had now started college at the University of Pennsylvania but lived at home.

One weekend, Dianne told me Ros had asked her to spend the next Sunday down at Atlantic City. Having told him she'd go if he took someone else, he was going to ask Keneth, and she said maybe Keneth would ask me. I waited and hoped, not so much for the date, but the shore held a fascination and Atlantic City had so many things to see on the boardwalk. It would be a fun outing.

Well, he *did* ask me, and it was our first big date.

Dianne and I talked over what we'd take to wear. She said we'd maybe dance to Mal Hallett on Steel Pier in the evening. Such exciting plans!

The day dawned rather misty, but it wasn't raining. I had a pretty, new white crepe dress piped in bright blue and so wore that. We had a merry holiday feeling riding down. We rented two lockers at the beach, one for boys and one for girls, side by side, with a partition between, to change into bathing suits.

The ocean was rough and misty with spray, and the lifeguard whistles blew constantly, keeping people close to shore. Just before we came in, I had reason to know why. We had been jumping waves and swimming when all of a sudden a wave rolled me over and under. I pushed up with feet on the sand, but before getting a breath of air I was rolling and twisting again on a wild chaos of churning water. It seemed to go on for such a long time and no way out. About the time of feeling panic-stricken, a firm hand grabbed mine and pulled me into the clear.

It wasn't the casual Keneth I had to thank but rather Ros. He was a very responsible fellow. I felt shaken and we decided to change. It was near suppertime anyway.

The partition between the lockers was about a foot above ground level. While we were changing, a bottle appeared in that open space with a hand holding it. "Here, have a nip of this." I looked at it as if it was a cobra, but Dianne had sampled it before, so she took it and poured herself out a capful. "It's delicious," she stated, "taste it." And we were cold. A very sweet, fine, oily feeling spread over my tongue. It was Apricot Brandy. Not as bad tasting as I'd expected, so I took maybe a half a teaspoon taste. Didn't know what it could do to you, so not liking it all that much I stopped there. But the idea! Now it could be said I'd had a drink. Wicked. I *was* over twenty-one!

Seeing how Dianne said we'd go dancing after supper, I'd brought along my pretty, long blue Woodstock dress and one for her. It was white with small crisscross lines of green and black with black tape trim. I gave it to her then and was furious no time later when I found she'd cut it off to wear as a short dress around home.

I don't remember supper. We probably had sandwiches because Keneth, I know, had no money. He had paid $5 for the white suit he was wearing. He wore corduroy all winter to college, for which he received much kidding.

What a big beautiful floor to dance on, and the orchestra was such fun to stop and watch periodically. It wasn't very crowded, but we could lose each other sometimes because the ballroom was so huge.

After such a full day, we decided we should be home by midnight. With so much fresh air, walking the boardwalk, and all the rest, we were pleasantly "done in."

It was chilly in the back seat of that open touring car, and Ros had brought a nice big wooly blanket to wrap around our knees. Actually, it was up around our ears. Ros kept saying he'd like to be a backseat driver with Dianne beside him. Keneth made moves to be a bit snuggly, but I would have none of it! Several times I asked him to move over nearer his corner. Dianne told me later that Keneth had told Ros what a good time he'd had, so I might be seeing more of him. It was OK by me. I liked the idea of double dating, and Ros was full of ideas of things to do.

Not long after this, I was walking home one night up that same black path when Keneth again came along in his little black car. I had the same white crepe dress on with pleats across the front and was hurrying home to beat a rainstorm. So I jumped into his car, and this time he whisked us on up the Pike, past the gates of Cairnwood, for a ride. We'd gone no distance when it began to pour rain. The top of the car kept it off the top of us, but it beat in the sides and the pleats disappeared. We soon turned around for home, and I walked into the back hall with the crepe dress three inches shorter in front than back. There were no synthetic nylons in those days. We'd have to see what the cleaner would do, but the fun was worth it.

Keneth had reached out a hand on that ride, and I'd slapped it and said, "I thought you didn't like girls who necked." He said he didn't, and I had the feeling he'd ask me out again. But he was in no hurry. Once in quite a long while we went to the movies or some such with Ros and Dianne.

Just around this time, I had a horrendous experience with another fellow. I'd been invited to my old classmate Eleanor's house for a Sunday night supper, just like way back when I first came to school. Her two older brothers were there. I'd seen them only once or twice before; the stepmother didn't seem to like them and they lived away from home.

The oldest one was a senior when I came to Bryn Athyn. I never saw him at school. Now he lived and worked up country on a farm that his father owned. We'd driven up there one Sunday afternoon for some reason. He was a big, extremely quiet fellow. I didn't know it back then, but he was filled with emotional problems and he came to a sad end. When Eleanor had given me a small Christmas gift, he'd sent a hankie. She said he liked me because I took a bit of time to talk to him. I was happy, however, that he wasn't usually around because I'd not want to have to go out with him. When I saw him again, I cut the conversation to a "Hello."

The next brother was as dark as the older one was light. He was handsome and more talkative. We had a pleasant supper with chit-chat and I forgot the whole thing. A couple of weeks later, he was again in town and asked me for a date. He'd driven miles on his motorcycle and told me all about it. I told him how they were so dangerous "you wouldn't catch me going near one." He borrowed his father's car to go to the movies. We talked coming and going.

Perhaps a month went by, and he showed up with a car of his own. We again went to the movies, and I wondered how come he'd gotten rid of his motorcycle, but he didn't say. Little did I know what was in store or that he'd decided that night at supper I was to be his girl. He asked if I wouldn't like to learn to drive a car; he'd teach me. "Sure thing." Maybe someday I could earn and save enough to buy one of my own. The housekeeper had bought herself one that year, and it was wonderful. Some Sunday afternoons she'd take a couple of girls who were free for a bit for a drive. It was a real outing for her, and she'd take her old mother, who was dependent on her, along.

All in all, I had four dates with this fellow, maybe five. I know we had two driving lessons that weekend and that was that on the driving. I'd never remember it all!

I was at an "up in the air" stage. Work took most of my time. I went to Friday Suppers and church and accepted dates as they came along. Sometimes there were two on a weekend, other times none. The kids in school who had gone steady were pretty much all married, and I began to feel I was going to be an old maid after all.

Next time he, E.C., showed up and asked for a date, he said he had something special in mind. Had I ever been on the boat ride down the river? That sounded like great fun.

We drove down to Philadelphia early one evening in his car to where the boat was docked. It looked like the steamer paddle boat right out of the movie *Showboat*, all alight with people jostling each other up the gangplank. It was sunset time when it pulled out and headed down the river. A band played, popcorn was for sale. We walked the decks to see the sights and danced quite a bit to the band. Then, on the way home, when the stars had come out, he asked if I'd not like to go up to the top deck and see the lights along the riverbank. Up we went to the very front of the ship with the breeze blowing our hair back.

This fellow talked more than the oldest brother, but that did not mean he was talkative. He was on the bashful, reticent side anyway, and I'd noticed he'd become harder and harder to talk with, but I was completely taken by surprise by what came next.

He grabbed me in a bear hug and said, "Will you marry me?" He was tall and strong, and the whole thing almost scared the wits out of me. I mumbled right away, "Oh, let go of me," and he begrudgingly did, but he was shaken by his own audacity. The thought then crossed my mind again of my mother saying, "Watch out for men." This always had the effect of making me think hard and fast and being careful.

So I acted as blithe and pleasant as could be and said I'd no idea he felt that way because he'd told me about some little Polish girls he had dates with up-country. He was still going to college at Cornell, so why not a date or two when he asked? I was worried about getting home, but when we got to the car I talked away about any little thing that came into my head. Chatter can ward off all kinds of things.

Thank goodness we finally got home; he'd said hardly a word all the way. That was the last time I went out with him, but such a time that followed!

I told my friend Karen about it, and she scolded because she said I'd led him on. I couldn't see how. Next, his stepmother phoned and said to be very careful, he'd be looking for me and was really berserk. So there was nothing to do but tell the other girls. If they answered the doorbell, I wasn't home.

He wrote letters and picked wild flowers and left them for me.

One night a bunch of us went to Cairncrest for the evening, and there he was when we got back, sitting outside waiting. It was a miserable time to get through, and I was glad when we went to the mountains for the summer. Letters followed there, too, and one day a box of wildflowers came in the mail, all dead to the point of being almost dried up. I felt sorry that he was so upset.

That was the summer of 1938. It had been over four years since I visited home after finishing school, and I'd been saving carefully for another "sit-up" trip back for my two weeks of vacation. Irene was almost through school, but brother Leslie was not yet ready to come. Why wasn't there more money somewhere? They were still so poor at home, much worse than I'd imagined even.

At the time, I felt going home would give me a reprieve from my problem with this fellow. It turned out the other way; the problem overshadowed the whole trip. A letter just before I left said he'd follow me out West, but I didn't believe him.

I'd had so many plans for the nice time of seeing the family and old schoolmates again. After a couple of days of being home we went to town, and I remember buying grapefruit to serve for breakfast as a treat. I thought it so good. The family didn't like it at all. It is true, people like what they are used to.

The house was just gray inside; everywhere the paint was worn off. The wooden kitchen chairs looked a sight and were all wired together. There was poverty everywhere. Dad saved enough money, rather set it aside, for the family to go to the movies once a month. I think he was a smart man.

Lots of people left the farms, dust drifted like the snow, and cattle died. Dad had been fortunate enough to have some life insurance so borrowed on that and, what with my sending clothes home and a tiny bit of money, had managed to hold on.

Cars had been turned into Bennett Buggies, pulled by horses, long before. (Bennett had been Canada's Prime Minister.) But our old green Chrysler supposedly still ran. That once-upon-a-time beautiful car in 1928 was a now sad sight.

The other thing I'd decided was the family should go on a little driving trip to see something of the world besides home. We'd go see the Rockies at Lake Louise. I'd always wanted to see them myself, and we could drive there in less than a day.

When we'd gone to town, there was a letter from the fellow, E.C., saying he was hitch-hiking and working his way out. He'd gotten as far as Minnesota. I felt rather panicky and told Dad we'd start off on our trip the next day or two. Dad, in his true stubborn fashion, didn't believe me. He said I was just anxious to get away from home.

Having been home a total of perhaps four whole days, Mom and Dad and I started out on the fifth for Calgary. The car gave us a bad time because the radiator leaked constantly. We found sloughs along the way to dip water from. Then it began to fail alarmingly, so we stopped at a garage. The garage man sold us some stuff to pour in that was guaranteed to stop the leaks. It did for a matter of minutes at a time, and we finally limped into the city of Calgary. In finding a garage there, we were told nothing would do but a new radiator at the cost of $60. I didn't have $60.

Dad suggested we look up Dr. Swatylander, who had been in

Oyen for years when he first went out there and had been the doctor through the time of Eva's death. Dad had always paid his bills to him, and they had been big ones. Surely he would lend us some money. He wouldn't, but he did help us to telegraph back to B.A. for some, so the trip was saved.

Dad then wished to go the few miles north to Didsbury, where a family he knew lived. They used to live near home. I wasn't of a mind to go, but then this outing was for Dad and Mom.

When we arrived, their two grown-up daughters were home. The youngest was my age and we had pleasant talk. Dad invited the two daughters to come along with us to see the mountains. It spoiled the trip.

They packed within the hour and were only too glad to come. It made a problem of places to stay; we had the barest amount of money and could rent only the poorest places for $2 a night. We went out to buy food to cook, and they weren't forthcoming in anything extra for their food. In a way it was pleasant, but I'd hoped so much for a chance of good talk with Dad and Mom. This way Mom just held back and did not enjoy it, I know. It would have been fun to show her things and get her reactions, but she was as quiet as a mouse, and it was strenuous for me. Two things came of the trip.

Frieda, the one my age, has written to me at Christmas every year since, though I've never seen her again.

Dad got home and said many times, "It was a waste of money. You could look at pictures of Lake Louise in a book." But the funny thing was he scrimped and saved to take the whole family for an automobile ride there the next summer! He's gone to the city of Calgary many times since, when the farm seemed to be too confining and he wished a change or felt he needed something he couldn't get at home. Of course, my mother was delighted to see something different.

When we came back to Benton for me to take off for Bryn Athyn, no more letters had come from that E.C. fellow, and I felt sad not to have seen more of the brothers and sisters.

I'd planned to stop overnight in Glenview, a suburb of Chicago, on the way home to visit a school friend. Upon arrival, there was a letter from Keneth Simons with pictures of a flood B.A. had had. Water had risen in the creek clear up to the station.

I figured Keneth was getting to be quite a friend if he'd taken the time to write a letter. He didn't usually bother with such things. The minute I got back, he asked me for a date and did each weekend from then on, or most weekends anyway.

That other fellow, E.C., was on the phone, too, to ask me to go out. But I'd tell whoever answered the phone that I wasn't home. He wrote letters. He said the reason he'd tried to go out to my Canadian home was because he felt sure I'd like him if I got away from the fancy people of B.A.

He hung around outside a few weekends, and I was house bound. His stepmother was worrying about him so phoned each time and said to be very careful, he wasn't himself. Within two weeks he was picked up by the police with a gun. He'd gone "overboard" and was looking for Keneth Simons. Someone must have told him I'd been going out with Keneth. Because he wasn't himself, he had been looking for Keneth with a gun in a nearby town instead of right here at home, thank goodness.

They locked him up for a good while, and he has had a sad life. I caught a glimpse of him twenty years later at a wedding of one of his relatives.

I was sure Keneth would be scared off by all this, but we weren't at all serious, so he wasn't fazed by it. Soon I went out to the movies with him. Then it was a date every weekend. Often it was a double date with Ros and Di.

Christmastime came again at Cairnwood. Keneth was considered pretty much my boyfriend by then because I'd gone out with him most. After all the hustle and bustle of preparation and the big day, he arrived that night for a date. When I came down to the back door and answered the doorbell, there was a bushel basket of potatoes to the side against the wall. Keneth was in no hurry to come in but stood and talked on the step.

I made some remark about it and he mentioned the potatoes. I'd paid no attention to them because baskets of vegetables were always arriving on the back porch. Then someone came out of the girls' dining room right beside the back door and said, "For goodness sake, shut the door."

Keneth said, "She doesn't like her Christmas present," so we both looked around and there was nothing but the potatoes. Funny joke. I didn't think much of his humor.

He finally had to tell me to go look in the potatoes. There in the middle was a cute little brown radio about as small as you could get them in those days. It was a most lovely gift, and a big one for him to give. All the girls oh-ed and ah-ed; no one had such a thing. I debated about keeping it and what everyone would say. No one kept gifts if you weren't *very* serious, and he'd showed no signs of such and neither had I.

GLENCAIRN

For years Mr. P. had been dreaming of the home he would build for Mrs. P., and it took him years to build.

When they had married in Atlantic City (because they were cousins and couldn't in Pennsylvania), he brought her home to his father's house, which was Cairnwood. His mother had died, but his two brothers and a young sister Vera lived there. Vera, about 18, died of appendicitis. The two brothers, Theo and Harold, later married and built big houses for themselves. Harold chose to build on land adjoining Cairnwood, and his house was called "Cairncrest."

All the help at Cairncrest was black, with the exception of a housekeeper, a nursemaid, and her helper. We girls at Cairnwood were good friends, and the two nursemaids often entertained us in the Stone Room there. (They didn't call it a game room.)

When I went to work at Cairnwood, the big new house was nearing completion. Planning it had taken most of the time, but the stonework was well started, and what perfect work, done by artisans.

We were taken to see a beautiful model of Glencairn, as it would be called, in one of the church work sheds. At that time, the Cathedral building was surrounded by wooden work sheds that had been there for years. The metal, stone, and woodworkers worked there.

Mr. P. had models made of everything. If he liked it, fine; if not, he'd try a new idea. We felt he couldn't make up his mind, but years later we realized why everything turned out so beautifully. He was very much an artist in his own way and worked hard over color and lines and form.

The house he was building was nothing short of fabulous and will go down in history as something very special to see. There was a tower seven stories high. A big scaffolding of wood with an elevator that was only a square platform with ropes to pull it up and down stood on one side. Mr. P. offered several times to take us up in the elevator to see the view. It was a most frightening procedure, but most of us took the chance and went up a time or two because we thought it was nice of him to take the time to ask us.

I didn't pay much attention to the floor plans then, but it was interesting to watch the building's progress. After we finished work in the mornings, Mr. P. would send word he wished a couple of girls to come over and sort very beautiful, small half-inch square tiles into their separate piles of color. There was much mosaic work to be done besides tile borders in the baths.

Mrs. P. saw to it that several of us went over at one time; she didn't wish us to talk to the workmen. But some of them were fun, especially when the house was more finished and specialists came in on lighting and the like.

By this time, one of the waitresses had left and a new girl who had come from a farm in Illinois to go to school had joined us to work. She, Shirley, was just a year younger than I and was something else! She plucked her eyebrows and wore lipstick! She was full of old sayings and kept us quite amused.

Quietly, everyone set about to reform some of her ways, like the eyebrow plucking. I was delighted to have her about, and we became quite a twosome when it came to being out late and stepping out to do things. She was going steady. More of her later.

Two and a half years after I started at Cairnwood, the new house was finished enough to move in. It was done over a period of time, so there was no one big day of moving. The only sudden change came when we all walked over and slept our first night there. We had moved!

None of us felt quite the same. All the coziness of living like a family had gone. This place was so huge that much of the day would have gone before you saw anyone. Some of the family might not be seen for days unless you waitressed at meals.

There were phones in every room, and lots of time was spent locating someone wanted on the outside phone. No more being in our room when on doorbell duty. We had to be downstairs in the back sitting room near the door.

The girls in the family seemed miles away. Each and every one had her own room, girls as well as family. Some were on the same floors as others; others were miles apart on different floors. Nothing was the same, except each other's faces when our paths happened to cross. In a sense, moving there gave the feeling of a family growing up suddenly. Everyone seemed more formal and removed, I suppose because more alone.

We'd been told ahead of time which rooms we girls would have. The housekeeper probably had had some say. I don't know. She had a rather small room in the back. My little Illinois friend and I had the best ones, we thought, and they were the biggest. They were also nearest the front.

I was tickled with my round room on the second floor, with a huge walk-in closet and a big tile bath. I shared the bath with the older nursemaid, Bea Ashley, which was easy and pleasant. She was always off to bed so early. I often brushed her long hair for her before she retired, which she enjoyed. She was fun to talk to, but I was warned later to tell her no secrets. They went directly "up front." She'd come from England and was entirely devoted to her adopted family.

My Illinois buddy, Shirley, had a big square room right across the hall from me, most convenient for running back and forth. Her room was considered more special because the windows looked out on the front lawn.

I worked hard to make long (mine were very long), lined pull drapes with pipings and trim for all the working girls' bedrooms, and after 27 years the drapes were still there!

I couldn't quite decide how I really felt about Glencairn. We got so much reaction from people on the outside, all the way from curiosity to disapproval. The biggest fuss being made was about its tower being higher than the church.

But I remember being defensive about it. If Mr. P. wanted to build a house a certain way, that was his business and his money. "He didn't mean the tower to be so high when he started, it just turned out that way when finished, so the proportion with the bottom would be right." I don't know whether I was told that or not, but I used the argument to shut the critics up!

We were asked how many rooms Glencairn had, and some of us roughly guessed about two hundred, counting all the closets, as they were so big. It was quite lonely being on doorbell duty, especially at night, because no bedrooms were near, nor was there the sound of chatter and the occasional in and out of others as there was at Cairnwood.

Another big change was that we didn't each have our own key to the back door as we'd had at Cairnwood. At Glencairn, the housekeeper handed one out when we expected a late evening; we'd ring the doorbell otherwise. There were only two keys in her possession.

One memorable New Year's Eve, Shirley and I hadn't asked soon enough and found ourselves without keys. We were often late home on outings anyway and knew we'd not give up dates with parties after to get home early. We thought and thought and finally left a downstairs casement window open a crack, to crawl in later. How it didn't set off a whole elaborate burglar alarm system I'll never know. Perhaps the very tolerant housekeeper watched till we were all in that night, but it was awful late. We didn't ask but expected to get the dickens.

Scattered around the walls, and especially in the Great Hall with its high blue mosaic ceiling with gold stars, were invaluable treasures from all over the world. Many were built into the stone walls. Previously, they had been housed for all to enjoy at the big Philadelphia Art Museum.

I think the part hardest part for me to get used to was the gray stone walls everywhere. But there were such beautiful things to enjoy seeing here and there. The stairways had beautiful colors from crushed glass that had been dusted over them. Silky-feeling, carved teakwood doors with beautifully done handles of beaten Monel metal were only some of the sights. My favorite antiques were the lovely old chests, some carved, and the round tables of a color no one finds in the regular antique shops. They were silky smooth, too.

One thing that was very impressive to me was a picture in the Great Hall. There were a number of big tapestries, and this looked like one. Mr. Pitcairn told me all about it one day. All I remember was the huge amount of work it must have been to move it. It was what is known, I think, as a "fresco": a picture painted on plaster, colored, done in some old church or chapel in Europe. The whole very thin layer was taken off the wall and made into a picture to be moved.

Ann and I had a favorite statue. She was slim and about life-size, a smiling princess standing beside the open arch in the Great Hall. There were many other beautiful things.

At Christmas, a large painting done by an artist in the Catskills was put up. It was a copy of the nativity scene. This was put over the fireplace, next to the dining room table. It would dwarf the average home.

Christmas in the new house was not nearly as enjoyable as in the old. There were the same sort of preparations, but they seemed more spread out, and I lost track of how they were handled. Everything was done on a bigger scale, and I guess extra help came in.

Ann and I still made all the beds, but that was about all that was the same. I didn't often pass her in the halls when on the way to feather dust. We each had our own areas. I cleaned Karen's pink bath and her bedroom, which was mostly pink, too. There were such pretty spreads on the two beds, lovely closets, soft rugs, and pretty white antiqued furniture trimmed in gold. Bethel's room was even bigger. Her bath and room were done in pale green. It was nice but not nearly as cozy as Karen's. I did her room, too.

Then there were all sorts of odd tower rooms, etc., to dust. This job I never liked. Nothing ever seemed to need dusting, and yet if I ever missed any of it the housekeeper was sure to find dust.

I still did the two days of substitute waitressing and spent plenty of time in the now remote sewing room. The little sewing lady still chewed her gum and tapped her foot. It was so quiet up there, I was twice as annoyed with her habits!

The one happy thing that didn't change was tying a sash or helping to fix Karen's hair when she went out. Bethel came in for some of this, too. Karen and I still talked about life, books, and who we'd gone out with. I think she sort of kept an eye of approval, or otherwise, on what I did. I know she felt freer to question me than I did her.

I appreciated it all the same and figured there were some things she just wouldn't understand, so didn't tell her everything.

Reta in the dress she made like Ginger Rogers'

Reta in an unknown year. She wrote cryptically on the back:
Another of me in my white suit. Like him? I'm so glad!

Glencairn in Bryn Athyn

Written on back: Left to right Bill, Margaret, Mabel, Leslie, Ted, Dad, Bea, Mom, Aunt Kate, Uncle Nelson and Norman with our car 1927 Chrysler
Reta's siblings, parents, aunt, uncle and cousin

Reta's father William Evens, Reta and guest Frieda at Lake Louise

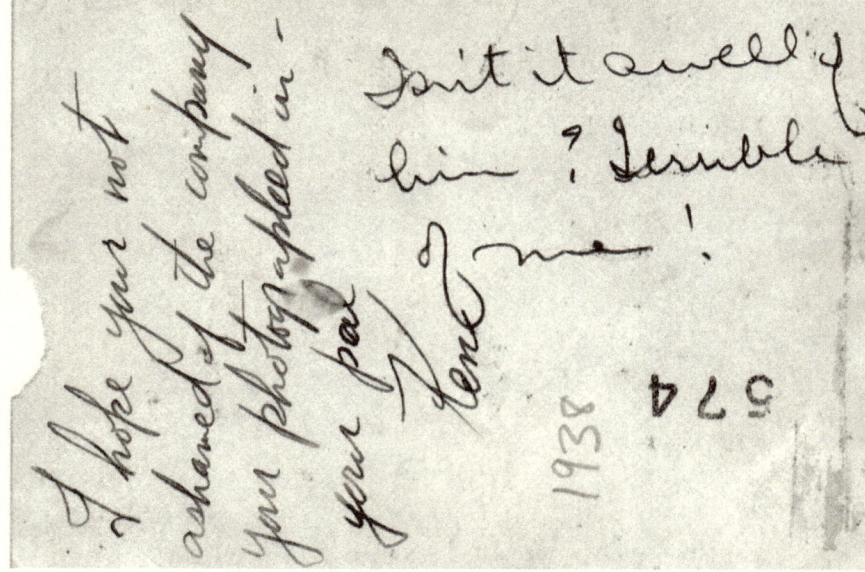

Reta and Keneth in 1938 with writing by each of them on back of photo

Chapter 8

MY FIRST DOUBLE DATE

The first double date I ever had turned out to be quite an occasion! This happened after I came back to the D.'s to work.

I had finished school and had just come back from the ill-fated visit home, where I broke my leg. Ros's brother Eldy asked me for a date. He had a car. Keneth had asked Dianne for a date. Keneth was Dianne's cousin, and he had taken her to some school affairs, so they were very much at home with each other. Ros, Dianne's future husband, hadn't discovered her yet. Eldy was his younger brother.

We were going on a real outing, our main plan being to dance. Everyone seemed to like to dance then. I wasn't very thrilled about my date; he was smaller than I, but I couldn't be choosy. This was my only chance at social life!

Binky Heath had an orchestra of his own, and he was playing regularly at a restaurant in Glenside known as the "Casa Conti." One part of it had a room used in the evening for dancing. All of us knew Binky, so that's where we went.

When it came to spending a night on the town, we were four of the greenest greenhorns in the world!

I can still remember walking into that darkly-lit room filled with cigarette smoke. There was beer on the tables and little else that was notable, excepting the jazz band. I wasn't thrilled; I felt involved in dark and dingy doings. For all the difference it made, I could have been stepping into a dope ring!

We hadn't told any elders where we were going, and no one asked. I was just nineteen. No one said that what we were doing was wrong, and I didn't know that some people might think it was. We were eager to sample the "big wide world" in those days, breaking out of the confines of Bryn Athyn.

We wanted to dance. To stay there, we had to sit down at a table. Soon a waiter came and asked us what we wanted to drink. We didn't know the names of any drinks. After looking at the list, we chose whisky sours. It was awful stuff, but everyone ended up drinking it, and no one said much about it.

When the waiter came around again, we decided to try something else. This time we had rum. We danced and the evening wore on. Next we had gin, and by the time we left for home we had had four different drinks, all terrible. We laughed and talked. When it came time to leave, I felt sort of wobbly on my feet but figured it was because I was tired from all that dancing!

We got into the car and drove home, and I *did* feel strangely dizzy! I was sure glad to be going home! On the way home, Dianne was as sick as she could be. I thought maybe she had a sudden attack of grippe! I can remember Eldy taking my arm up the cinder block steps at the D.'s and being very glad of his support.

Now that I was "grown-up," the D.'s did not check up on everything I did. When I arrived in the dark house, I just went quietly to bed, and there were no bad effects.

Years later when we told this story, we could laugh at how well we'd done on our first drinking date, except maybe Dianne. Eldy took me on several more dates but none to match the first!

I worked at the D.'s for about six months. I particularly remember my Charter Day date that year. Someone had given me a lovely, fine, crisp white taffeta evening dress. It was a little too old for me but at night was still pretty. The top was made of white taffeta. Also of taffeta were the big white petals sewed to the waist, reaching half way down the skirt. The bottom half of the skirt was white tulle (net). The skirt was very full. The big bow on the back was lined with red taffeta. I thought it was a beautiful dress.

Nathan P. had asked me to the Charter Day dance, and I was so tickled I had something pretty to wear.

The D.'s were all in a fluster over my dating Nathan.

He came in his convertible, which was fun. It was all shiny and new. All the other fellows I knew had rattle traps for cars, and we never knew when to expect a flat tire or a breakdown. That would never happen with this lovely car!

I was happy to be going with Nath, as we called him, but didn't feel very much at ease. I was sure that his mother didn't approve so did little more than answer him.

Later he asked me for another date, and we went to Willow Grove Park. I enjoyed the Park, and he was great company, but I was still afraid. Liking his mother, I did not want to displease her, so I felt awkward with her son.

In those days, I had no thought of getting serious with any boy. I did not have the feeling that every date was a potential step towards a serious relationship. I just accepted dates as outings and had a good time. I certainly had no idea that Nathan's attentions were serious. I just didn't look at it that way.

On the way home he stopped the car, probably to talk. I right away said, "Oh, aren't you going to take me home?" With that he started the car right up again, and we were both awkward.

That was my last date with him.

KENETH SIMONS

By the next Charter Day, I was working at Glencairn and had dated this one and that one and was feeling generally at loose ends.

Nathan owned an autogiro. His Uncle Harold was in the business. One weekend he asked some of his brothers and sister Karen if they'd like to take a ride. My friend Ann and I were invited, too.

We went to what is now the Naval Air Station. He took us up, one at a time, and flew us back over the Cathedral.

I was scared of the ride and told Nathan, "No dips!" He said, "Aw, no fun then." We did take a dip or two, and I looked back and frowned at him. He said he wanted us to get a better view, but I felt it was his excuse to be a bit of a tease. He enjoyed it.

It gave me the uneasy feeling of sitting on a chair with nothing solid under it. I never did like heights, and there were the trees right underneath and, goodness, would he miss the telephone wires? It had an open cockpit, which just made things worse. At least he didn't go as high as some of the other planes I saw.

Flying then was a new thing and not to my liking. There were no big airliners yet and jets hadn't been dreamed of.

Again it was time for the Charter Day dance. This time it was held in the Auditorium of the old de Charms Hall. It seems so small in memory! It was decorated as a garden. That was always the easiest sort of decoration.

No one had asked to take me to the dance. I was rather cross about this because I had been out with several fellows. I felt that they didn't ask because they were afraid of being labeled as "steadies," and that made me cross. Boys always seemed to care so much about that. So I went anyway with a couple of girlfriends. Even though there were many more girls in town than boys, there were a few boys who showed up solo at dances. I used to tell the girls, "Why not go and see what happens?" Something always did.

Halfway through the evening, they brought out a basket, two in fact, with slips of paper. I dove in like most everyone else, and my slip said, "Meet someone at the fountain." It was to be a dance to mix everyone up.

When I got there, a tall dark fellow was standing with a slip of paper in his hand that said the same thing. I'd never seen him before nor knew of his existence.

He was Ros Coffin's older brother, Al. I don't know where he worked.

Well, it turned out to be great fun. We danced and danced. It had a bit of a fairy tale flavor, and I wished he'd be just the one. He danced so well and was so easy to talk to. He seemed to know just how to handle himself with a girl. He had a nice car, so we went for a drive after we danced and then home.

He took me on one or two other dates and showed every sign of being very serious. I liked him very much but not enough to get serious. I was wondering how to cool things down. Only a couple of weeks after I met him, there was horrible news. He'd been killed in a car accident while driving to work with someone else.

As before told, Keneth was here and there in the picture. Everyone, including me, called him Kenny. At home he was called Gick, a name I detested. When asked, "How come?" he said his older brother Elmer had nicknamed each family member after his father died. (Keneth's father and oldest brother had died within the same week, just before I came to B.A. in 1929.)

Elmer's nickname for Elmer was "T.G.," which stood for "The Great." Elmer was good-looking and most sociable, a big wheel with the gals.

When he was a child, Keneth liked to take alarm clocks apart. He wanted to know how things worked. Elmer, whom everyone called Bud, thought of cogs in connection with Keneth. Cog backwards became Gock (relatively speaking), and the name ended up as "Gick." Later, when Keneth became interested in ham radio, the family often called him Dit-Dah, but Gick was the name most used.

Bud named his younger brother "Sook" because as a child he sucked his fingers. He was David, who grew up to be a minister and principal of the elementary school.

The youngest brother, Hilary, was called "Pups." That's because he was the baby and still a pup. Buddy kidded him most. Poor Hilary still tells sad tales. When he carved, Bud always gave Pups the pope's nose of the turkey "because it was the last bit over the fence." Being the youngest, that's what was left for him.

Over the years those nicknames were used less and less. At family gatherings, Uncle Bud is the only one left now who still uses them. Most others have forgotten them.

After the Christmas of the little brown radio in the potato basket, I felt Keneth was more a steady than less. He'd never be the sort to go to the bother of a gift if he wasn't quite interested, even though he'd not want anyone to think so (including me).

Most young men don't want to feel caught, up to the last minute. I did not feel any differently than that about him. I did begin to feel he was the best friend I'd ever had in all kinds of ways. I felt at home with him, could be comfortable being myself, and could talk about anything.

He and Ros were just getting to be real buddies. One Sunday, Ros invited Di and me to go along to some small airport near Hatboro. He was going to take Keneth up for a ride in the Piper Cub he flew sometimes, when he could afford it. He'd bet Keneth he could make him seasick. We went to see.

After fitting themselves out in parachutes, they took to the air. We saw them disappear and then come back into sight as they circled higher and higher. My, they were far up. Ros then went into a spin and did all sorts of things. We girls weren't enough involved emotionally with them to be at all anxious. We did feel glad we weren't up there. They finally got back down, and Keneth did not look quite himself. He still had his 50 cents (the bet) because he said Ros had not made him sick but had only scared him half to death.

Keneth had gone to work for a couple of years after high school to save money for college. When he once got started at the University of Pennsylvania, he won a scholarship for being the brightest freshman.

Having finished another year of college, Keneth was asked by a classmate whose father was chairman of the board of the United Gas Improvement Company, to go on his father's yacht as radio operator. They were going to fish for marlin off the Island of Bimini, for one thing.

This yacht trip was most exciting and added some glamour to my feelings about Keneth. He seemed very easygoing, went along with things in general, but now something like this was a big change. He was finally excited about something. He could tell you tales of how he was to be part of the crew and yet not.

His classmate's name was Britt Chance. He was a distinguished looking fellow. His favorite hobby was sailing, and he later won a gold medal for it in the Olympics. Besides that, Britt was devoted to his work. Britt and Keneth both went on to make important contributions to their respective fields. (Note: Keneth later worked with Britt when they were both in their 80's.)

One of his favorite adventures on the trip happened when they got to Havana. They moored in the harbor. Cuba was not Communist then. Keneth was invited by the family to the Yacht Club for a party. Before he had shipped out on the yacht, Keneth bought a white cotton suit "just in case." It cost all of $5. He hurried this only suit off to a cleaner and got it back again just in time. When he went to put it on, he discovered it was missing all of its buttons. Men's pants then had no zippers. With Mother Chance's friendly help, he found enough straight pins to hold it together. He danced and sat carefully the whole evening. For partners he had a couple of Cuban girls. One taught him a little Spanish, "La luna es muy bella," in the moonlight.

Keneth wrote me letters and mailed them when they made port. He had always enjoyed swimming and was entranced with seeing beautiful little colored fish around a sunken ship in shallow water off Bimini.

In those times, ordinary people didn't take winter vacations in Florida. The Caribbean was a place you heard about. So even though it was in summer, this trip was high adventure.

Keneth came back his same self.

Britt wished to have Keneth work for him, but the pay was poor. It was to be "a love of the use," but Keneth needed more than that to exist.

He worked during all holidays and kept on winning scholarships. He finished college and was offered a scholarship for his Master's Degree. He felt he'd starved long enough. His mother needed money, too. He was never one to give up books, but he left them formally behind for a job.

IN THE MEANTIME

Ros was most anxious by now that Di would say "Yes." She still hung back, and most often would not date him unless it was a double date. So Ros would always ask Keneth, who would always ask me.

In well over a year's time, more like two, we did lots of fun things. Ros was for high adventure, but Di held back. I used to wonder why but guess now it was because she did not want to be too beholden, in case she decided to say "No."

Once, the three of them came to pick me up on a lovely, warm evening, and Ros said, "Let's go to New York. I know a wonderful place called the Merry-Go-Round Bar where we can see all sorts of sights."

"No," said Dianne.

So we drove and drove till Ros remembered another place a friend had mentioned. It was up in Jersey somewhere and was called "The Chicken Barn."

Such a fun place.

The story went that the owner had inherited it on the condition he leave the farm the way it was. He almost did. The bar was in the oat bin, and we sat down to supper at a wooden table in a stall. I remember we each had a tiny roast chicken. This was before Cornish game hens were invented. A little flag on each chicken had a number on it. A lucky number meant a free meal. Also, if you were taller than the very tall owner, there'd be a free meal. Best of all, you got a free meal if you came in a sleigh!

In the hayloft above, the center was cut out with more tables around the edges. Up there was also a dance orchestra. We danced in the middle of the barn floor. Outside one could play horseshoes.

We had a delightful evening

KENETH'S COLLEGE FRIENDS

At the University of Pennsylvania, Keneth had two college buddies. The three of them (Simons, Smith, and Samter) ran the class and held all the offices. Samter was an especially lively character. He introduced us to the Melrose Riding Academy, a picturesque eating place where many young people collected.

Melrose was only about six miles away from B.A., and we thought it the best of all places to go. The fellow who owned it collected all sorts of junk, and the place sprawled in all directions. On the way in, we passed horses with their noses out of their stalls to be patted. We never did any riding.

One building had some little and some big dining rooms. The first time we went there, we chose a little Chinese room, romantically lit by candles. It adjoined a central room with a jukebox for dancing. World War I mementos hung from the ceiling, literally covering it. There were German helmets, bayonets, and other war gear.

Downstairs was the most delightful of all. Sawdust covered the floor. Walls were stucco with dark beams. In wintertime there were lots of bright burning fireplaces. In summer there was an outside brick terrace for dining after a hayride.

From the building where meals were served, we walked across a little courtyard to another building. It, too, was full of mementos and had a bar and a big fireplace. Around the room were pinball machines. On a little balcony decorated with horse collars was an orchestra.

The owner later added a roofed pavilion with one open side, and around the other three sides were wagon wheels as open windows. We danced there. On one side of the terrace were old stagecoaches. My but those stagecoach drivers rode high up on their perches!

One time Samter called Keneth at midnight. He had a date with a blonde and they wanted to climb the Cathedral tower in the moonlight. Keneth, of course, called me. We had a wonderful time. But I sure felt like a country cousin next to the glamorous blondes Samter dated.

In 1938, Keneth got a job with WCAU radio as a studio operator. Part of his job was to go to various night spots around town to put orchestras on the air. The big name jazz bands were the "in" thing then. Every young person wanted a chance to dance to them.

In Philly there was a nightclub called the "Arcadia." A lovely broad stairway led to a room with a circular effect. It was a lovely and luxurious place.

Gene Krupa's band was playing there. He was an outstanding drummer and a most handsome fellow. Keneth was sent to put him on the air for broadcasting. All the dials were set, and then the moment came. Krupa came on with a thundering roll of his drums.

The needle on the audio meter banged to the right, and WCAU was off the air. Imagine Keneth's embarrassment! Because he was awed by the famous Krupa, he had failed to ask for an "opening level."

When Keneth was about to graduate from college, we went to the Arcadia with all of his college class. Classes were quite small then. I felt very elegant coming down those stairs in a long, embroidered, crisp white organdy dress with sparkly buttons down the back. Samter was there, too. He was all over the place, doing everything except trying to play Krupa's drums.

Would you believe it, I'd gone with Keneth for at least two years, and we had never so much as held hands?

Most often, when we had dates, we went for a walk or down to his house. On Sunday evenings we most often went to his house and listened to the radio. It was, of course, best after all the family had gone to bed. Mother Simons discouraged this solo dating and called down every little while to be sure we were behaving. After many such dates, she became more tolerant.

Then one night we were sitting on the couch listening to a particularly nice symphony and Keneth's hand crept over to mine under a pillow. The lights were very dim. They had just announced the title of the music, and the fire had burned low. We just sat listening, and in what seemed like only a few seconds they finished playing. It was the most outstanding short passage of time in our whole lives!

GYPSY VACATION

Keneth and I were dating pretty often now, almost every weekend. It was just a pleasant round of outings. Keneth never was one bit serious. I found it rather difficult as to what kind of stand to take. I wasn't all the way sold on him. So I had other dates, too, some of which I enjoyed very much.

Vacation time was coming up. Everyone else on the job went home. I had Irene in school and couldn't afford to go. The train ride would use up most of the two weeks anyway.

Ros and Di came up with a suggestion. Dianne's family, the Will Aldens, were to spend their vacation up at Lake Wallenpaupack. Her uncle Karl Alden had a nice cabin on the lake, and in his backyard was a big back-to-nature tent that the Will Aldens could use. It was screened halfway up on all four sides, which was fine as long as there wasn't much rain. The cooking was done outside over a pile of rocks. Beside the tent was an iron pipe with a spigot from which came cold water.

Ros loved to camp, so he owned a little pup tent with a canvas floor and two little cots. This he took up for Di and me to sleep in. He and Keneth would be up for weekends and sleep close by, on the ground. The weather was perfect. Keneth drove me up early one morning on his way to his job at RCA in New York City.

It was great fun living in the tent and waking with the birds and sunshine. Brushing our teeth under the faucet and washing our faces in such cold water was invigorating. The fellows didn't find it so good for brushing up lather for shaving. There were no electric shavers then.

Keneth came to spend the one weekend, and that was fun. We swam and roamed. I wore a real full skirt, and we danced barefoot to "Begin the Beguine" at some little mountain retreat. We rowed one night across the lake, which was all wild still, and talked by the edge of the water in the moonlight.

The next weekend, when it was time to go home, Ros came alone. Keneth had told Ros that he couldn't get away. It was awkward. Worst of all was driving home with them. Naturally they didn't want me along, and the family car was overflowing. It was a most unpleasant ending to a lovely vacation. Ros was irked and let me know it. Di didn't like it either. It made me wonder why she didn't make up her mind about Ros.

One other little episode comes to mind in relation to the lake. It was very embarrassing at the time. The K.R. Aldens had an oldest son, Guy, who was about my age. I still dated him occasionally. His parents allowed him to invite several fellows and girls to spend a weekend at their lake cabin.

Keneth was invited and asked me to go along. It was a weekend party with the senior Aldens as chaperon s. There were few rules. Each couple chose what they wished to do much of the time. Most always we stayed as a group and talked, played games, and helped with meals. Sunday we all decided to take a walk. The lake was very wild then, even on the White Beauty side. The long and the short of the story is that Keneth and I got "lost" and were hours late for Sunday dinner. For some reason, no one believed our story about getting lost!

MORE KENETH

His cousin Guy still asked me out, but he didn't much like it when I slipped and called him "Kenny, Guy"!

I went out with other fellows, too, because Keneth made it clear he wasn't ready to get serious. I was also still unsure. Much time and wondering was spent thinking about such things, naturally. Getting married was such a final step, and how could one be positive? I hadn't fallen madly in love with him like I'd heard others did with each other, so it seemed good to wait.

Keneth finished college, and I went to one or two affairs with him in town. The Electrical Engineering Department at the University of Pennsylvania was certainly small for such a big college.

Keneth graduated with honors, and he was offered a scholarship to go on to take his Master's Degree. He felt he'd been poor long enough, and, being older when he finished college, about twenty-six, was more than ready to have a steady job. Because he was president of the honorary society, Tau Beta Pi, he was sent to a convention in San Antonio in the wintertime.

He was voted by his professors "most likely to succeed," which won him the A. Atwater Kent award: two hundred and fifty dollars and his name on a permanent plaque in the school hall.

With the money he bought a bright blue Ford sedan. Now he had a car of his own to go to the movies, and he was very proud of it. His family was happy he had it. His youngest brother, Hilary, who was about eight years old, didn't like me around. He was afraid big brother Keneth would get married and there'd be no more car, as had happened when Bud moved out.

Now I was invited to the Simons' house for Sunday dinner quite regularly.

A young couple, Flo and Dick Lynch, rented an apartment next door to the Simonses. They were not members of the church. They were very up and coming. He did photography to fill the gap between jobs. They were most friendly, and we sometimes visited them. He took a lot of good pictures of Keneth and a classic one of Mother Simons peeling apples. She canned much in those days.

She got him to take a group picture of her family and made it into her Christmas card. The next year's card showed the family's old brown house after a pretty winter snow.

I particularly remember a couple of very enjoyable evenings. I'd gone to visit Di early on one summer's evening. Having run out of conversation, we decided to go for a walk. We walked up around The Loop, and there was Keneth's car parked outside his house.

The light was on in his upstairs room, so I said, "Let's throw pebbles at his window. Maybe he will take us to Hoglan's to have a delicious ice cream cone." Hoglan's was a little place built up where White's store is now and the Sorrel Horse Inn used to be, not much more than a tiny stand. This Hoglan family made unusual varieties of ice cream, at least a half a dozen flavors. Drug stores carried only chocolate, strawberry, and vanilla, and, in those days, one never got ice cream at a market.

Keneth finally heard our pebble and opened the window. He came out, and Dianne quickly made excuses to get away, leaving us together. It was a middle of the week date and all the more fun for being different. We usually had our social times on weekends.

Another time that was fun was about the end of May, the next year. Keneth came home from his RCA job in New York every weekend. He tells me now that he came down to see me. At the time, I thought it was to be with his family. They were a tribe that liked each other and had a good time together.

It was a lovely evening, as May evenings can be. I was busy working on a Friday Supper committee when he walked in to find me. He said, "When you take your apron off, let's go somewhere different." I had to stay for supper and felt guilty about skipping class.

The society was small then, and we had to slip out carefully not to be seen.

But we did. We drove and just at twilight time arrived at Bowman's Tower up along the Delaware. We sat in the car and talked at the base of the tower. There were only one or two other people there. Crowds were not what they are today.

Then we decided to climb the tower and up we went, round and round the circular staircase.

Coming down, I got scared. Oh-oooo...such a nice wide stairway, but I hesitated part way down.

With that, Keneth swooped me up in his arms and carried me the rest of the way down. I was tickled with the idea but felt wicked to let him act so boldly. I jumped to my feet the minute we got down!

That incident seems minor compared with our next adventure. I planned to meet him one day in New York, on my day off. I felt sure Mrs. P. would fire me if she knew about that! (She might well have done so!)

Keneth told me what train to take and very carefully gave me instructions about the New York subways. He even enclosed a map of the subway system. I was to meet him at Radio City. It all looked very simple ahead of time. I made out OK till I got to my first subway. I went downstairs from Penn Station. Down there, there were layers and layers of subway. How did anyone in all that throng know where they were going? I needed help but didn't know who to ask.

Finally, a nice-looking fellow saw my plight and asked if he could help. I showed him the map. He said he'd take me to Radio City, so I said, "OK," and followed him. With all those people, I'd be safe.

Keneth had a fit when I told him. However, I'd quietly asked someone else sitting next to me if this train went to Radio City and was assured it did. It took time to find the place of meeting, and it was mighty good to see Keneth standing there.

We finally got to his nice little apartment. That was what he wanted to show me. We had something to eat. Then he opened the door of the refrig. There sat a couple of cans of beer! It made me sort of leery of him. He bought *beer* to have at home!

We stayed at his apartment only a short time. It was right under an elevated train, but it was rather nice. We then drove home to B.A.

Now so many things are involved with Keneth I can't keep them all straight.

When Keneth was finishing his last bit of college, he would call me once in a while to meet him in town on my day off and have supper. I paid for my own.

We went to the Italian Gardens, a little basement restaurant that was under $1 for supper. Neither of us had seen spaghetti eaten Italian style before, and we had fun trying it. No one around town served such things then nor the nice long loaves of Italian bread.

It took until many years later for people to come out of their shells and try all sorts of new things. People did go on picnics, but charcoal and cookouts at home never had been heard of in this part of the country.

Keneth and I still had a most loose-knit setup in relation to each other.

Then he was off on an oil tanker trip. He took several such trips to study automatic steering. He wrote travelog letters of sailing down the coast, through the Panama Canal, and on around to California. These were the adventures of Sinbad the Sailor or some such fairy tale.

He went to the movie studios when he arrived to see the glamour spot of the world, Hollywood. There wasn't such a thing as TV then, and movies were the big thing. The movie stars ruled supreme. Next came the big band leaders to listen to on the radio. Some crooners were also coming into their own on radio, such as Bing Crosby.

I had lots to tell my friends about Keneth.

He arrived back in early September. He called. There was a wedding that night I wished to go to, so he said he'd see me there. I came out of the church, and there he was, all very tan and slim looking. He was a sight to see, and it was a thrill for the very first time.

We wandered off down to Mrs. P.'s little house in the woods to sit on the wooden bench by the pool and talk.

From such an auspicious beginning, the evening turned into being most disappointing and somewhat of a shock.

While he'd been on the tanker, he'd decided to put himself through a regime. He'd been so easygoing that he'd put on weight. He'd never cared much about the clothes he wore or about his appearance in general.

Now he'd decided to snap up a bit, the only time he ever did such. While doing all this, he began to think of his old girlfriend and informed me he was going to ask her for a date. What a blow.

When he first started high school, he'd had a crush on a dark-haired, attractive girl whose parents were Austrian. Mama had edelweiss pressed behind all her pictures and made the old country goodies like Fastnach. They were a quaint and charming older couple. The youngest daughter really was different.

She was my friend, Ann, from the mountains. My first summer there right after high school was when I got to know her. Much had happened since then, and we were now working together at Glencairn.

I knew she'd been Keneth's only "crush," but she'd long since been going steady with another fellow. We talked about everything, and she *was* on the fence about her boyfriend. I could *never* see how she ever happened to even go out with him, he was so undesirable as to his outlooks and behavior.

She was very kind and reticent. She had a bad time telling me Keneth had asked her for a date. I had a feeling she liked him still, and I said, "Why not?"

I felt terrible about the whole thing. Here it was the first time I'd seen Keneth again and felt maybe we'd get serious and that I could like him very much. Now I felt there was nothing to do but pretend the reverse.

Who could ever care for someone who wanted somebody else?

While making beds one morning, Ann finally came right out and asked me if I liked him. I said, "No." I knew she'd never go out with him otherwise. If she was so on the fence herself in relation to her boyfriend, she also had better find out.

The other girls around wondered just what was going on when

this came about. It was mildly upsetting. Everyone knew Keneth and Ann had liked each other once upon a time.

The long and the short of it was that her boyfriend got good and mad. Keneth had his one date and time went on.

After several weeks, I think two, Ann talked again to me. She was in a stew. But in the meantime, Keneth had decided that was that and again asked me out. One date had decided him to leave the past.

That Christmas, the present from him was a cute little wooly lamb made of real lamb's wool in a yellow beige color with a bright blue ribbon around its neck.

I put it carefully away. It was the only hope chest item I had.

My son Kurt may remember it; we gave it to him when he was still a bit of a thing.

A VISIT TO GAY'S

The eldest P. daughter, Gabriele, known to everyone as Gay, had married the bishop's handsome son, and they had been sent to Pittsburgh to run that Society.

Up until then, Gay had been a happy homebody and trips to the mountains with her family were the extent of her travels.

Now she was whisked off to a new city and sudden responsibilities. She was very homesick, so once in a while she spent a weekend back home to visit.

Gay and Willard did not live in the then impossibly dirty city itself but instead chose a rural setting. The steel mills of the city left dust and smog around for miles. White curtains scarce could be kept white with care.

Young minister Willard would have to make pastoral calls on other cities, which meant leaving his bride alone in a big house. Instead of going home, she decided to stick it out for one extended trip of her husband's.

The first I knew about it was when I was approached and asked if I'd go out and stay with her.

I'd like that now. We could have such a good visit. But back then I didn't feel as though I knew her at all, and her newly-acquired status, besides her background, added to the gulf.

But I went. I was completely in sympathy with her, too. I could not enjoy being alone all night in a big place with no nearby houses.

I often wondered why I was chosen; she had some good friends among the girls. Probably I was the least important there.

The house was beautiful. A big, rambling stone one with fields and wooden fences, green lawns, and spreading trees. Inside was spacious and gracious, lovely soft carpets, fireplaces, and big winding stairs with a landing part way up.

My guest room was soft and pleasing with a book ready to read until you fell asleep.

In the morning a breakfast of choice was served by a butler. He was impeccable and could have served a king. Made talking that much rougher for me. Big white linen-covered table, shining glasses, and sparkling silver.

It was a strange land to be living in.

The day went by, not very fast, and we lit a fire in the living room to talk, read, and stitch beside after supper. There was a chill in the air. I can't remember whether it was spring or fall, but I believe spring as the trees were green.

Why does one always hear noises at night? I'm convinced houses *must* creak as much during the day, but no one is aware.

After being settled in our respective bedrooms, somewhat distant from each other, and my light being turned out, I thought I heard a voice. It was Gay. She crept across the hall and whispered, "Did you hear anything?"

I hadn't, except for creaking stairs and the very sort of sounds one hears when afraid. It was her house, and I was depending on her.

After talking it over a bit and not being able to say what she heard was nothing, she suggested we creep down to the landing where several guns were encased on the wall. Now I was bothered. She fumbled down a monstrous thing looking like a shotgun to me. "Here, you hold it, too," she said, and down the stairs we went with the thing at least pointing in front of us.

I'll tell you, I learned something. Our hands were shaking so bad any burglar would have laughed outright and been as safe as safe. The chance of a near aim was pretty slim.

We wandered around a bit with chattering teeth and finally got back up to bed.

I wonder if she ever told her husband of her escapade?

THAT MAN

Summertime came and we left Glencairn en masse to go to Tonche in the Catskills. I loved it up there, but it meant no social life, which meant just girls for friends.

In the middle of the summer, Keneth wrote to say he was going to come visit me Saturday night and would stay some place at the bottom of the mountain. I tried to dissuade him, but he'd not listen. I was 24. I knew the P.'s would not like it.

I rushed to tell Karen. She didn't say anything, but she told her mother. Mrs. P. then was very cool to me. I liked her so very much that it bothered me. Then at the dinner table she made some remark in front of everyone.

I rushed out of the room bawling.

Soon Karen came to talk. She stayed away from the subject, so I felt in a bind.

Keneth called next day, and I told him all about it, but he was undaunted and said to walk down to the first bend in the road and he'd meet me there. We went to a Saturday night movie. Ordinarily, the P.'s were most cordial and invited anyone in to Sunday dinner, etc., so this was rough going. I *had* decided in spite of everything I had to lead my own life and so would put up with it.

Sunday afternoon, Keneth suggested we go for a walk on that pretty mountain. What should happen but Mr. & Mrs. P. go for a Sunday drive. Keneth and I had walked a long way down the road and then decided to cut across the zig-zagging road. Just as we took off into the woods, they came along. It sure looked bad. There were no smiles. If only a minute had gone by, we'd have missed each other.

Well, we got by, but it was an unhappy remembrance.

Sometime in about here, after going very steady, Keneth and I got down to brass tacks about talking. It wasn't about us as a couple but about how we looked at things. We agreed quite a bit. I had no good answers for him. He'd been to college, and some of his professors liked to talk of many things besides their regular classes. It was a liberal education.

Keneth enjoyed such "chews" with me, but I didn't.

Finally, one night while standing outside the door at Glencairn, I told him I was wasting my time, "Goodbye."

It took some doing to say it; I was very inexperienced still in being grown up at all. At the time, I saw the next generation almost all going steady, down at the high school level, and I could understand the feeling of security it gave them.

I sure felt adrift.

Right away, though, I decided to not miss any society doings and would accept any date that came along. I had some pretty funny ones and some very good times, but I missed Keneth. I'd gotten so comfortable with him. Now I had to be on my toes again.

My pal Shirley across the hall had broken up with her steady, too. Actually, she was engaged at the time, though it hadn't been announced. She was very unhappy. All of us felt he'd not been right for her at all so cheered her on. She had no family in B.A. either.

We went looking for trouble.

The beer cellar at Mrs. Heath's had turned into the Civic and Social Club, now in a stucco house on Alden Road. It was rather attractive, and it was a shame to have it changed. However, to help carry expenses, the downstairs was turned into a little grocery store by a B.A. resident. Now B.A. had its own commercial spot.

Upstairs was the Clubhouse and it has stayed so ever since. It was enlarged much later. Being over 21, we could go there. We were not encouraged to, but we were allowed. We'd been to similar places around.

I can remember being in a car full of dates when we went to the old School House in Ambler to dance. It was about the only time the waiter asked our ages. I was just over 21 and Shirley was still 20. The waiter believed the reverse, much to everyone else's surprise, which made me mad. We didn't go back there.

My pal and I decided to try the Clubhouse one evening. We felt sure Mrs. P. would not approve so didn't tell anyone. She heard most things, so we went only a few times with a good spell in between. I had Cokes and she had sloe gin fizzes. She thought them the greatest and vowed she'd have them at her wedding someday, along with hamburgers, her favorite snack!

The trouble was that any fellows who hung out at the Club were not ones we cared for. This once, there was quite a crowd, and we each had a date by the time the evening was over.

Mine happened to be that old flame from way back in high school, Cedric King, who was visiting town. Sure gave me mixed feelings. We spent the evening riding in the back seat of my pal's date's car. I was intrigued to find out how he'd turned out, but as luck would have it, I very soon needed to get to a ladies' room and could scarce think of anything else!

He got very chummy, which made me not too unhappy to go home early. I felt I could like him again if he'd been his old self, and I would have liked to have seen more of him.

As it turned out, he did come to see me later. He was having a very hard time trying to get through medical school. He came to see if I would lend him some money. I was busy helping at home and still had Irene in school. Brother Leslie was due to come as soon as she finished. I was torn and felt if he liked me I'd probably give him the moon and forget everyone else. But I saw no signs of it and didn't want him beholden so said, "No."

Gold discovered in California

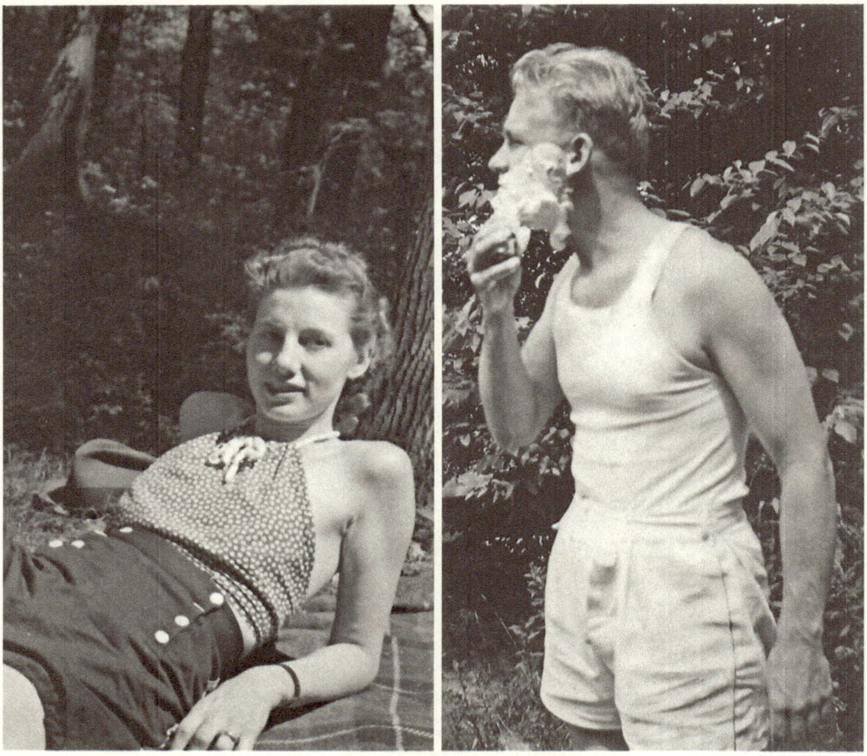

Reta lounging and Keneth shaving while camping

Keneth and Reta camping

Keneth Simons on the yacht Antares, sailing to Cuba

Back of Reta wearing dress illustrated on page 212 and, on right, Keneth Simons at graduation standing by plaque of A. Atwater Kent award recipients at Moore School, University of Pennsylvania.

Keneth and Reta with Ros and Di

Chapter 9

THE ANCHORAGE

Along in here, maybe three odd couples would manage to scrounge a car from a parent for a Saturday night outing. Most had been out only to a movie or Sunday drive on their own.

One night we were in a gay humor, it being about May, and the warm weather made us wish to wander. After driving around to talk up plans, we headed down Roosevelt Boulevard toward the city. Someone had heard that the "Anchorage" was a good place to go. By this time, it was dark. A band was playing, the lights were low, and we'd be able to dance and waltz, our favorite outing. Almost all young people loved to dance back then. The music was not so fast as the Charleston had been.

None in the car were the least bit sophisticated. I happened to have a date with Guy. I don't think he had even heard of nightclubs, let alone been in one! The Anchorage was a place that had no cover charge, which was why it was chosen. We were all poor.

The waiter found us a table near the dance floor, and we were all disgusted that the dance floor, as usual, was so small. Clubs were interested in selling liquor, not amusing people. He asked us what we'd like to drink. Some of the boys chose beer, which the girls didn't like, so we hemmed and hawed around trying to decide. We didn't know the names of drinks; cocktail parties were rare in their parents' homes.

We wished to look like we knew. The waiter looked disgusted and gave us the feeling we were "mighty poor pickin's." We chose whiskey and water. It tasted terrible, but a pretense was made at sipping it. Mostly we tried to dance in the crowded space. It was poorly lit, not pretty and gay, as we felt. The old waiter asked and hovered about for more drink sales. We snuck out and poured a couple down the john in the ladies' room for fear he'd not let us stay if we couldn't drink up.

Soon there was a noisy rolling of drums, and a spotlight flashed on. An M.C. took the mike and began to talk. He told jokes, *dirty* jokes. Most of us didn't understand and, if some did, they were quiet about it. We giggled.

The high spot announced was to be a fan dancer act. Oh wickedness! We felt we should leave, but then it would soon be over and there'd be more dancing.

In scuttled an old bag with two big white feather fans, one before, one aft. Cheers all around! The music started up, and she made an attempt at dancing and waving her fans. She was so inept we were hilarious, but nervous. She at least pointed her bare toes out in front. She was so busy trying to use the fans, dance steps went by the board.

She stayed fairly modest, but when one caught a glimpse of a large part of bare leg it was so saggy one could think of nothing but how she should go home and dress it up with stockings. We almost felt sorry for her, which I guess is better than being embarrassed over some young thing having to be in such a performance. My date was *so* embarrassed over all of it, he blushed to the roots of his hair. No one felt comfortable, but as long as the dancer stayed decent, and she mostly did, I felt it was an education.

After the show was over, we fast lost interest in the place, and when the waiter came around for another drink order, we left. We'd go for a car ride.

Next night, we heard the place was raided. Was I ever glad it had not been when we were there! Whatever would Mrs. P. have thought or done if she'd known where I'd been! We all kept it secret.

BETTY'S

Growing up, there are always some "scampy" things that have to be tried. My small nucleus of best girlfriends were all very proper and well-intended. Not once did any of them go to town without permission, and they could hardly quarrel with parents over the style of clothes worn anywhere. Clothes, like the people, were proper in style. Skirts below knees and Oxfords for school.

Betty was Betty Childs, who lived in the big green house on South Avenue overlooking the "point" down Station Hill. She had large, jovial parents who graciously entertained. While a senior at the dorm, I'd come to know her because one of my pet dorm friends, Katy, was a classmate and pal of Betty's. We often went on a walk to Betty's and munched on her cookies and drank root beer while exchanging tidbits of girl gossip. Tryn Rose, my classmate and friend of the summer before, gravitated to our outings sometimes, as did a couple of other classmates of Betty's who lived nearby.

Betty's family built a beautiful swimming pool at the foot of the yard (a house is built over it now). The Harold P.'s had one, but that had been the only one in town. Now many who had never been in a pool hoped to have a swim in this one. So it was an exciting event. The water was such a pretty color, and the pool was nice to sit around. A natural pond would be better for swimming. The water in the pool was nasty tasting, and one could be swamped when anyone else dove in. With others swimming it was always splashy, but it *was* readily available.

Betty's parents were swamped with children's friends clamoring to be included. Others watched through the fence. All in all, they must have found it a busy experience. Betty had her chance to invite us, and a couple of times we went.

Her family had strict rules for occasional visitors. This brought about an episode we were to giggle about for years. Three or four of us were invited down one evening and, after dark, when the pool was off limits, Betty suggested we go try it in our skinnybares. We walked down to its inviting edge and milled around with the idea. Then someone said, "Aw, come on." Shoes and stockings came off very tentatively, then hesitation. It was pretty dark, no moon. We must be quiet or someone would hear. Who was that giggling? Betty encouraged and called softly to each of us to hear progress reports.

Finally, someone slipped into the water. Car lights slid down the road and we flattened out, dresses handy to at least cover ourselves. Cars coming up the hill were worse. The main light of them bypassed us, but we could then see each other, and it seemed to add to the hazard. Betty maintained that, if we once got in, everything would be all right. We were even careful to be far from each other, being modest creatures.

Well, I'll tell you I did not enjoy it. After being the last to slide in, the water was unbearably cold. I'd been in and out of my dress a couple of times, in fright, having put a foot in the arm hole in trying to pull it up and on instead of over my head, which a car light might see. I did get wet and had the feeling of being terribly bare. Some of us managed a quick swim across the pool and back, and by this time another girl said, loud enough for all to hear, "The boys are coming."

After the false alarm about the boys, I got dressed. Being in the water was noisy, and who knew who might catch us? Betty probably had been the one to mention boys, just for the fun of seeing us all react.

It seemed a hit and miss affair as far as the swim was concerned. We soon all headed back to the house, tucking in wet bits of hair. Collecting on the porch, we sipped root beer and exchanged reactions noisily, until someone would again remind us to be careful or parents would hear.

ODDS AND ENDS

An old town bachelor asked me out once, and we went roller skating. I could scarce stay on my feet, but it was fun. It was enough of him though!

The best thing to come along was a very handsome, dark-haired Swede. He came to college and was only a year younger than I. He'd seen me at church and had asked another schoolmate to be introduced to me. We met pretty often for about a month. He was talkative, freely met anyone, and seemed completely at home in any spot he happened to land. He was invited everywhere. Some of the girls really envied me, and one asked if I couldn't get her a date with him. It was quite a whirl to go out with him but, not being my type, not as much fun when alone. We went on walks and to parties. He was pretty funny sometimes in his use of the English language, and some of the girls felt it was planned rather than accidental.

In the meantime, Keneth had his car and a job and had picked up with a girl older than himself. Berith had been a senior when I was a freshman. She always had a touch of glamour and to me was very good looking. She had come to teach in grade school.

Andy Doering's family had offered their Water Gap place for a weekend party. He was going with a nurse, Peggy, from Delaware County so asked several fellows to bring girls. Keneth was one, and he took Berith. I felt gypped when I heard about this. I also began to wonder about him. If this gal liked him, he must have something I'd missed! I was keen to hear all the exciting things they did.

What got me was that I had dated him all through his poor times. Now that he had a job and could do much more, he had chosen someone else. All during this time, I didn't happen to run into him once. We tried to avoid each other. There was one exception.

Keneth's older brother, Buddy, had married and, after living in New Jersey for a time, moved back to B.A. They were living in an apartment in the old Colonel Wells house. It has since been torn down for the house Bob Asplundh built.

Buddy's wife, Jackie, was and is an incurable matchmaker, but I didn't know that then. I was invited to a Sunday dinner. I didn't know them very well and thought they perhaps hadn't heard I'd broken up with Keneth. It would be awkward to explain this, so I went. There was Keneth! Such an awkward meal! As soon as possible, I left. They said years later they preferred me to the other girl and were helping out!

Came school opening time and the first dance. My Swedish friend asked me to go, and I had a pretty new dress. He was very attentive and danced well.

When the evening was just about half over, there was Keneth

with his glamour-puss; he'd exchanged a dance. It was a surprise. The thing he told me was he'd exchanged dances with every foreigner hoping to find the right Swede. Now what to do?

I think it was at this time, right after Labor Day, when we'd come home from the mountains, that Keneth and Ros took a trip out West in the blue Ford. They had a pup tent to sleep in. Ros had wanted to take Di along, and the idea was for Keneth to take me. They figured I'd need a chaperon because of where I lived. Ros had suggested Mother Simons but, of course, it was all impossible. The idea of travel was one of my fondest ambitions, and I sure wished it could have been. They covered 7700 miles in two weeks, in a car that had nothing compared with now. They ate much Spam, which Keneth could never face cheerfully again.

I spent quite a lot of the time thinking about Keneth. I figured now if I accepted a date he'd probably be very serious, and I'd better be ready with an answer.

After a few days, he did call and sounded quite sparkling. When I saw him at the door, he even looked that way. We had an inconsequential date; nothing was said of importance. I think we sat and talked out under the pergola because I remember the misty night. It was such a pretty place with all the wisteria vines growing over it.

On that occasion, I called him Keneth and not Kenny. I did from that day on. In a couple of days, he again came up to see me and suggested we walk down to Mrs. P.'s little house in the woods. It was a very romantic place.

We were halfway down the path when he stopped and said he wasn't going to wait any longer to ask me.

Probably typical of women, but I wondered why he hadn't asked on the previous date? It would have been much more of a surprise. At least I felt it would have been the right timing after not seeing him for a while. Accepting the date was naturally a big occasion. But Keneth was never to be hurried into anything.

We talked by the pool at the little house for a long time! He first told me how he'd thought to bring a ring and all his plans for it. Then we talked of wedding plans for the following June.

It was October 13, 1939.

We wanted to tell the world! Mother Simons was, of course, first on the list. We walked down past the church to her house. She was sound asleep in bed, so we went upstairs and woke her. She sat up, momentarily looking very sleepy, and said, "Oh, I'm not surprised," and humped over and went back to sleep.

When I got back to Glencairn, the first person I thought of was Karen. By this time, it was well after midnight and Keneth had gone home. I tiptoed up to Karen's room, and it was really fun telling her. She sat up, so sleepy, and then jumped out of bed for a big hug, and at once she started scrambling under her bed. I couldn't believe what she was doing because she was scarcely awake and still looked so sleepy.

She pulled out a box and handed it to me. In it were four plates, a pitcher, and I don't remember what all, of beautiful, hand-blown blue glass with little air bubbles through it. She then said she'd bought it that summer at the mountains because I'd admired its color. Because Keneth and I had been seeing so much of each other, she had figured it would come to something. So she'd bought it and kept it under her bed since coming home. After we had returned from the summer and broken up, she'd been wondering for six weeks what she was going to do with it.

It was a delightful ending to the day and so typical of Karen's thoughtfulness.

THE FALL OF 1939

Irene had finished school, and Mrs. P. had asked her to come up to work at Tonche that summer. Irene was a bit too independent to make out very well up there, and I was sorry she went. Perhaps she could have stayed on to work in the fall in B.A. and had a good job.

Granny Glenn was sitting beside me one day at the tennis courts and asked if there was another one at home ready to come? Yes, there was a brother, Leslie. I'd been wondering how it would be possible to get him to school. With keeping one in school there was no chance for the next to come except over the summer. I had enough for his tuition at the end of that but was stuck for his railway fare down.

Home was still under a carpet of dust. Another thing, there was another brother, Bill, just a year behind. Leslie and Bill were inseparable, and the ideal thing was to have both of them come at once. Irene had had four years of high school. Leslie was only two years behind her so was plenty ready to come. Bill was, too. I knew it was impossible for both to come but was most sorry about it as it did very much change their status with each other.

Shortly, Granny Glenn looked me up to say Mrs. P. would talk to me about it. She then offered to pay Leslie's way down, and happily he arrived for school in September. He made out well and was liked at once. He had a good sense of humor, besides being very serious minded. He was lots of fun and came calling when he could.

He had been down here for only six weeks when Keneth and I became engaged. He was most tickled about it and offered his help. He was very anxious to help with the wedding and wished to be head usher. At that time, he was so new and hadn't yet learned "the ropes." I felt we should have a more experienced person, so we asked Uncle Will Cooper, an older man, to do the job. I was so sorry to have disappointed him, but he seemed *so* inexperienced! By the time we were married in January, he probably could have done it. We made him an usher, and he did a fine job, besides being all smiles. He felt all set up in his black tux. Don't know where we got him a black tux and white shirt, but he certainly enjoyed being "all dressed up"!

For the next long while, there was little time to see as much of Leslie as I'd have liked. He played football in the afternoons, evenings were for study, and weekends I spent mostly with Keneth when off duty.

Irene was then working in peoples' homes in B.A.. I believe it was for Miss Phoebe and Margaret Bostock at this time. It was her first chance to earn money, and she wasn't about to want to part with it by way of helping out. I'm sure she did later.

Upon hearing we were engaged, Mrs. P. said, "A year ago I would have congratulated you, but now I wish you happiness." Having tremendous respect for her and wishing always for her liking, I was a bit put out. She'd apparently felt I'd run after Keneth, at first, which I'd firmly deny.

She still wasn't at all chatty with me but from then on would appear in my room with a gift every so often. The first time it was a half-dozen big linen face towels like she used in her own bath, those soft, thin ironed sort. No ordinary home used them, and it was an elegant gift. I treasured them. Next it was a half-dozen fine percale pillowcases and next sheets. Before long I had a dozen of each. They were all hemstitched.

Imagine having all the happy prospect of the future plus a Christmas and birthday aspect added to it. I felt rather overwhelmed with gifts before I was through.

THE SIMONS FAMILY

Time rolled on apace. I now felt more free to be at the Simons household.

Along about in here, it might be right to try and tell a bit more about Keneth's background.

When I lived at the D.'s, I went sledding down Station Hill a few times. The Simons house was one where young people were invited afterwards for cocoa. I could never go. Christmas Eve would find Wynne at the piano playing carols with young people, singing till they wore out. When years went by, she did the same at the C&S Club instead.

Mother Simons was the eldest of William Hyde Alden's six children. They lived in Philadelphia, and he worked in the book room of the Convention Church. When the Academy movement got under way, he joined it. John P. had moved out to Alnwick Grove, what later became Bryn Athyn, and bought a large parcel of land for New Church people. William Alden bought a lot on Alden Road, which was named for him, and built a two-story white frame house with a front porch. This took some years to do, and by the time the house was built his family had grown up. It now belongs to the Williamsons.

Mother Simons, whose name was Gertrude, had been very carefully brought up, as most young ladies were. She felt most fortunate to be allowed to go to the West Chester State Teacher's College, but she still lived at home in Philadelphia. Just at vacation time her family got the mumps, and special permission was given to her to go stay with a friend she'd met at school, Elizabeth Simons. Gertrude was about seventeen. She was beautiful. Elizabeth's older brother Sam took one look and fell in love with her. He decided immediately that she was the one he would marry. Imagine the parents' consternation!

Sam very much went for the Swedenborgian Religion, and his sister Elizabeth also joined. She married Mr. Iungerich, the minister who came to visit us out West so many years later.

Gertrude and Sam were engaged for six years. They were married in Benade Hall in the old chapel. This has since been replaced, but the new one doesn't have stained glass windows or as much light. The floor in the old chapel was flat, too, and there were chairs on the side. I liked it.

Sam and Gertrude had three children in three years: Alden, Elmer, and Wynne. Sam was a dry goods clerk and very poor. He and Gertrude decided that enough was enough! All her other children were three years apart. She then had Keneth, Una, David, and Carolyn. Carolyn had a twin sister named Keruah, who died. Then came Hilary.

The oldest children were born in Philadelphia. Keneth's birthplace was 3648 North 62nd Street.

In the meantime, Gertrude's parents, Grandpa and Grandma Alden, had built their house in Bryn Athyn, and the young Simons family often went out to visit in the summer for a week or two. They picnicked and loved the country.

When Keneth was a year old, his parents bought a house on South Avenue on The Loop. It was a brown-shingled three-story house that had been built for Professor Vinet, a little bearded Frenchman who joined the church and taught French in the new schools. The house was perhaps fifteen years old at this time, had no electricity, had a coal stove, and a very dingy kitchen. Nevertheless, they were happy about it and paid all of $1,500 for it!

Father Simons dearly loved flowers, and his fond dream was to own a greenhouse. The nearest he ever came was cultivating every inch of his backyard that sloped down a hill and was small, as yards go. Here he raised as large a vegetable garden as possible to help feed his family. Sam actually had a greenhouse business before marrying, but it went bankrupt. Keneth remembers children being forced to weed and to this day won't touch a thing by way of gardening.

His father was not a strong man. He suffered very badly with asthma and spent much of his nights sitting up in a chair. He loved people and was kind and thoughtful. So the Simons family grew, the jobs got worse, and so did his health. He ended up commuting two hours to work down in Chester at a dark, nasty little store, being a dry goods clerk. He was coughing more at night and, being run down, caught a cold and then pneumonia. With asthma it was too much, and around about Christmastime he died, not yet fifty.

All the family got sick. Una was the one not expected to live; she did, though, but was never very well. She, too, had asthma. Oldest son Alden had come home from Antioch College for the holidays, also worn out from earning his way, and with no warm coat. He got back to college and died there of pneumonia, too.

In one week, Mother Simons had lost both her husband and her eldest son. In addition, her house was full of sickness. She was about forty-four. Neighbors and friends rallied round. Mother had been a loved and protected person and now took years to learn how to "really stand on her own two feet."

Mrs. Raymond P., who was Mother's age and a friend, helped the family. Most of the Simons kids objected, including Keneth's older brother and sister, but goodness knows what ever would she have done without the help? Keneth was appreciative, I'm proud to say. Mother baked her homemade brown bread twice a week for years, as a gift to show her love and appreciation.

She then launched a pre-kindergarten school. This she did twice a week from 9 a.m. to noon for years, but, outside of giving her a feeling of being useful, it brought in little money.

When her children were grown, she took in boarders to help the budget.

She was in charge of making ministers' robes, and, for years, a circle of ladies came in one afternoon a week to sew with her.

She made the Holy Supper bread for church. She belonged to a reading group that got together one night a week to read aloud.

The Will Coopers, who became neighbors, always came, and he was "Uncle Will Coop" to the family. He did the reading aloud.

One summer they formed what they called a "Gray Matter Club" to read Swedenborg's Writings, with pretty much the same people. It was held at different members' homes, with a nice supper first. They could invite guests! Keneth would hear stories of the interesting discussions and delightful times they had.

Mother was not a widow to be left out. If invitations were slow coming in, she cooked up a social affair of her own.

When I arrived in town, she soon came down to the D.'s for a quick call. I didn't remember this, but she told me much later. She did this on the request of Mr. Iungerich, who was her brother-in-law. He'd had to move to Pittsburgh as the society's minister just before my arrival.

Keneth was sixteen then and a junior. He was around, but I hadn't noticed him much. After Keneth finished high school, he took a year at Bryn Athyn's College. It was so small then, and scarce any credits at all were allowed at outside colleges.

He rode a bike to Glenside and worked at the new little radio station, WIBG, that operated in the basement of a church. Working for twelve cents an hour, he quit when they owed him over three-hundred dollars in back pay. He then went to work for RCA for two years to save money for college.

At RCA he happened to find a man's wallet. When he returned it intact, the fellow thought him so honest that he said he'd give him a job anytime. He was an RCA Department Head. Eventually Keneth went to UPenn and, when he was done there, he went back to work for RCA and stayed with them for a number of years.

When he started college, he'd bought himself a dark blue corduroy suit. College was attended usually by the well-to-do, and not many ordinary boys had the opportunity to go. Girls rarely went. Keneth was kidded constantly about his suit. The trouser legs were cut wide, and when he walked there was ever present a washboard sound effect as the fabric swished back and forth against itself. It was bulky looking also, with its double-breasted coat. He was nicknamed "Butterball."

Keneth lived at home and rode the train each day, so he was home on weekends. When he was at UPenn, I was dating him more and more by the end of his junior year and all through his senior year. One of our first real dates, not an accidental meeting, was on a Sunday afternoon. We went down to the Simons household. Keneth had voiced no warning. There all the family sat in the living room with the radio on. Sh-sh-sh. It was "the" Sunday afternoon concert of the New York Philharmonic Orchestra. They looked forward to it each week. It was "number four" for me to sit all afternoon and, of course, not appreciated aesthetically either.

As I came to know the family much better, I was particularly interested in stories about Keneth, as all girls are about boys they know. Keneth did not seem to enjoy social life as such.

One day I asked Mrs. Simons about who he played with when young. She told me a story that is the type I still get indignant about. She said, "Oh, he didn't get much time to play." When I asked, "How's about recess at school?", that, too, was booked!

In front of de Charms Hall was a bit of a turnaround with a rock in the middle. Mr. Otho Heilman was the principal. Although a man who did all kinds of good things, he was not cut out to be a principal, at least it did not keep his full interest. While teaching a class, he might be off downstairs setting the type for the weekly news folder, the *Post*, sent to B.A. people. Or he was ordering up the food for one of the numerous banquets held in town. He did a far better job on all the extras than he did at organizing the school. Even I heard kids tell about what fun they'd had in classes due to his wandering off into other ventures.

The ten of eight train in the morning brought mail to B.A. and another did at five o'clock. School began at 8:15 a.m. Because Keneth's family needed money so badly, they did any odd jobs they could get. Keneth carried mail for several older ladies. He'd go down to the station to pick it up, deliver it, and then on to school. He was several minutes late each day.

Result: Mr. Heilman made him walk around that little loop with the stone in it during recess as punishment.

That is the way he spent his playtime. When I asked Mother

Simons why she hadn't talked to Mr. Heilman (she forever avoided any unpleasantness), she said she was too busy and hadn't known about it.

To this day, I have no respect for that man.

Keneth took that routine as part of his job, but he did dislike Mr. Heilman for one other thing he did. If he was behind on typesetting for the *Post*, Mr. Heilman asked kids to help him after school. One day he asked Keneth and said he would pay him. School was over at twelve-thirty, so Keneth spent a couple of hours working. When he'd finished, Mr. Heilman paid him in "play money." That didn't happen again. Keneth was a most trusting person, and it was hard for him to learn to look out for himself, but he did after that when it came to getting paid.

When the Simons tribe were older and sat around the Sunday dinner table, lots of stories were told and laughed over. Uncle Buddy loved to tell them, and they grew in the telling.

Mr. Wells, who was Mrs. Donald Rose's father, known as "the Colonel," lived in a big old brown-shingled house on Alnwick Road. He was a dapper man about his person and raised a sizable family. Everyone liked to tell stories about him because he was such an adventurer. His life was a matter of ups and downs. I don't know where he came from, but he married into one of the town's first families.

At one time he had plenty of money and bought a big Stutz Bearcat car. During this affluence, he thrilled his friends by taking them for rides.

Before anyone knew it, he was poor again. But one thing he always kept was a horse. Behind his house overlooking the church was a bit of a barn where the animals lived. He hired boys to clean out the barn. It was as unorganized as everything else. Bud Simons got the job and kept it for a year or two. He hated it and the horse, too. Sometimes he was paid and sometimes not, so he quit.

Keneth fell heir to the job. For anyone who suffers from hay fever, as he did, there was no pleasure to be had from the work! He curried the horse, too, but never cared for "Minnie" or any other horse. He kept strict account of his working time and, when the end of the week came, sat on the Colonel's doorstep until he was paid. To hear the story told, Minnie the horse must have liked *him* because it died when he quit the job.

Mother Simons told a story about Keneth and the yearly oratorical contest. Mother's red-haired brother, Karl Alden, was principal of the boys' high school and taught Elocution along with English. Each spring, the boys wrote papers to learn by heart and present to the society. Three judges were chosen to pick the three top speakers.

Up the road about fifteen miles was another private school run by Quakers, known as George School. Our school and theirs had many friendly relations, and competition ran high. We played them in football on our biggest holiday, Charter Day. They, too, conducted an oratorical contest, had three judges, and chose three speakers.

Then a night was set for all six speakers to present their efforts. One year everyone was invited to have it at George School with their judges presiding, and the next year the affair was held in B.A. with our judges.

Keneth had been chosen as the winner by the Bryn Athyn judges for his paper "My Ideals." The finals were held at George School that year. After the speeches were over, the spokesman for the judges came to the stage to announce the winners. He began by saying the speech of Keneth Simons was excellent. So good that it couldn't possibly be written by a boy that age, so he was disqualified. Mother Simons never went to another oratorical contest. It was unlike her as she never carried a grudge all the years I knew her.

That was Keneth's nearest claim to fame in B.A. When he went on to the University of Pennsylvania and was showered with honors, his uncle the high school principal said he wished he'd noticed him a little more.

I might add a note about that red-headed uncle. We as students saw him every day at school. He sat up front in one of those old chair seats and out of the corner of his eye kept watch on the boys during morning chapel. He was short and pleasingly plump, with wavy thick red hair, freckles, and a most ready smile. He could be very serious, but most of the time he was exuberant. He had a soft husky voice, radiated pleasantness, and had the appeal of a father confessor. He was an affectionate person, inclined to be sentimental, which the kids made fun of, but oh! so kind. Many boys who had laughed at him in school, years later and far away, chose him as the one person they liked and wished to remember.

He took time to listen and be understanding. One never felt hurried by him, and yet he accomplished all his work as minister, principal, teacher, and father of a large family. He and his wife doted on one another. He loved to sing; a favorite song was "I Want A Girl, Just Like the Girl That Married Dear Old Dad." It was he who took us all Christmas caroling.

He was fond of young people. He put up with the boys' pranks, sometimes giving them a little talk later, perhaps about thinking of others. His outstanding trait was his enthusiasm for all of life and how "easily met" he was. For that reason, he was good at missionary work and meeting with new concerns.

He was one of the very first people to buy a lot at the new Lake Wallenpaupack. In fact, he owned five lots. His good friend Harold P. helped him build a cabin there, and he shared it with many. Many were the times Mother spent up there with her brother to "get away from it all."

For some reason, the Simons children didn't "go for" this uncle. They much preferred Uncle Will Alden, who, like his father before him, lived on Alden Road. He, in fact, built a sizable house almost across the street from his father. That big white house came from Sears Roebuck!

Uncle Will was very quiet. He liked to play chess with the Bishop de Charms, and he liked to join the young Simons men on the golf course. He chuckled over his favorite jokes, and I always think of him with his nose in some new magazine when he came visiting Mother Simons and the family was about. He was a good audience, and perhaps that is why the family liked him so well.

As the years went on, some of the best times were Mother's Sunday night suppers. They just seemed to happen most of the time. She encouraged her family to stop in, and they were always welcomed with a big smile. When we walked in the door, she'd be there in a minute. Up went her arms, and we'd be enfolded in a big hug amid cheery chatter. I felt so welcomed. I feel sorry for undemonstrative families but suppose it can be overdone. Not so with Mother. If it was late afternoon, she'd serve up wine and Rye Crisp or perhaps a thin slice or two of her brown bread. Conversation was tops. She was a walking book of knowledge, and time flew by. Along about now she'd say, "Do you have to go home?" Out would come a can of tuna, and with no bother there would be supper. She collected a few or many of the family for birthday suppers. It's delightful to not have to cook one's own birthday supper. There was always a clever gift eked out of savings.

Her sons doted on her, and in Buddie's stories she was "the Queen." Might seem silly, but it wasn't if you knew Bud. It was all in fun. I felt that the Simons' family parties were very enjoyable. Serious talk and thought happened as often as the nonsense. The individuals were as different in outlook and living as any cross-section of people. Being very loquacious, it was all very refreshing and stimulating, and homey besides.

I'm sure that none of us really did our share for Mother Simons. I will say that even those who had families of their own felt it a privilege to take her along on vacations to the shore or mountains. She loved to swim, and she was game for any adventure.

THANKSGIVING

The misty fall and pleasurable, casual walks of the past years were gone. This fall was filled with excursions of one sort or another.

Keneth had said it would have been most fun to surprise me with a ring, but he hadn't the faintest notion of my finger size. Being anything but an affluent society then, the young people were most unaccustomed to buying things. Eighth graders now are as sophisticated as many high school grades were then! So he set up a time when we both could go downtown to a wholesale jeweler that Uncle Will Cooper had been connected with way back. A lovely diamond was chosen. I'd never been so very fond of them as stones but liked this one because it was my engagement ring. The stone had its history with it. It had come from a South African mine and had been cut in Holland. Mrs. P. commented on its beautiful cutting.

At this time, I wanted all the standard things: a white satin wedding gown and "Here Comes the Bride" for music.

I can't say as how I especially enjoyed this period in one respect. I didn't know so much and was uncertain as to many procedures. I didn't think I should bother Mrs. P., and she played a tentative role. Did she like me or not? Besides, I felt she was so good, I could never quite live with her outlooks, so it was easier to try and find my own.

Mother Simons was pleasant enough but not that sold on me as a daughter-in-law. I admired her, in that she was staunch in certain things. She might not like the girls her sons chose, but after they once chose, she never was anything but affirmative, regardless of her feelings. She did not utter a critical word, and she did pleasant small acts to endear herself, such as bringing a loaf of homemade bread, etc. But at this stage I was not fond of her. Keneth had been the mainstay of the family as far as she was concerned, and she depended much on his steady way.

For the first time since graduating from college, Keneth had a steady job at RCA with no strings attached. Before that, he'd helped the family, but anything he could save went for college. So during the summer and the early fall months, the Simons tribe had enjoyed a car, the blue Ford Keneth had bought with the money he won for outstanding scholastics. Mother Simons had charged bills at Strawbridge's Department Store. I was mighty irked that she owed a hundred dollars at the time we got married, so Keneth hadn't been able to save a penny.

Whenever I had a Sunday off, I went to the Simons' for dinner.

Sunday dinner at their house was a fun affair. Mother Simons enjoyed good meals and was handsomely plump and a good cook. Much of it was a pinch of this and a handful of that. On this account, her homemade brown bread, for example, varied drastically. She made a loaf twice a week for Mrs. P., who ate sparingly, but always that brown bread.

Keneth kidded about it. Nothing was wasted in that house. If mother forgot the yeast, the dough was cooked up as pancakes. They went all out for Sunday and always cooked a roast. Whatever was left over was used on the weekdays following. The dessert most often served was Bavarian Cream, with strawberries over it in season.

Oldest brother, Buddy, was gone, Wynne had just been married. She lived in a Rose apartment, which was seen from the Simons' back windows, and often visited with her new husband, who never "went" for the Simons. He would leave as soon as the meal was over.

Mother Simons had one of those big round oak tables with a central pedestal with lions' claws on it and umpteen leaves so that she could seat up to about twenty-five people. It filled the whole dining room and was wonderful because it had no legs and everyone could see everyone else. On it was always a white linen tablecloth and napkins, silver and cut glass.

Mother Simons, very soon called Nana, was death on dishes, so the patterns varied. When she got to the jelly glass stage for drinking glasses, they were again put on her Christmas list.

Keneth, Una, David, Carolyn, and Hilary were still at home, so there would be a minimum of, say, eight for each meal. Jackie and Buddy would sometimes come from Jersey and soon moved to the old Colonel Wells apartments.

Dinner was a jolly affair. After the meat was carved, the subject of the sermon was discussed, and the talk covered everything after that. Not gossip. Mother Simons was very good that way. They were all bright and quick and so very different. They rubbed the corners off one another, being very frank. A Simons could never keep a secret!

Then came Thanksgiving. Every meal was a bustling affair, but quietly so, and interspersed with dry wine being served (no money for cocktails) before sitting down. Afterwards there was much fun stacking, clearing, and washing up. This could take quite a while, as no one hurried, except Nana, who splashed away at the dishpan in a little dark sink.

She never gave one the feeling of hurry, though she seemed to accomplish so much. When the big holiday came, one was introduced to the fact that Mother Simons had been an Alden. This meant there were traditions that had been handed down in her family, and very pleasant ones.

We heard stories of how there was a John Alden desk that had come over on the Mayflower. Another branch of the family became the happy owners of it. When I finally saw it, I could hardly believe my eyes. There had been a lot of rivalry over it. The thing consisted of little more than a couple of wee drawers, the whole being so small that it could be sat in the middle and on top of a dresser.

Mother Simons was the possessor of a lovely big silver loving cup, all fancy. I have a feeling it was the sugar bowl and someone else had the cream pitcher, but I thought it most handsome. It was used once or twice while I visited, and I do believe one time was Thanksgiving Day and the other at the time the first grandchild was born. Later such things would be considered unsanitary, so it sat in the semi-round glass cabinet in the dining room with other special things. Some of the silver had been Nana's grandmother's, and I especially remember teaspoons and a big turkey stuffing spoon which was given to us and lost in the fire.

The Thanksgiving table was prettied and filled with food and happy faces. The menu was always the same, except the green vegetable could vary. There was the big brown turkey, lots of giblet gravy, white mashed potatoes, candied sweets, creamed onions, olives, and prettily fixed celery. Dessert was pumpkin and mince pies. Ice cream was ladled onto the mince pie, and the pumpkin pie was pricked with a fork, and then some whiskey was poured on it and also whipped cream.

Everyone always ate too much. They went for a short walk sometimes and, in later years, all men and a favorite uncle, Will Alden, played golf for an hour or two before dinner.

When all was tidied up after the meal, everyone was seated comfortably in the living room and the fun began. Each person had to do something by way of entertainment. Uncle Buddy began. His was always a long poem. The young ones sat around cross-legged on the floor and were entranced. They knew what was coming and could not wait. He walked to one end of the room and, with an expansive feeling, he tugged up his trousers and stuck out his chin while talking to his audience. Sometimes softly and sometimes loud and scary. "The Shooting of Dan McGrew" was most often his poem.

Later, when there were grandchildren, the program started with the youngest, even if they could do no more than a somersault with assistance. It was such fun.

The family were quite musical, although the whole as an orchestra often went awry. Wynne studied piano and David studied the clarinet, so we always had to sing "For Peace and For Plenty" with them playing.

By the end of the long afternoon, no one's interest had wavered because best was saved for last. Nana stood and, with everyone's hands joined, they circled around the room and then sang "Johnny Schmoker." They performed all the actions and built up to a grand crescendo at the end. Everyone kept a close watch on Nana to see what came next. No one else could seem to remember it all.

Left: Gertrude Alden Simons, photo taken by Dick Lynch
Right: Gertrude demonstrates Johnny Schmoker for her granddaughters Andri, Nanette, and Gillian in the 1950's

Simons family: Carolyn, Keneth, Hilary, Wynne, David and Una

Carolyn, Gertrude and Hilary are in front. David, Keneth and Una are in back.
Photo also taken by Dick Lynch. Photo of Samuel on mantle.

Chapter 10

WEDDING CLOTHES

Keneth was working in New York, which seemed very exciting. He came home for weekends.

We'd become engaged in October and had decided on a June wedding. But not long after being engaged, we decided that June was *such* a long way off! So we pushed the date up and finally settled on January. January 13th was a Saturday, so Keneth suggested we choose that day because it had been October 13th when we had become engaged.

It was no chore to decide all the fun things right away as my thoughts were full of them anyway. Blue was my favorite color, so the bridesmaids would wear blue.

Who to choose was quite a problem as there were so many girls that had been friends. I decided that Irene would be Maid of Honor. Dianne, of course, would be a bridesmaid, and then there were a couple of others hard to decide upon. Lib Walter was chosen because she was a friend of both Di and me. Karen had been such a good friend, and I very much wanted her as a bridesmaid. I felt a little anxious about asking but decided to do so in the end. Shirley Cracraft was the little Illinois friend who'd shared so many escapades, so she had to be included. That seemed like an awfully big wedding, but they were all people I wanted. For flower girl we would have Jackie and Buddy's pretty little blonde baby, Barbara, called Babby, who was only a few years old.

No one had any money, so I chose pale blue taffeta at 59 cents a yard and bought enough for all the girls. They paid for the material, which was under $3 each. A simple pattern was chosen and a bit of deeper blue velvet ribbon for trim. Then I got busy. Every spare minute was spent cutting out and sewing. Di and Shirley helped willingly. They had done much so much, and so often came for advice. I made Irene's dress. Karen had her dress made, so I did not have to worry about it.

Then I just cut and fitted a dress for Babby, the flower girl. It was a white organdy with little white flowers printed on it. The yolk was tucked with a full skirt and puffed sleeves with lace whipped around the sleeves and neck and a bow sash. She looked so pretty and did perfectly.

As soon as Karen told her mother of our wedding date, she said she would buy my dress as a gift. Karen would take me into town to pick it out. That was most wonderful. I'd figured I would have to make it. We went to Bonwit Teller's, no less! I'd been there with the P. daughters when they went to shop for dresses and often got ideas for ones I made myself. To have my wedding dress bought there was a gift indeed!

I must tell a story in connection with that store which added to its "awesomeness." Shirley Cracraft had seen all the pretty dresses that came from there. The evening clothes were particularly beautiful. Having come from an Illinois farm with no goodies and then having a full-time job with money of her own, she was going to buy an evening dress from Bonwit Teller's! She chose a beautiful black velvet. All dresses were floor length and had full skirts, either flared or gathered.

The most shocking thing to come out in style was strapless evening gowns. This Shirley chose. It was for the Charter Day dance. She had begun to go very steadily with Roy Rose.

Such a bustle that night when Shirley finished waitressing supper and at last donned her pride and joy! Shirley sure had courage! The girls felt it was rather shocking for her to have spent so much money, especially the older ones. I was secretly pleased so didn't say a word. I'd have liked to do exactly the same thing if I'd not had so many commitments!

I helped snap Shirley up in her bowed top and hoped it would stay where it was meant to. Much speculation went into the discussion of strapless tops. If attention was what Shirley wanted, she got plenty. Every girl came in to see and comment, and we guessed what all they said when they left. The ritzy store from which the dress was bought, as well as the style, were equally a source of comment. Even Mr. P. came over to see Shirley in it.

Next I went over to tie Karen and Bethel's bows and heard their reactions, too. Shirley must have told them; I would not have but would have just appeared at the dance if I had nerve enough to do such a thing.

By this time, she was launched on a second startling new idea. A gardenia corsage had arrived for her. Every corsage was worn on the shoulder; she had no shoulder strap and did not wish to mar the velvet, and also, why not go all out and do something different? She'd wear it on top of her head! That's just what she did, and it started another whole round of head shaking. It certainly seems funny and tame today with all the miniskirts, tight mannish pants, and long-haired boys.

The order of the day now is to be way-out instead of just an odd few. Colors and prints and combinations of color are exotic. I must confess to liking much of this latter.

Karen and I arrived at the store to be taken to the Wedding Salon. I lacked background in this kind of place. What was the proper thing to do? I had my heart set on a shimmering white satin dress. That was what almost everyone had. I knew of one white velvet from way back, and in summer there had been maybe something else.

The saleslady brought out a dress to try on, took it back, and I tried another. I so much wanted to get my hands on a rack and look them over and choose what to try. All in all, as I remember, she brought out only three. The third one was a lovely, heavily-beaded, brocaded satin, which was more expensive, too. I didn't even wish to try it on, but Karen thought it was beautiful, so I did. It fit perfectly.

I even asked to try the last plain white satin one on again and did. It wasn't as elegant but was what I'd always wanted. Dear me!

Karen really left me in freedom, but I knew exactly how she felt. I worried about it being more than her mother had allowed, too, but she didn't! So the brocade was wrapped up in folds of white paper to be delivered.

Next they brought in veils, and we chose a lovely, handmade French lace tiara. It was the only one that looked right with the dress. Because it was so expensive, Karen asked if I could buy the veiling and attach it myself, so I did. Everyone wore them as long as their wedding dress.

This dress of mine had big pleats in the back and was a long trailing affair, besides being so full. The long pointed sleeves must have lace, so Mrs. P. said I might add some of her French lace that was one-half inch wide. This was also put around the neck and softened it.

After we'd finished with the wedding dress and my mixed emotions, Karen informed me she was going to give me a housecoat. I was to pick one out. It was the same sort of procedure. In those days, housecoats were not the exotic affairs of today. They were all made like bathrobes and belted at the middle. All went to the floor, and the usual was flannel for winter. The elegant ones were velvet or satin.

I right away saw a white satin one with blue velvet ribbon and a bit of lace. It was the only one I truly wanted. Karen picked a pale blue satin one with embroidered white organdy trim and asked me to try it on. That was it! I was lucky to get such a beautiful thing, and the color was more practical. I hated being practical *all* my life.

I'd never seen a wedding dress arrive. All items from stores were delivered. It was only an odd thing that shoppers carted home themselves. After opening the brown cardboard box, there, amid much paper, was a huge silver box tied in an enormous white bow of satin ribbon. My name was written in black script on the box. Remember, too, that gifts then did not have all the pretty papers and ribbons of today; it was not then an affluent society for most people. Every step along the way to wedding preparations was such an adventure. I'd never been that involved in a wedding before, having no family or relatives about and being the first of my crowd to get married.

P.S. I came to love that wedding dress and consider it much more beautiful than the white satin.

APARTMENT HUNTING

After we decided, "Why wait?", we rushed ahead to get all matters settled. One of them was where to live.

Keneth, who had been working in Camden, New Jersey for RCA, was told that he would again be working in New York. The company would pay $75 a month for living expenses. That seemed a wonderful lot. I'd been making $60 a month, considered very good pay in B.A. Keneth was making about $35 a week, and his family thought him rich!

For a month I had either Saturday or Sunday off, and we'd drive to New York to hunt all day for a place to live. I wasn't as thrilled as I could have been; I was scared. The *idea*, though, of living in the big glamour city was so exciting. We bought a newspaper and studied the ads. Keneth didn't know the city as well as he liked to pretend, but he did pretty well.

The blow came the first place we stopped! Even in unpretentious neighborhoods, a living room with a separate bedroom was way above $75 a month. It was the first time I'd seen Pullman kitchens. This was like double closet doors to open. A person would still be standing on the living room floor with a tiny everything in front of them. A refrigerator to the left and under the counter, a stove to the right, with a sink in the middle. Overhead were a few cupboards. Where would one put everything?

No room here for Sunday drinking glasses and that kind of thing!

The reason $75 was inadequate was that we were looking for a furnished apartment. Keneth expected to be there for perhaps six months only. Besides, we didn't own a stick of furniture and hadn't a cent to buy any. We'd have to save for it piece by piece.

Going up one day, Keneth mentioned that the Dick Lynches lived almost in New York. They had been Mother Simons' neighbors up until very recently and had been very friendly with us. Dick had taken us down to his darkroom, the first we'd seen, and showed all the stages of developing and printing pictures. He took "candid shots," too, a pretty new idea. He was excellent!

They were a very snappy, good-looking pair. Dick seemed to know his way around everywhere and knew a bit about many things. His wife was very, very smart, knew how to handle waiters and was sophisticated.

I liked this couple but never, never felt at home with them. I felt most inadequate. How could they enjoy us? They were so worldly-wise. They'd accidentally stumbled on B.A. and didn't wish to belong to the church so were lonely, hence the friendliness when living there.

In those days, I never hesitated long over anything. If asked to do this or that, I'd go try it; even if I didn't know what to do, at least I'd go see. This worked fine for most things. My biggest gap was in the social graces. All older people were awesome, plus teachers, ministers, etc. It was many years before I felt that most of them were people, just like me. Of course, many were cleverer than I, which only made them interesting, not frightening!

We decided to stop and visit Dick Lynch and his wife on the way home from New York. They lived in a big second-floor apartment with their two young daughters. It turned out to be an awkward time. They welcomed us warmly and insisted we stay for supper. Dick had a good new job, and they didn't know anyone yet in the area and were glad we had stopped in.

But – everything was so stiff. Keneth, who usually could kid easily with Dick, was quiet as could be. The apartment had very tall ceilings. The living room was big, which added to the austerity, and a maid came in with a drink on a tray. She was dressed all in black, with a little white apron and white ruffled cap. She looked just like the picture of a maid from the turn of the century in a rich home. Not a smile or sound, just silent service.

When we sat down to a tall glass and silver set table for supper, conversation died all the way. After the Simons' most informal, but nice, living Keneth seemed lost. I remember that when coffee was served, Keneth left his spoon standing in his coffee cup after he'd stirred it. I was mortified. He didn't even do that at home!

Probably, like many girls I'd felt one could expect the man in the family to know most things and how to handle situations. To suddenly have to watch out for him, even at a small happening, was rather a letdown. It probably opens the door, too, for bossy wives. Sometimes I sympathize with them.

We didn't repeat the visit. We had enough other things to tackle.

Then one weekend close to our wedding date, we did find a brand-new apartment. It wasn't such a good neighborhood and was a walk-up of four or five floors, but everything was new, including a plush couch and two plush chairs. Awful colors, but clean. I felt I'd for sure have claustrophobia in just one dark room, like we had seen many times before. This place had two rooms. Now I'd feel as if there was something to keep house in. To live in one room in a big strange city, with no job and no one to visit, was unhappiness. What would I do?

We were very happy about our good fortune and signed up for this new apartment. They wanted a $50 down payment, which took us greatly by surprise. Between our cash and a check, we managed, glad to have it settled.

We never lived in the apartment and, worst of all, only got half the money back from RCA!

THE END OF 1939

Each spare moment was spent sewing. Some bridesmaids couldn't sew on their dresses and some wouldn't. Then there was the little organdy dress to make for the flower girl and the veiling to be sewn onto my tiara.

Keneth and I went looking for a flower shop and found one up Southampton way. As I remember, it was on a farm; at least it was off to itself. It had been recommended by someone married recently.

Wedding parties carried big bushy bouquets, nothing like the formalized cascades of carefully wired arrangements they now wear. Pink roses were chosen for the six bridesmaids and white ones for me. The bill was $45. A fortune! This included a corsage for Nana and white carnations for the groom and the best man.

In recent years, the Charles Doerings had finally realized their dream of a bigger and better home. They had moved almost directly across the street to an enormous white house of three floors with a portico, long halls, and broad stairways. There was also a porch and even a back kitchen. It was so big that the first-floor hall had a fireplace in it.

Now most of their children were gone, and it seemed like such a big place to keep. True, many times family came to visit, but it was a shame not to have had it when raising those nine children.

One Sunday afternoon, Keneth and I were invited down to tea. This didn't seem too unusual because Keneth's classmate, that blond Andrew, had just been married, and we'd have the chance to meet and talk with him and his wife. She was a nurse he'd met while studying to be a doctor.

We walked in the door and, surprise, surprise! It was a shower! I'd wondered why there were so many cars! I bet to myself they'd asked both of us because I was so tongue-tied when faced with onlookers. My two friends who worked at Harold P.'s had organized it. In those times, just about the whole town turned out for such an affair.

We got many beautiful things. There was a dozen of everything in sterling silver, plus many odd pieces like a honey spoon. I didn't know what *that* was for! It was hand-beaten in our pattern, Simplicity. We also got soup spoons and demitasse spoons. I loved these. They were so cute and small. Having been given demitasse coffee cups also, we could serve coffee to guests after dinner! Such fun to have something like that; it seemed to be like playing house. I loved the table all set with pretty things for company. We used the new stainless steel for ourselves carefully set. There were linens, glasses, almost everything to start housekeeping. The town insurance man even gave us a $1,500 policy for a year or two. We'd never have thought to have had any otherwise because it was money we did not have. I didn't know what to say, so we both just stood up and said, "Thank You!"

In the mail came a beautiful large white linen tablecloth and a dozen napkins from Mom. Such a beautiful-looking damask cloth and a big gift from my hard-pressed family! I couldn't see how they'd managed it. Mom probably thought we'd have a wonderful home to grace it, and I can see her pleasure in sending it. The beautiful thing was carefully saved and, in the end, never used. We'd never managed that sort of a home before everything was lost in a fire, years later.

Mom would have loved to come to the wedding, but there wasn't a chance. It so happened she had no chance to see any of her four daughters married, nor the one son. She'd have been so thrilled to see this, the long white dresses in our beautiful church. Her son Bill was married down East, too, in Ontario. How very "left out" for her! Weddings are such milestones in people's lives and such a happy time for all.

I tell you, it seemed overwhelming to think that when one good thing came along so many others followed. Every day seemed like Christmas. There were gifts to be opened, with onlookers anxiously waiting to see the contents and share in the "oh's and ah's." There were more pretty clothes and invitations. From being a single non-entity one slips into belonging to a family and becoming a unit in society. Such a lot of things to cope with!

Lovely Christmastime came, and you'd never guess what Keneth thought to give me and did all on his own! A sewing machine! It was the handsomest little portable Willcox and Gibbs chain stitch. For some reason everyone in B.A. used them, so they were the kind I felt at home with. I loved to sew and had made dozens of things over the years for other people and almost all my own clothes. I'd not talked sewing with him but was overjoyed to have him think of it. We'd never have afforded it for years! Imagine him thinking of it!

Jackie and Buddy gave us a wardrobe suitcase and, along with the two I'd been given for birthdays by the girls I worked with, we were well supplied.

The biggest surprise was to have a letter come from my old schoolmate Richard from back home. He was coming to the wedding! What would I do with him?

He saved and worked his way here, arriving several days early. I'd mentioned it to my girlfriends, and no one invited him even to a meal. I was too busy to do much about it and don't know where he slept or how he got around. He managed a couple of afternoon visits and gave me a strange feeling of a tie with the past. Everything about home was long ago and far away, besides being very alien to my present way of living.

I remember the first afternoon he came. Having him come was about as strange as seeing a man entering a harem! Being a stranger and an "outsider," which was a big thing in those days, the girls stayed away. Leslie came to visit and, shockingly, I took them both up to my round room at Glencairn and served tea. We sat cross-legged on the floor and talked and had a great time. I'm sure the girls were shocked, but there was nothing else to do. The atmosphere was impossible anywhere else. I'd decided I was leaving anyway and wasn't going to care. I did, though, but didn't know how else to handle the situation. I showed them all my gifts. Richard saw that, like the scenery, the things I'd written home about were not lies, or, in nicer language, "exaggerations."

I told Richard where the wedding was to be and the time. He said he was looking forward to seeing a "society" wedding for the first time. Anything as fancy was no less than what they did in high society in his eyes. This was partly true.

WEDDING PLANS

One of the first things we'd thought about and settled on was to ask our favorite minister, Bishop de Charms, to marry us.

Reverend Elmo Acton had come back from South Africa and given Young People's Class for two years. We'd enjoyed the classes very much and didn't want him to feel left out, so we asked him to do our betrothal service. It had been six weeks before in the Little Chapel. I'd made myself a deep blue velvet two-piece dress, and it turned out very pretty.

The feeling of the service didn't seem to be there, and I don't know why. It was a dark chilly night and the room so bare. There seemed no happy feeling about it, and I was glad when it was over. The whole thing was something you were supposed to do, and so we did. I think I expected Keneth to say something special, and he probably expected me to, and neither of us did. We were terribly green on so many things.

It was about this time that Keneth gave me a yellow topaz pendant on a little gold chain. My first piece of real jewelry, and I loved it!

Anyhow, it was nice to go afterwards down to Mother Simons' and sit in front of her fireplace, where many, many pleasant hours were spent over the years, and have cocoa and talk.

Meanwhile I, of course, was just full of wedding plans. They had to do with what I'd wear, colors, and who I would choose to be in the wedding. When I think of all the things in connection with it now, I often wonder who took care of many of the other details I didn't even know about. In putting on a wedding, there are so many people to be called and so many arrangements to be made. I guess it was simpler then, as regular Chancel Guild girls lit the candles and set out the flowers.

I know Mother Simons did nothing to help. She did no more than listen to anything I told her about it and she never offered a suggestion. Mrs. P., I'm sure, was the mastermind.

Mr. P. loved to play the violin. Sometimes we would see and hear him walking about in the music room, "sawing" away at practice. Other times he had three other men who came to the house, and they were known as the Flonzoli String Quartet. They often put on concerts on Sunday nights and invited B.A. people to attend. When practicing for a concert, we would find him walking around playing in the upstairs living room and hall. He'd cock an ear and listen for a particular tone. We kept out of the way.

One day at the dinner table, he asked if I'd like him to play at our wedding. I was speechless for a while! His offer had taken me completely by surprise. This austere, removed, lofty, untouchable man was still a complete stranger to me after five years in his home. I'd never had one single conversation with him. We'd often all gone to the chapel after supper and seen him while he gave worship. I had served him with meals so had asked a question or two requiring the simplest answers. But that was all. He was such an intelligent man who didn't waste words. I did nothing more than make out very badly so only answered him if he asked a question. He'd probably ask what he was to play, want to practice, and goodness knows what! I didn't want to get involved with him over the wedding and be awkward but was very happy about his offering. Besides, I felt that his talent should be reserved for important weddings!

I hate to think now of how rude I was to him, but I never knew how to explain things in those days, let alone be diplomatic. I said, "Oh, no," that was all. No "Thank you" or anything. I wonder what he thought? My thoughts raced on about how alone I felt trying to get everything ready and knowing how long he took fussing over the taking of just one picture at the mountains. He'd for sure gum up the works!

We just told Bishop de Charms the date and, outside of clothes to wear, didn't work on anything else. Wonder who got the wine for the reception?

Keneth's brother Buddy was in the bakery business and I guess donated the cake! There again, I would have loved a little bride and groom on it. Always thought they looked so special. But I wouldn't dare say so. I'd heard others talking about how distasteful that was. So on the top was the little archway with a simple silver bell, shaped like the glass kind often seen on Christmas trees. It was a pretty three-tiered cake. We kept the top layer for a while as there were no freezers then and enjoyed it by ourselves.

Two days before the wedding, I got my yearly attack of the grippe: aches, cold, and high fever, especially aches. Nothing to do but call off the wedding. The flower man was not very happy but was very obliging.

In addition, Keneth was told at the last minute we weren't going to New York after all, so he went apartment hunting near Camden by his lonesome in the snow and managed to find one.

The first possible new date for the wedding was the following Thursday. We kidded about it being "maid's day off." The only calamity was that a special boyfriend from school days, who was studying to be a doctor in Philadelphia, showed up at the church that Saturday night to find it dark and locked.

OUR WEDDING DAY

January 18th, 1940, Thursday night, 8 p.m.

Such a long, odd day it was. Half my work was taken away, and the hours crept by in the morning. I didn't feel happy but only unsettled. What would it be like moving out of the town? Would I die of nervous fright? How nice for some who were surrounded with helpful family. I was mostly glad Dad and Mom wouldn't be there, as they would never have known what to do.

The old adage was that you should not see your betrothed on your wedding day, why I'll never know! So I didn't see Keneth, and the day was much too long. Sometime late in the morning, Mrs. P. sent a message to meet her in her boudoir. All it did was scare me. She'd never had cozy little talks with me, but that room was connected with talk from her when several girls were called in to discuss entertaining at Minister's Meeting time or "late nights." Having never given me a warm friendly feeling, I thought it must be some kind of lecture! I still admired her from afar.

Well, I went, and we sat and talked. It was a most stilted conversation. She had a knack for saying things in most subtle ways, but what she said that morning passed me by. Perhaps she'd been kind in inviting me to chat in case there was anything I wished to ask. She lived in another world, and so her way of doing many things would never be practiced as far as I could see.

When she'd wished us all in bed so early, I'd known it would have meant giving up the best social life, dates. If work was finished late, dates would be later, and I wasn't about to change that. It was true that we could have been home earlier, and I don't blame her for feeling responsible then. But you know how young people are. I felt that I was working on my own then, and my life was my own. I was almost twenty-five.

So lunchtime came and it was afternoon. About the middle of it, Ros Coffin, who was to be best man, stopped in to say he'd come to take me for a ride, bless his boots! It was a most nice thing to do, although I knew he'd have much to say about Di and how he wished she'd marry him. He'd been after her for a long time, and now his buddy Keneth was getting married first! That fact made him rather unhappy because he'd known his own mind so much longer. But it was nice to get out and break up the day.

I don't remember eating any supper. Next, we were all at the church, everyone fussing with getting dressed and made up. Does my hair look OK, etc.

I remember thinking bridesmaids weren't much of a help. I had trouble trying to bobby pin on that long veil so as it would stay put if the end of it caught on the rough stone going down the aisle. Each girl seemed completely absorbed in her own get-up.

Next, we had to get everyone and that long wedding-dress train under the church and over to the far side for picture taking in the minister's Meeting Room. There were steps and a black railing where all bridal pictures were taken. It made an attractive setting. Dick Lynch came from New Jersey to take the pictures. He'd taken such beautiful pictures of people.

There was a huge white glassy box with the wedding bouquet. Much to my surprise, the bunch of white roses had white ribbon streamers dangling down with bits of maidenhair fern tied on every so often. I wasn't too sure it didn't cheapen the whole thing with my elegant dress being brocade. But I thought it was pretty and softened the flowers. The florist had muttered he'd have to make the bouquets simpler due to the wedding date being changed. Perhaps some of the flowers ordered for the earlier time were a loss. So, I wondered if he'd have fancied up the bridesmaids flowers? Was glad to see he didn't.

Now Mother Simons arrived, and everyone got their best smile photographed. I'd forgotten that Dick's idea was to take candid shots whenever he felt like it, so when I suggested Keneth try putting the veil back off my face, which he found anything but simple, pop went a flashbulb! No one we knew had had candid shots, and they were fun to see afterward.

Then we returned to the back of the church, which by this time was filling with people. It was such a dark labyrinth down under the nave! There were pipes all over to stoop under. Then the dank little room was crowded and darkish to wait in. It was wonderful to come up the narrow little winding stairs to open space in the back of the nave.

Then we all lined up to stand and stand. The church was full of guests, such a crowd! Everyone went to weddings as there were so few of them. The chancel was prettily decorated. I remember seeing ferns. Only later in remembering, I figured it couldn't be anybody else but Mrs. P. who had seen to that.

I felt so anxious to get down that long aisle. Keneth seemed as calm as could be. It was good to take his arm and feel it so steady. There was brother Leslie looking very pleased. I tried reciting what I had to say at the chancel and didn't forget it.

Going up the aisle was easy, and it was rather cozy and private when one reached Bishop de Charms. He had such a kindly sphere about him, too, it was quite reassuring.

Then Keneth completely surprised me, and it was somewhat unnerving. When we got to the part where he says his piece, he took a step back, facing to the side, and in a big voice said, "With this ring...." It sounded as if he was making a speech! Weddings are usually so quiet, and part of them are scarcely heard by the audience. It does make it feel as if it's between the couple and the minister, which is kind of nice. I wanted to grab him by the coattail and bring him back. In asking him afterward why he'd done it, he said he'd run the sound system for weddings and could never hear all of it. So he was making sure everyone heard him!

He was full of surprises, if one can call something like that a surprise. I felt a little cross to be startled so. Then there was that long walk back down the aisle, which was hardest of all. My face felt stiff from trying to smile. I love to see the few brides who come down looking relaxed and happy. My sympathy was all with the bride who, in a wedding after ours, made it down the aisle and then fainted dead away!

I only remember a few parts of the reception. Bishop de Charms was the only one to make a speech. He started out by saying this was all sort of like a fairy tale. Then something to the effect that a poor girl had gone to live in a fairy castle and a knight had found her. It was pleasingly done, and that is all that I can recall.

Richard came along near the end of the reception line with sparkling eyes. He thought it a grand occasion and whispered in my ear that Keneth had said to him, "The best man won." He also thought he'd happened to be in one of the flash pictures and hoped I'd send him a copy. He was sure it was going to be in the newspapers! I never saw him again. He joined the merchant marines soon after the wedding and later went down with his ship.

The cake had been cut and served and we'd shaken hands with everyone and stayed quite a spell to visit. Most people visited with each other. Keneth and I wondered a bit about when to leave the thinning crowd. We then went to find his car.

We drove down to Mother Simons' to change. The house was all dark with only the porch light on. Di came along and Ros and later Mother Simons to say goodbye.

I had no trousseau or special going away suit, so I don't remember what I wore.

THE HONEYMOON

Keneth had Friday off, so we had only a long weekend. I'd not the faintest idea of where we were going to spend it. We got in his blue Ford and he tucked a blanket over my knees. After we'd driven a short piece, he reached to tuck it down again beside me. I wondered why, and then he asked me if I hadn't noticed something? I couldn't imagine what as it was pitch dark. Then he said, "the auto robe." He'd splurged and bought a pretty blue plaid one with fringe on the ends. I didn't much see the point of it but thought it was nice. He wanted to be sure I'd be warm enough!

We seemed to drive and drive, and I got the idea we were on our way to New York. This was just what Keneth hoped I'd think, and he'd gone out of his way so as I would not recognize any landmarks. Then there shone the red letters of the PSFS Building on the corner of 12th and Market Streets in Philadelphia! I didn't say anything, but it was a letdown. Then we drove up to the Bellevue-Stratford, which had always been considered the best in old Philadelphia tradition.

I had no feeling of something special. I knew it was wise because I supposed we were tired, even if we didn't feel so. It wasn't very late.

Well, it was a gloomy old place. Why did everyone think it was so great? The main hall was old and musty. Little white tiles, like those in old-fashioned bathrooms, made the flooring, and all about were dark high ceilings and low lights. You had the feeling everyone had gone to bed. An old man asked us to sign our names and another took us up dark halls to a room.

I was sure when he opened a door we'd see a change. But no! The room looked as bad. There was one bright spot: on the old dresser sat a lovely bouquet of flowers of several kinds. I remember particularly the blue iris. I took for granted the hotel had put them in each room, but Keneth said, "No." Well then, "Who had sent them?" He had to tell me "I did, of course!" Then they became something special. He'd never sent flowers before!

Keneth suggested we have breakfast in bed. This seemed the height of pure laziness and elegance, so why not? He picked up the phone and finally discovered the right place to call. I wasn't the kind to ever go back to bed. After getting up to wash my teeth, it seemed silly to go back to bed, but I might as well play the game.

Promptly there was a knock on the door, and Keneth opened it wide. An old grey-fringed duffer came staggering in with a long table twice his size on his shoulder. This table was long and skinny with four bulbous legs on the end. He put it down at the foot of the bed and slid it up over the bed. There weren't enough pillows to make it comfortable to sit. In front of us was white linen and what seemed like dozens of silver-covered dishes. I felt so sorry to have inconvenienced the poor old man. It was no fun at all.

So we ate breakfast, and I felt I'd much rather eat the regular way. (Boy! would I like to go back and enjoy it now!)

As soon as it was over, Keneth said, "Now we go to New York." It was a nice, sunny, clear but cold day. We landed up at the moderately priced New Yorker, a business hotel and bustling, and a small room. We had a light supper, again in bed, because we didn't feel like getting dressed to go out.

Any number of Simons relatives had come to the wedding but

mostly Alden relatives from away. Grandfather Alden had had a brother, Ezra Hyde Alden, who was in the railway business. He was the only well-to-do relative. Grandfather and Grandmother Alden had been gone for a number of years, but Hyde was still alive. He slipped Keneth a fifty-dollar check at the reception.

Now in New York Keneth suggested, "Let's go to the Rainbow Room as our one special occasion to celebrate." We'd go for supper Saturday night. It was very new and considered the top nightspot. We were very much in awe of the idea.

During the day we walked the streets to do some sightseeing in the big city. We spent the longest period of time in Macy's looking at all the things we'd like to buy. I had exactly $8 in my purse. That was the sum total of any money left from my working days and after starting brother Leslie in school. As we walked through the store, we passed a beautiful fluffy gold satin quilt. It was luxurious-feeling and looking, but it cost a lot of money. I spent the whole $8 I had on it. We carried it back to the hotel. It was a disappointment in the end. We woke up to forever find the light but slippery thing on the floor.

I always bargain-hunted for clothes and then re-did hems by hand, took off cheap trim and poor buttons, and had something pretty nice looking when through. I'd been lucky buying an evening dress for the New Year's dance that year. It was a long, heavy white crepe with about four pleats in the center front and straps over the shoulder. With it was a thin red wool jacket that went down to a point in front and zipped up the very middle. It had long sleeves, rather like the jacket of the little Philip Morris ad fellow who was dressed as a bellhop. It fit perfectly and had a sprinkling of elongated gold beads from the shoulders down the front. This was most unusual; only the stage people wore bangles and beads. All that dress had needed was a new hem. I loved it and felt elegantly dressed. Keneth had liked it very much, too.

He had a black tuxedo given him by Mrs. P. for his senior dance. Her oldest son was in the same class, and she gave a couple of his friends tuxedos to wear along with him, which was much appreciated.

We learned that the Rainbow Room required evening dress and were glad we'd brought these along. All banquets, weddings, and dances meant long dresses. People dressed far more formally for all occasions back then. We'd had a very good time at that New Year's dance, so getting dressed in the same things gave us a happy feeling, and we looked forward to it with great expectations. It was nice to feel as if we'd at least be one of the crowd in appearance.

We took a taxi! Then a swoosh of an elevator ride to the top floor of Radio City. We stepped out into a plush, dark, carpeted room, a sumptuous-feeling place with low lights and soft chairs.

A waiter bowed, led us to a table and left a menu. We unhurriedly looked about and almost next to us sat Louise Reiner, the movie star, who had played the lead in Pearl Buck's story The Good Earth. How exciting!

Another waiter went by holding aloft a tray on which sat a fair-sized Scottie dog made of ice, with coal-black eyes. The clear ice was all so perfectly frozen that the hairs were seen. It was just decoration on the tray! In front of the dog sat a nest of spun sugar, which we watched them serve with ice cream.

Then we studied the menu! Bread and butter was seventy-five cents. An uneasy feeling crept over us. We didn't belong here! Such unheard-of prices! What could we have? We couldn't even make out what some of the items were. Fish, naturally, was the cheapest thing, so we chose that and with it came a vegetable. It was Pompano. I've never had it before or since. I just have not seen it anywhere, but it was good. It came baked in a little brown paper bag. The vegetable was braised lettuce. A sad, wilted, ungreen sight to my eyes. Then Keneth decided to order a split of wine, whatever that was! The waiter had told him about it. It came to the table in a huge silver urn all packed in ice. A treat lost on me. No kind of drink tasted any good with the exception of the first whiff of something like Apricot Brandy.

Supper, after seeing the prices, wasn't as much fun as it could have been, and we skipped any dessert. In fact, we left feeling almost hungry.

The waiter announced that coffee would be served in the lounge. This was fun. We walked out to a spacious room that had unusual couches, which were low-backed. There were long coffee tables in front of the couches. We set our cups on them and looked out the big glass windows all around, with the city lights sparkling below. It was a dramatic sight. With our big experience almost over, we sat and enjoyed this part very much.

Then back to the hotel, and we decided we were anxious to get home. I was dying to see the apartment Keneth had found for us to live in.

We'd leave first thing in the morning.

Reta and Keneth practicing

Keneth and Reta Evens Simons

Karen, Shirley, Lib, Keneth and Reta with Babby in front, Ros, Irene and Dianne

Simons women at the wedding: Buddy's wife Jackie with son Brian, Una, Wynne, Jackie's daughter Babby the flower girl, Gertrude and Carolyn

Roscoe Coffin and Keneth

Reta Evens Simons

Reta and Keneth's marriage license after 1952 house fire

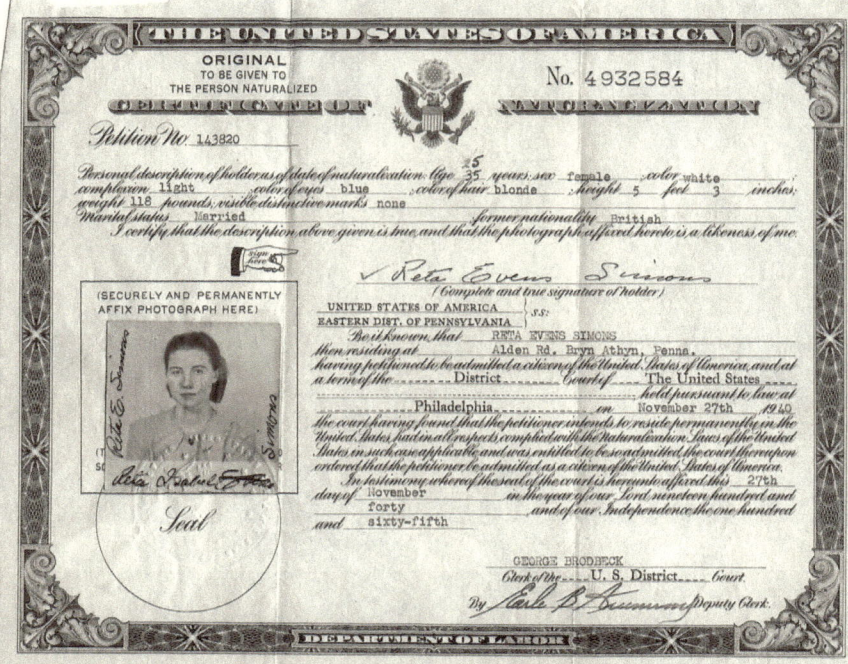

Reta's naturalization paper

Reta's brother Leslie, a sergeant in the Royal Canadian Air Force, who died in World War II. Here with Reta's son Kurt in 1944

Back row: Reta, Bea, Irene's son Leslie, Irene, Bill (also in the RCAF), Margaret
Middle row: Reta's parents William and Rose
Front row: Reta's children Kurt and Andri at Christmas in 1945

Reta with her daughter Andri in 1944

Reta Evens Simons with daughter Dona on the Staten Island Ferry in the 1960's

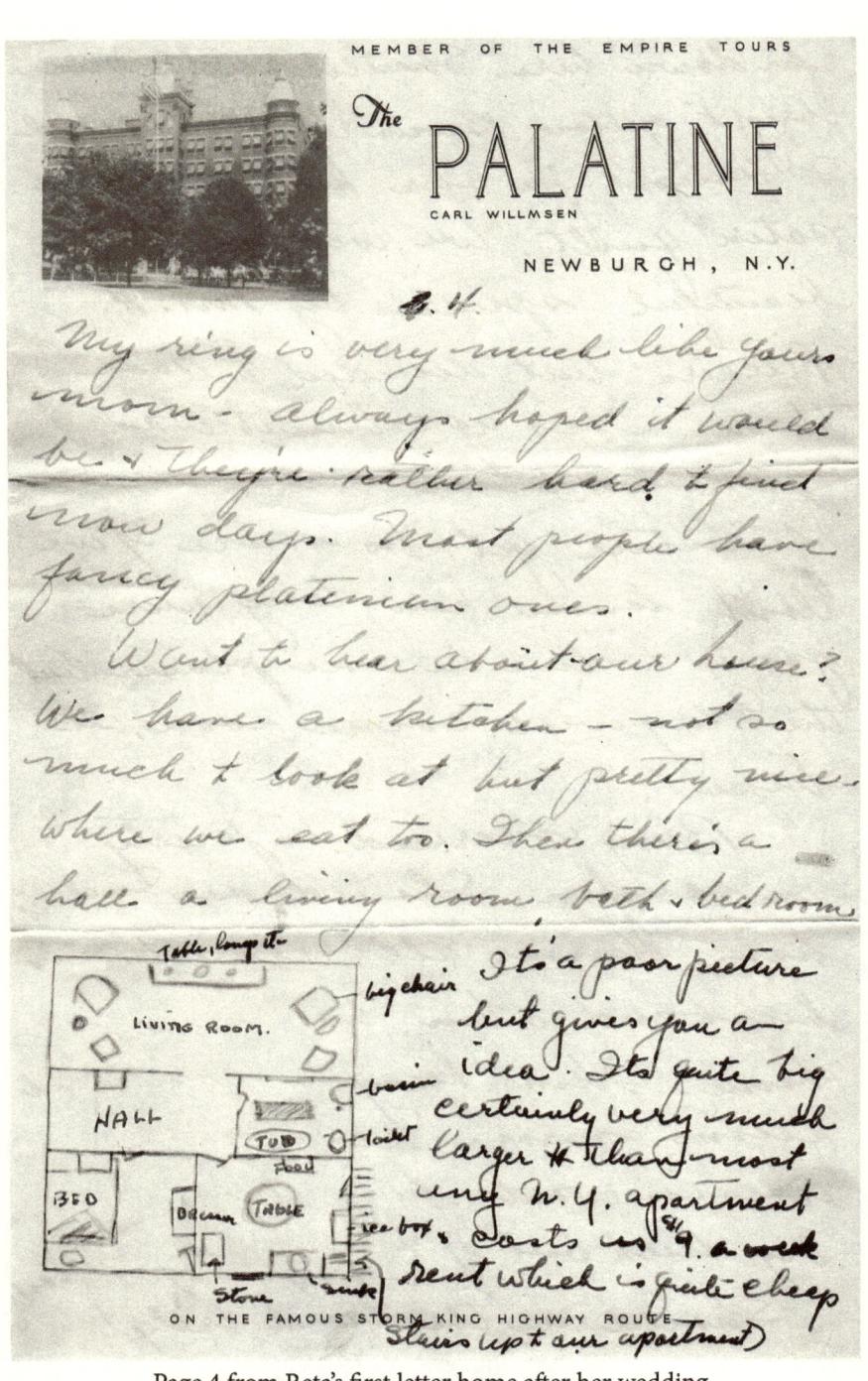

My ring is very much like yours mom – always hoped it would be & they're rather hard to find now days. Most people have fancy platinum ones.

Want to hear about our house? We have a kitchen – not so much to look at but pretty nice. Where we eat too. Then there's a hall, a living room, bath & bedroom. It's a poor picture but gives you an idea. It's quite big certainly, very much larger than most any N.Y. apartment & costs us $9. a week rent which is quite cheap. (Stairs up to our apartment)

Page 4 from Reta's first letter home after her wedding.

Epilogue

The following is the first letter Reta wrote after her wedding.

Jan. 26, 1940

Dear Family,

Here I am at a hotel way up in New York state. Keneth had to come up early yesterday morning for a couple of days so wishes me to go too. It seems he will have to do some traveling around like this and as long as the company pays most of the expenses the budget doesn't suffer too much. It's nice being with one's husband as much as possible.

His old company says one thing & in two minutes something else. Anyhow this inconvenience of traveling etc. is partly why he's so well paid.

My hotel room looks right out over the Hudson River which is a very pretty sight. The town across the river is all lit up & the mountains (Catskills) are up behind that.

They're pretty but nothing like the Rockies.

You know I have about 200 'thank-you' letters to write for wedding presents from all over. You just never saw so many presents in all your life & I couldn't possibly tell you about them all.

We haven't seen our wedding pictures yet – the photographer lives up by New York & we just haven't seen him. We did manage to mail you ½ of the top layer of wedding cake this morning & here's hoping it's intact – even though a little stale. It's white cake – nothing exciting in a way but what all brides seem to have here. The fruit cake is my idea of a scrumptious wedding cake. It looked so pretty – it was very big and had layers with a cute design standing on top with a big silver bell. (Hope you get it O.K.) The wedding went off very successfully & you'd have been proud of how pretty it all looked. The church was beautiful with all the candles and flowers. Mrs. P. went down herself & helped supervise all the flower arrangements. There were all kinds of white potted flowers & easter lilies besides pine branches along the choir stalls. Too bad we couldn't take a picture for you.

Guess Irene has written to you about some of it. The bridesmaids carried yellow roses & mine was gardenias & lily of the valley. Um–um! Here's hoping for a good picture or two.

We have a whole second floor apartment over in Jersey & are only about four miles from Ken's work so he comes home for lunch which makes the day seem much shorter. Afternoons are longest.

Our address there is 167 Elm Ave, Woodlynn, New Jersey so I hope you write soon. I'm usually quite busy so haven't had too much time to feel lonely but it does seem awfully quiet after living with so many people.

Mom & Pop I was very touched with that lovely table cloth & napkins & it just means so much coming from home – you've no idea. It was just elegant & I needed a set like that. If you were anywhere near I'd sure have you for dinner & use it along with my lovely new set of dishes from the girls at Glencairn & drinking goblets (an amber color) from a Simons (not in church) relation of Keneth's. In fact we could have steak & cut it with the swell silver steak set and serve vegetables in the twin silver vegetables dishes Bishop & Mrs. de Charms gave us. The bishop is the most wonderful man I ever knew & it's not just because he's a bishop either. We were so glad we could have him marry us – I guess Uncle Karl Alden even forgave us not having him.

The P.'s certainly were lovely & Mrs. P. practically burst into tears when I said 'goodbye'. Always hoped she'd like me!

Well I feel so thrilled at the way the wedding went off & how pretty it was & all the luck we've had I feel sort of tongue-tied. It certainly will be something to remember.

My ring is very much like yours Mom – always hoped it would be & they're rather hard to find nowadays. Most people have fancy platinum ones.

Want to hear about our house? We have a kitchen – not so much to look at but pretty nice – where we eat too. Then there's a hall, a living room, bath & bedroom.

It's a poor picture but gives you an idea. It's quite big certainly very much larger than most any N.Y. apartment & costs us $9 a week rent which is quite cheap for down here. Should see the nice bright yellow, brown & orange spread I bought for our bed & the gold satin quilt. We were given two beautiful spreads by Mrs. H. P. but decided to save them. This apartment was furnished which means we've no furniture yet. No sense if we don't know how long we're going to live in one place – but the day will come soon, we hope.

Being married is pretty much fun. Should see me have dinner all ready for my husband when he comes home. Him being my husband seems more real than it does in words but I get a very big kick out of saying "my husband".

Should see the landlady! She's sort of big and rather uneducated. She talks a mile a minute but seems to be quite kindhearted. She's very clean & tidy & loves bright things so our apartment lacks anything like a color scheme but is quite colorful I assure you!

Ken is out checking on television sets up here so the government can make an inspection. It seems Philco & some of R.C.A. competitors are jealous of us (R.C.A.) putting television on the market (they've been struggling hard to do the same) & so are bringing up a case & the government is looking into it. They claim television isn't ready for the public – of course it is new & is steadily improving & one must start sometime.

It's good to be able to write – cause it's like talking to someone – had to go down and eat dinner all by myself in the big dining room. Ate about seven – but it's not much fun alone. Ken called and said he couldn't get back.

Being married is swell too because you're your own boss something I'd never been since hitting B.A. You're head of a household & besides you've something better than anything in the world – namely a husband. It's swell too because I'm starting to appreciate little things again – that on my last job were pretty well taken with little thought.

Our honeymoon was perfect – went to Phila. For the 1st night very much to my surprise. Ken decided we'd be too tired after the wedding as off we started – I was sure we were half way to N.Y. When all of a sudden we were right in Phila. He'd taken me all round about ways. We stayed at the Bellevue Stratford – Phila.'s biggest & had breakfast in bed next morning, packed & were off to N.Y. There we shopped – loafed – and had swell fun topping it with the most wonderful time. We went to the Rainbow Room for dinner about 10 o'clock. It's on the 70th floor of Radio City. It's a scrumptious place, big squnchy chairs, rugs & such service. They have two big rooms outside the dining room where one may be served after dinner coffee & smoke. It looks down over Central Park, has fountains & the cities lights are even reflected in the ceiling which is all mirrors. The ballroom is a large circle with big carpeted steps & tables on tiers all around so one looks sort of down on the ballroom. We had a most different supper – brazed lettuce with wine sauce – pompenou (a special sort of fish) with quarters of oranges baked on top– and a bottle of champagne! It cost us $15. for supper but we were given some money for a wedding present & we wanted to do something special. It was worth it but of course probably won't happen again in years. It's a place of celebrities. The floor show was very cute.

 Well, about enough of this – I wasn't trying to impress you but just tell you about what fun we had.

 We could have stayed another day but thought it had reached a very fine climax – so home we came.

 There's just dozens of things I feel like bubbling over about but guess I'd better stop before I wear the pen down – must save something to write all those 'thank yous'.

 Thank you again for that very swell present.

 Lots & lots of love
 Reta

When I became 18, and felt very grown up, I decided to write a book. How to go about it never daunted me. Its title was to be "It Rained at Harvest Time" and naturally it was to be the story of my life.

—Reta Evens Simons

About the Author

Reta Evens, later Simons, grew up on the Canadian prairie almost 100 years ago. In many ways her life there was very different from what most of us experience today. In other ways, related to human nature and behavior, we are all too much the same. You can read about her early life in her first book titled *It Rained at Harvest Time: Memoirs of the Forever Prairie*. With a charming and conversational manner, Reta takes us through the realities of life with a pioneering family farming wheat on the seemingly endless prairie of Alberta in Western Canada. While conditions there were often difficult, Reta adds levity with her impromptu illustrations, sprinkled throughout the text. At the end of the eighth grade, there were no high schools on the prairie and she faced the rest of her life working on a farm. A combination of events, along with the fact that it happened to rain one harvest time, changed her life forever. And that brings us to the beginning of this book.

Reta was born in 1915 and died in 1973. After marrying Keneth Alden Simons, she had three children: Kurt, Andri and Dona.

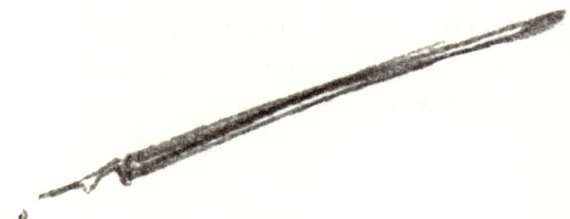

About the Editor

Dr. S. Leigh Matthews is a Lecturer in the Department of English and Modern Languages at Thompson Rivers University in Kamloops, British Columbia. She reads, researches and publishes mainly in the areas of Life Writing and Canadian Literature and has published a book titled *Looking Back: Canadian Women's Prairie Memoirs and Intersections of Culture, History, and Identity* (University of Calgary Press, 2010).

www.ingramcontent.com/pod-product-compliance
Lightning Source LLC
Chambersburg PA
CBHW030431010526
44118CB00011B/592